GEORGE GISSING
GRAVE COMEDIAN

GEORGE GISSING

GRAVE COMEDIAN

Mabel Collins Donnelly

HARVARD UNIVERSITY PRESS · CAMBRIDGE

1954

Library of Congress Catalog Card Number 53-10869
Printed in the United States of America

TO JOHN

PREFACE

Mr. Alfred C. Gissing, son of George Gissing, has given kind permission to quote from manuscripts as listed in the footnotes and from *The Letters of George Gissing to Members of His Family,* Constable and Company, 1927, and to him I am particularly grateful.

I am also indebted to an admirer and devoted collector of Gissing, the late Arthur Pforzheimer, whose kindness I wish to record. Like her husband, Isabel Pforzheimer has also been helpful and gracious. Mr. Stanley Wood has summoned memories of Gissing's boyhood at boarding school and has shared those memories.

The courtesy of the curators of the principal manuscript collections of Gissing is gratefully acknowledged: that of Dr. John D. Gordan, Curator of the Henry W. and Albert A. Berg Collection of the New York Public Library, and Mr. Paul North Rice, Chief of the Reference Department. Also Mr. Robert F. Metzdorf, Curator of Manuscripts of the Yale University Library.

Thanks for permission to quote are also due the Boston Public Library, Mr. Richard G. Hensley, Chief Librarian, Division of Reference and Research Services; to Jonathan Cape, Ltd., for an excerpt from Virginia Woolf's Introduction to Gissing's *By the Ionian Sea,* the Travellers Library, 1933; to Constable and Company for excerpts from Thomas Seccombe's Introduction to Gissing's *The House of Cobwebs,* 1906; to Chapman and Hall for material from *Memories* by Edward Clodd, 1916; to the Columbia University Press for an excerpt from a chapter by Angus Burrell in *Modern Fiction,* 1934; to the Odyssey Press, for an excerpt from the Introduction by Robert Shafer to *Workers in the Dawn,* 1935; to the Sunday *Times,* London, for an excerpt from a review by Cyril Connolly, "The Legacy of Gissing," January 25, 1953.

Grateful acknowledgment is also made to Professor Howard Mumford Jones and to the American Council of Learned Societies and Radcliffe College for help along the long way. To Dr. John Donnelly, too, special thanks are given.

M.C.D.

December 28, 1953

CONTENTS

Chapter 1

REVALUATION

George Gissing, in his own day a man "ahead of his time," has suffered the fate of appearing old-fashioned in the eyes of a later generation. When fervor is interpreted as futile and passion judged as puerile, a man can be taken seriously no longer. In late Victorian England, Gissing was scourged more than once, but by implication men who are scourged are, at least, taken seriously instead of regarded as fussy "obsessives." Indeed, in 1885, *Punch* was so irate over Gissing's iconoclasm, particularly his attack on prudery in the novel, that it thrashed him soundly in print: "Praised be the gods for thy foulness, Gissing, but also, that, as we fondly hope, there are not many like thee." [1] Few publications adopted so censorious a tone toward Gissing, but all the literate journals were united, at least, in regarding him as a formidable member of the *avant-garde*. Today, by contrast, his life is described in terms of "doing dizzy circles around himself in futile gymnastics of escape," [2] while his talent has been criticized as not of the first order. [3]

Recent diagnosis of the futile compulsiveness of Gissing's life has been made largely on the basis of data now known to be bowdlerized to a grave degree. The precocious childhood, the scandal-ridden adolescence that left a bitter misanthropy as its legacy, the two disastrous marriages, the sorties into the sharply separated classes of Victorian England, sometimes as maverick and sometimes as accredited ambassador, the final stoicism — these experiences have not been fully exposed as the sources of Gissing's iconoclasm. It has been hinted darkly in several quarters that Gissing's life had moments as lurid and powerful as those of eminent Victorians whose biographies have been finally brought forth in all honesty, but full consideration of the crucial experiences in Gissing's life has been wanting. In spite of the fact that when Gissing died in 1903 he left behind him reams of diaries and letters in manuscript, the mass of the material did not see print until 1927 when a volume of excerpts was published,[4] and even this long-awaited book lacked many of the man's most characteristic utterances. Orthodoxy was at last forced upon a dead man even though the garment did not quite fit; passion was tailored to suit the tailor.

The shroud refuses, however, to remain in the conventional folds. Heretofore unpublished material reveals the extent of Gissing's iconoclasm, his sharp observations on mores with which he was sharply at issue. While most men exulted in a naïve concept of democracy, equating liberty with *laissez faire* and equality with mediocrity, Gissing pointed out the dangers lying in wait: government by petty men, cruel and wasteful wars, mediocrity of culture, perhaps even a return to barbarism. Nor could he join the ranks of the religious revivalists who urged humility and thoughts of otherworldly blessings, for he decided from his experience that humility and meekness were most likely to survive when preserved by the more aggressive members of the community. As for the conventional views on marriage and the family held by the average Victorian as the last preserve of the pure-in-heart, Gissing dared to discuss the differences between marriage and sexual fulfillment, the often conflicting demands of the race and the individual in the matter of propagation. In short, in a day when cultural anthropology was a very new science, its work almost unknown even to the "intellectuals," Gissing dared to trespass upon forbidden ground.

A man who dares much is liable to the charge of mere brashness; a man who spurns not only sentimental paraphrases of the Christian virtues but the very virtues themselves, is liable to the charge of arrogance. Gissing has been charged with both. There is no doubt that he is not a figure readily lovable; in his lifetime he received so little of that benefaction that he scarcely learned to dispense it. But there is also no doubt that he was an honest man who learned slowly and painfully that brashness is not an adequate substitute for suffering. Thus in his youth he began his campaign against religion with diatribes against ritualism; he ended his campaign, in the painfilled days before his death at forty-six, with an essay upon Christmas which has in it nothing of sentimentality but all of the *lacrimae rerum*. His problems and the new set of values he tried to work out in dealing with them are among the most challenging of those confronting Englishmen of the end of the century. Perhaps his most admirable quality was fairness, a rejection of bigotry even when bigotry was fashionable. Thus when Bradlaugh was most maligned, Gissing was among the few who recognized a stubborn, possibly erring, but certainly honest, man.

George Gissing deserves study not only as a skilled surgeon at work on Victorian orthodoxy, but also as a novelist of skill. The limited appreciation of his work comes in large measure from the lack of a standard and readily accessible edition and to the assumption that his work is all of one piece, that is to say, all tainted with the obsolete style of the Victorian three-decker. In fact his craft of fiction developed remarkably well between 1880 and 1900, between *Workers in the Dawn* and *Eve's Ransom*, a development all the more laudable when contrasted with the pattern of so many Victorian novelists who found a recipe for easy and successful production and followed it slavishly in order to make a profit. Gissing was one of the few novelists aware that a revolution in both the technique of fiction and the mode of living was taking place, and slowly he emancipated himself from the old Victorian conventions.

He began writing in the seventies in the only tradition of the novel that was popular, the three-volume giant complete with "moral thesis, plot, underplot, set characters, descriptive machinery, landscape coloring, copious phraseology, Herculean proportions. . ."[5] He interrupted the narrative in order to comment upon characters and action, frequently digressed, and devoted whole chapters to the antecedents of characters. His earliest model was Dickens — as a boy he had read the Dickens novels in serial parts — and he had all the ambition of Dickens without any of the humor. But even in the early sprawling books Gissing showed the dogged honesty that would become the hallmark of his novels. He believed in 1880, as he believed at the end of his life, in writing to express truth as he saw it, not as interpreted by Mrs. Grundy. It is true that his escape from the old narrative conventions was neither sudden nor brilliant, but he did escape at last, after years of steady tugging at the fetters.

The difference in technical efficiency and point of view becomes clear when *Workers in the Dawn* is contrasted with *Eve's Ransom*. In the earlier novel Arthur Golding labors through three volumes to decide what he will do with his life. He first joins a workingmen's reformist movement; then he yearns to be an artist and to the devil with the life of a crusader. His wish comes true by dint of the favorite machinery of Dickens — the will of a conscientious man — but soon Golding becomes ashamed of his "selfishness" and marries a girl of the working class as part of his expiation. She deceives him most sordidly, but the letter of the marriage keeps him from union with the "angel" in the novel, a young woman who quotes Kant and Comte and who is not realized as an individual. The third volume ends with the suicide of the hero, as indeed it has to do, since the author at this stage saw life only in terms of the glorious gesture.

Eve's Ransom, by contrast, is a single slim volume. In it the provincial hero recognizes his limitations, knows that the sudden legacy he has received cannot change appreciably the probable road before him, and, attracted to a woman who is only mildly responsive to him, he spends his money on a trip to Paris with her. Were he Arthur Golding, he would digress on the beauties of the Louvre and would prefer two women to one, one a strumpet to arouse his feelings of guilt and the other an angel to provide an opportunity for sublimation. However, the young man of *Eve's Ransom* is now described by a much older man than Arthur Golding, and his trip to Paris has nothing in it of orgy. The couple return to London where the hero is promptly deserted, in the kindest way, in favor of a more prosperous friend who offers the lady not necessarily an ideal love, but at least a red brick villa in the suburbs. And by this time Gissing's heroines are real enough to appreciate the value of a red brick villa! As for the bereft young man, he is at first unhappy, but then, after an interview with the girl, goes off to the country.

"A white frost had suddenly hastened the slow decay of mellow autumn. Low on the landscape lay a soft mist. . . A perfect quiet possessed the air, but from every branch, as though shaken by some invisible hand, dead foliage dropped to earth in a continuous shower . . . the grasses by the wayside stood stark in gleaming mail.

"And Maurice Hilliard, a free man in his own conceit, sang to himself a song of the joy of life."

The flavor of *Eve's Ransom* is subacid. The style is concise, dramatic. The more noisome aspects of romantic love have disappeared, and with them Gissing's usual paralyzing identification with the hero, his prolixity and didacticism. Indeed a comparison with the urbane and dexterous work of George Meredith could be justly made.

Even in Gissing's own day few critics were aware of the gradual maturing of his work, and among general readers there was even less recognition of his ability. Gissing was no more a "popular" author at the end of his career than he had been at the beginning. 1897 was his "Year of Terror" because, after seventeen years of publishing, his income had dropped again to barely one hundred pounds, little enough to support a wife and two children.[6] His competence in telling a story had improved, but publishers continued to tell him that his work was too "pessimistic" or that it was too sharp in probing "the public truth," that body of convention which is not necessarily reality but which the general public prefers to consider as such.

It is a curious anomaly that Thomas Hardy's brand of pessimism became popular although Gissing's variety never did. However, Hardy gave the reader "strong" scenes, and, on the whole, was able to ennoble characters through suffering. He had been a clever apprentice in the school of the sensation novel as taught by Dickens and Wilkie Collins, and he made shrewd use of his skill, so that the reader was both titillated and purged, enjoyable sensations, like having one's cake and eating it too. But Gissing denied the reader such a pattern. Unlike Tess of the D'Urbervilles, few of the men and women of his novels are permitted to pluck the heartstrings of the reader in pathetic expiation of sins of passion. Even when loved ones die, like Alma in *The Whirlpool* or Lilian in *Denzil Quarrier,* the survivors must get on with the business of life with limited capacity to make speeches of protest or revenge. As Godwin Peak says acidly in *Born in Exile,* "In general, the more complex a man's mechanism and the more pronounced his habit of introspection, the less capable is he of loving with vehemence and constancy. Heroes of passion are for the most part primitive natures, nobly tempered; in our time they tend to extinction."

But the English reading public refused to concede that the type was almost extinct, and they retaliated by ignoring the notices of Gissing's books in the press. The *Athenaeum* summed up the peculiar impression left by the novels: "Mr. George Gissing is unable to write a book which is not powerful, and unwilling (apparently) to write one that is not disagreeable — that is, the writing is interesting, and often witty and full of insight; but he never creates a character, as far as we can judge, which he wishes one to admire..." [7]

Gissing realized, even from the beginning, that his views might alienate the majority, and he also foresaw difficulties with publishers. Of his first novel he predicted, "Its circulation — if it attains one — must be among the strictly intellectual classes." [8] Or again, "We are too apt to forget the deplorable state of the intellect of 999 out of every 1000 men, that utter absence of receptivity, that absolute lack of formulative power which renders the assault of a new idea as little effective as that of a cannon-ball against a feather bed." [9] The result of Gissing's feud with the general reader was that his life's work was never collected in a uniform edition. Not until 1935 was *Workers in the Dawn* made readily available, *Isabel Clarendon* has never been reprinted, and most of the other titles have appeared in haphazard fashion, with the reason for the publisher's selection remaining, in some cases, a mystery to the reader. Before his death Gissing foresaw the dismal prospect and tried desperately to have all the copyrights bought by a single publisher. Lawrence and Bullen nearly came to the rescue, until they plunged, like so many publishers of the day, into oblivion.

If Gissing has never enjoyed a large public, he has received some praises from far-flung corners. German critics considered him the founder of modern English realism,[10] and in Gissing's own England a critic acquainted with the new French naturalism was heard to pronounce Gissing's work "more valuable . . . than the whole De Goncourt series." [11] A comparison has even been dared, this time in the United States, between Gissing's *The Whirlpool* and Flaubert's *Madame Bovary*, with Gissing's novel faring better than one might expect.

"It is fair to say that the heroine of *The Whirlpool* is the English Madame Bovary, depicted with more conscientious art upon a larger and more crowded canvas. The carefulness with which Gissing has worked in the details makes Flaubert's treatment of them look patchy. Flaubert has, however, the inestimable advantage of sharp outline, vivid colour, and boldly simplified form. He remains far above Gissing in concentration, in 'interest,' though for all that *The Whirlpool* may be the more solid performance." [12]

Probably the best and the briefest comment upon the characteristic quality of Gissing's work was made by the *Academy:* "Mr. Gissing is in love with ideas and can illustrate them through flesh and blood: his work lives." [13]

Here lies the importance of Gissing's work, as Mrs. Woolf also has insisted, that he is consistently a novelist of ideas,[14] although he needed many years to learn to express them subtly instead of didactically. He is therefore one of those novelists who must be taken seriously when read at all; he always gives "a solid performance." He is not interested merely in attracting the reader's attention; he wishes to *engage* it.

Gissing's fiction, therefore, is well worth serious regard, but it is his life that doubtless holds most interest for the general reader as well as the student of Victorian psychology. This interest is all the more roused as formerly unpublished materials become available, for clearly Gissing's diaries and unexpurgated letters are as important in the Victorian period, as well as more frank, as are *The Autobiography of Mark Rutherford,* John Stuart Mill's *Autobiography,* Ruskin's *Praeterita,* or Butler's *The Way of All Flesh.* All of these reveal fundamental conflicts in thinking men of the day, conflicts that began in the family circle and acquired larger significance as the circle expanded.

The central problem for Gissing, as it often is for earnest, rational beings in a time of transition, was that of the solitary in search of a tradition and an allegiance. From the very days of boyhood Gissing found it difficult to identify himself with a group on terms which he could respect, a difficulty that stemmed, in large measure, from the example of his parents. Thomas Waller Gissing suffered from the conflict of ambition and necessity. He earned his living as a shopkeeper, a chemist, but he kept aloof from other shopkeepers and indulged his taste for serious reading and botanizing. Occasionally his observations were printed, an achievement that doubtless increased his self-esteem but drew him further apart from his neighbors. Gissing's mother, unlike his father, was capable of no intellectual distinction, but she too entertained hopes of higher social status and indulged her vexation over her limitations by scorning her commonplace neighbors. Both mother and father were rigid moralists, with charity and humor remaining qualities quite out of their reach, and scorn, masked under righteousness, their salient trait. In later years George Gissing idealized his father (never his mother) as a man without prejudice, but the reminiscences jotted down in 1884 suggest that Thomas Waller Gissing was in fact not above reproach in this respect. Thus scorn, imitated before it was understood, became second nature to young Gissing and brought loneliness in its wake, since the barrier of class seemed impossible to surmount. The premature death of Thomas Gissing removed what little security the family had enjoyed, and the eldest son was left with a nascent misanthropy, precocious learning, and little else. Thus the way was prepared for the series of catastrophes in which Gissing imagined himself, as Dickens in similar circumstances had done before him, alternately martyr and criminal. He felt isolated and rejected and wavered between scorn of his fellows and a vast inadequacy before them.

To the unwary bystander there would seem in Gissing a compulsive urge to self-destruction, a febrile refusal to make compromises and adjustments, but more careful study reveals gradual learning in which he slowly evolved a new set of aims and methods as he faced the intricacies of his own self-deception.

He began his dreams as a confused adolescent, weltering in a

tradition of romantic love in which he identified himself with
Palamon and Arcite and phantasied that a girl of the streets in
Manchester represented ideal love. Yet his mood was not consistent, for he chose to prove the depth of his passion by an act
savoring less of Palamon and Arcite than of Raskolnikov. The act
severed him from Owens College in Manchester and his one opportunity to attain distinction, the academic path, open to a man
without money and family. All he had left was the girl for whom
he had sacrificed himself, and, as she regressed through the
years, he learned to distinguish between reality and phantasy.
The final lesson was not learned, however, until one more unhappy adventure in marriage and more years of patience.

Just as in his domestic life he saw his ideal fade before reality, so
in political and social life he faced similar disillusionment. His
need to belong, to make himself important to other men, drove
him into partisan groups, at first Radicalism and then Positivism.
In his thick-soled boots he hurried to listen to speeches in workingmen's clubs in London and soon was lecturing to the workingmen instead of listening. In 1880 he described himself as a member of the "advanced Radical party" [15] which he defined as a
group impatient with the venal concerns of existing government
and hostile to "Ritualism." The group, which was not really a
party at all, was a heterogeneous collection of dissenters, with no
party discipline. Gissing shared its enthusiasms even when personal relationships with workingmen (among them some of his
London relations) disgusted him. However, Radicalism continued to seem loosely articulated, and soon Gissing turned his attention to a more tightly organized body of thought, the Positivism of Auguste Comte.

Positivism meant for him no less than "the science of social
life," which, curiously enough, he distinguished from "miserable
empiricism." Ultimately, Gissing believed, Positivism would free
men "from the state of social anarchy into which we are at present
plunged." [16] The Positivist method was to study the history of

knowledge and to deduce the general rules by which the future of the race could be predicted. The prediction was an optimistic one — no less than continued "intellectual and moral progress."

Gissing was at first quite certain that Positivism would make metaphysics unnecessary, and would undermine any theory of pessimism. By the end of 1882, however, his personal problems as well as his reading had so pushed him into scepticism that he forsook Comte's doctrine, abandoned "The Religion of Humanity," and advised his own brother to read Kant. The final stage reached was, clinically, depersonalization, in which Gissing looked at all things as phenomena and made no moral judgments.

By the mid-eighties Gissing had recovered from complete denial of the responsibility for making judgments, but he had also given up hope for comfort from philosophy or from any system. Now he devoted himself to reading the most daring writing of the period — Spencer, Marx, Buckle, Bourget, Romanes, eventually Frazer of *The Golden Bough*. He studied comparative religion and the new psychology, particularly the experiments in animal intelligence, which could have been no happy reminder of Positivism. To supplement his reading he roamed the streets of London and Birmingham, Paradise Street and Whitecross, with his notebook in hand, looking for raw material for the harsh novels that he was turning out two or three in a year. It was his ambition in this period to describe all London life, although he knew his method was different from that of most English novelists. When his brother remonstrated with him on the frankness of his fiction, Gissing reminded him that on the continent such work was anything but "startling." [17]

Gissing emerged from his lonely researches, from the libraries as from the streets, confirmed in cynicism. He had a poor opinion of the species as a whole, particularly the variety of his country and century. The new democracy that most men were acclaiming, as well as the fast-growing technology, augured, in his opinion, the rule of barbarians, with increasing possibility of colossal wars. Whether it is expressed in a letter of 1880, 1892, or 1902, Gissing's distrust of slogans is patent. For him the only hope of survival for the race was the realization of individual moral responsibility, without the need for supernatural guidance or mandate by the state. Yet the capacity for the lonely search after truth was to be found in only a few individuals. The age itself Gissing could describe only as "thoroughly empty, mean, wind-baggish. . ." [18]

Yet Gissing had to admit that he could not linger eternally in the past, but must cope as best he could with the present. The necessity sometimes made him feel as sick as he had been during a ramble in Greece, looking for ideal associations, when he discovered that the well of the Eumenides had degenerated into an ordure-ground.

The only kind of crusade for which Gissing could muster any enthusiasm as the years went on was the one for the emancipation of the novelist from Mrs. Grundy. Gissing knew that the battle was not likely to be won in his lifetime: he wrote in 1884, "English novels are miserable stuff for a very miserable reason, simply because English novelists fear to do their best lest they should damage their popularity, and consequently their income." [19]

It must be remembered that Gissing moved with the new currents of his era, away from the pleasant, though stagnant, places which the proper Englishman preferred. The jolly Briton was not so jolly as he saw his retreats invaded: in 1888 he sent the publisher Vizetelly to prison for publishing in England such "immoral" French novelists as Flaubert and Zola.[20] Rebels like Gissing reacted with like harshness against the Philistines, and he, with many of the rebels, finally went into exile in France. It is true that Gissing departed for France not solely because of disappointments in England, but because he wished to make a new beginning with Gabrielle Fleury, whom British law could not recognize as his wife. But even before he left England, he was for most of his years an exile from the social life of the English intellectual: although such men as Carlyle and Matthew Arnold and Frederic Harrison protested some of the hypocrisies in English society, they behaved with as much propriety as Samuel Smiles himself would have endorsed. Breeding and profession and success kept them decorous, though they might think daringly.

Nor was Gissing able to find comrades among the new crop of Bohemians flourishing in defiance of the middle class from which so many of them sprang. On the contrary, he regarded the antics of the precious young men — Moore and his boa constrictor, Wilde and his green carnation — as fatuous. In temperament Gissing was as earnest, as deadly earnest, as the older generation of the English statesman-intellectual, although his lack of worldly success had forced him into retreat from those clubs and drawing rooms where his intellectual attainments might best have been appreciated. He was an accomplished classicist who read Homer for pleasure after teaching Greek verbs to dolts; he feasted on elegiac poetry after a meal of split lentils; and he read Dante's *Inferno* to the accompaniment of gusts of smoke from the Baker Street Railway.

But to dwell overlong on the small ironies of Gissing's life is to forget that the importance of the life does not lie in such a catalogue, but in the search which a gifted and hard-pressed man made for a set of values. Gissing had all the varied interests of a Humanist without belief in God or the assurance that man's right reason is either commonly found in the species or prized when found at all. His groping for a concept of moral responsibility which should serve in spite of the absence of any divine canon of ethics was nobly pursued although he entered the world already dispossessed, and in the flush of youth threw away the little chance that he had for success of the conventional kind.

And, as he strove to make order out of chaos, in his fiction as in his life, the end-of-the-century world revolved wildly around him, with a near war with Russia, a real one with Boers, the Irish Rebellion and Trafalgar Square riots, and the great Reform

Bills. At the end of his life, although he had worked out a philosophy, Gissing still belonged to no man's party.

"I am able to look at both sides, and to laugh at the weaknesses of both. This is why the conservative organs have frequently spoken of me as if I were of their party. The uncompromising party of radicalism still regard me with doubt; I do not go far enough for them, or at all events do not speak with sufficient intolerance." [21]

Chapter 2

EARLY INFLUENCES

H. G. Wells, who became a friend only in the last few years of Gissing's life, was one of the canniest, as well as one of the most vociferous, Englishmen at the turn of the century: it was both his gift and his limitation that he evolved large theories from small acquaintance. In judging Gissing, as in judging most subjects (and Gissing was to him rather a "subject" than a dear comrade), he was able to make an acute observation although the evidence in support of it was scanty: Thomas Waller Gissing, he declared, was "the chief formative influence" upon his son's character.[1]

Today the central role of the father in shaping the child's aims and methods has become almost a truism, after the propagandizing of the psychiatrists; in Wells's day the remark must have seemed an affront to those who preferred to minimize the irrational, emotional sources of values. In any case, it is clear from the extant diaries of Gissing that Wells was right, but that he did not guess how important a role, unconsciously played, Gissing's mother had for her son.

Gissing's ambivalent opinions of his mother were seldom expressed in writing (although they were acute when finally made conscious), but his admiration of his father, mixed with wonder and nostalgia, was noted again and again through the years, at times in places where the note was almost irrelevant. Thus in 1902, only a year before his death, he interpolated in a commemorative article on Charles Dickens an appreciation of his dead father.[2] It is true that the personal touch made for intimacy in a journal admittedly not academic in its approach; nevertheless, Gissing's manner when contrasting his father's study and its "empty chair" with Dickens' study is that of a melancholy man who has not yet stopped thinking of himself as an orphan. That is to say, he felt deprived at his father's death of the one being who most supported his peculiar abilities, for his mother scarcely understood them.

The digging into memory went on constantly — in 1884, when he jotted down in the manuscript (which has never been printed), "Reminiscences of My Father," [3] phrases as vivid as if the death had occurred in that very year instead of in 1870; in 1896, when he searched in the British Museum through the Index of British Botanists and thrilled to see his father's name listed there,[4] reassuring him that the family was not "ordinary." Through the years when he wrote to his sisters in Wakefield, Yorkshire, he made regular requests for books from his father's library, the fine collection that preserved the family from classification with other tradesmen (and to the self-conscious Gissings this distinction was as important as bread itself). Indeed, in moods of depression Gissing turned over his recollections of his father as a poor man fondles pieces of gold.

The nineteenth century is rich in reminiscences of fathers in which deference rubs against defiance, probably because economic pressure forced the son to remain too long under his father's roof and domination. Gissing's reminiscences show the same mingled emotions.[5] His father's study and herbarium were ever associated in his mind with warmth and light — the recollections are strongly sensory in character — ". . . the smell of camphor always brings it back to me. . . In the same room stood an aquarium, and the sunlight, reflected in the water, used to dance on the ceiling, and often drew my eyes from a book." Days of reading and daydreaming were spent in a room which bore only his father's influence, the plants later described in botanical journals, the substantial volumes of Gibbon, Thirlwall, Humboldt, Hogarth, as well as the standard works of English literature — Shakespeare, Jonson, Burton, the major poets, the Waverley novels. But since George Gissing was precocious as a child, it soon occurred to him that his father was not a "learned" man in the strict sense of the word. Naïvely he felt shocked because his father "was not aware that the Greeks and Romans never rhymed," and later he realized, with some horror, that his father's taste in poetry was not cultivated, that it preferred commemorative verse of an obvious kind. It is irony that the fastidiousness which Thomas Gissing inculcated in his son was in the final analysis directed against the teacher, for the boy could tolerate nothing but the impeccable even in those he loved most.

Ambition and love of learning were among the finer values that Thomas Gissing passed on to his son, but equally important in the legacy were the qualities that brought so much unhappiness in the son's later life: fervent distrust of the mass of men, and rigid moral judgment. Gissing wrote in 1884: "We children did not associate with the children of any other shopkeepers in Wakefield. Of the other chemists my father had the poorest — even contemptuous — opinion." For, of course, Thomas Gissing considered his amateur botanizing and zealous reading insurance against classification with the tribe, although his means as proprietor of a small chemist's establishment scarcely permitted him to live in the style he preferred. The neighbors resented the attitude of superiority, and Thomas Gissing and his son were aware of the resentment without having the capacity to allay it. "When the shop caught on fire and we ran a risk of being burnt out, father said afterwards that the mob would have stood in the streets and 'cheered as each floor fell through.'" This must surely have been a traumatic experience for the boy, impressing upon him the hostility of the neighbors and emphasizing his isolation. Interestingly enough, some of the most powerful scenes in Gissing's novels, in *Demos* above all, are "mob" scenes, when the mob thirsts for the blood of one lonely fugitive.

Thomas Gissing saw to it, too, that his son was instructed in morality, although he denied any supernatural basis for the code he taught. His son recalled, "He once stopped with me at the top of Market Street to point out a drunken fellow reeling by — on the principle, of course, which activated the Spartans when they made a Helot drunk and exhibited him to their boys. I wonder whether he knew of the precedent." Such moral instruction left its impression, and years later George Gissing was never to finish a bottle of wine without the conviction that he was being libertine, or, at least, "a gay dog."

Whatever anxieties Gissing was later to suffer because of the influence of his father, fear of damnation and caviling before the powerful were not among them. It was with enthusiasm that Thomas Gissing described for his son the forcing by the barons of concessions from proud King John, and with enthusiasm he read the Radical press of his own era, *The Leader,* edited by G. H. Lewes. He had also read Lewes' *History of Philosophy* and approved its freethinking, and he knew the work of Darwin. His own freethinking, it must be admitted, was of the forthright, almost simple-minded variety: the son recalls, "I remember his ridiculing the belief of the world being created by 'a man standing up and ordering it to exist.'" It is therefore a tribute to George Gissing that in at least three novels—*The Unclassed, A Life's Morning,* and *The Emancipated* — he tried to understand the nature of the religious experience, even though his father's position was cynical.

Thomas Waller Gissing, born in 1829 in Halesworth, Suffolk, had five children in all, but of them George was the most precocious. His reading ranged from *That's It, or Plain Teaching,* a pedestrian summary of natural wonders, to J. Eastmead's Lecture upon Gladstone's book *Juventus Mundi.* His early interest in the classical past, an interest that he would pursue through a lifetime, is manifest in his construction at the age of ten of "a model of a Roman trireme, the oars moving by steam." On the same day that he built the trireme he experimented with a locomotive engine:[6] clearly he was not interested exclusively in the artifacts of antiquity! The reading list he drew up in his own hand and which still survives, is also eclectic: Shakespeare, Dickens, J. Fenimore Cooper, *Robinson Crusoe,* Wordsworth, *The Boy's Book of Adventures,* two volumes of Greek grammar.[7]

At the age of ten he was avidly seeking his father's approval by doing outstanding work at school. His sister Ellen tells the story of his running off to classes with a herring bone stuck in his throat rather than miss a lesson.[8] His sketching, too, pleased his father, and away on holiday he sent sketches home through the mail and gave lessons in perspective to his little brothers. Clearly he learned at an early age to be didactic!

He was unusually earnest and pensive, but before his father's death, at least, while he attended Harrison's school in Wakefield, he was gregarious enough to join one of the customary secret societies formed by young boys. Curiously enough, to this very day the boys' fabricated deed to lands in the Antarctic has been preserved.[9] However, as George Gissing approached adolescence he turned his phantasies from manly explorations in strange lands to ideal love. He began a story entitled "My Clerical Rival."

"She was the fair Emelye who appeared on that May morning to the mournful prisoner Palamon; she was the heavenly vision of the 'Sensitive Plant'; she was all these, yet more than any of them, so deliciously real and present before my senses." [10]

At the age of thirteen, the year his father died, the boy was ill-prepared to venture forth into the world about him. He was an insatiable reader, for had not his father told him that learning was all that mattered; he was wildly imaginative; and he was conscious of his own superiority. Now bereft of his father, he knew no other ways to secure approval than those which had been successful, at least at home, for so long. Prizes for their own sake did not matter to him; the important consideration was the approval of the "special" people in his life. Approval he received aplenty from his brothers and sisters, to whom he was now increasingly the paterfamilias. He never outgrew the role: at ten he gave them directions for sketching, at twenty he drew up reading lists for them, fearful that life in the provinces would render them intellectually slothful. When occasionally they disagreed with him, as Ellen did years later over his portrait of a religious woman in *The Emancipated*, he was beside himself with anxiety, sending long letters, half-apologetic, half-defiant.

At the death of Thomas Gissing, the three sons were sent to a Quaker boarding school at Alderley Edge in Worcestershire, the two sisters remaining in Wakefield. Here George became acquainted with Mr. James Wood, the headmaster, and his family, who attended Quaker meeting.[11] Most of the other boys went to Wilmslowchurch, however, so that there is little reason to ascribe George's habit of introspection primarily to the influence of Quakers; the trait was well established even before the death of his father.

Once again George plunged into his studies, classical studies above all, and in his leisure time he produced and composed plays in blank verse. A marked copy of "Love's Labour Lost," with stage directions, survives,[12] as does Gissing's original play, "King Richard I."[13] Fragment though the latter is, it testifies to the boy's precocious love of literature and to some skill in blank verse. In the spring of 1872 he was cramming for the "great exam, the Oxford. . . If I pass all I go up for, I shall have passed five this half."[14] He did more than "pass": he performed so well in the Oxford Local Examination that he won the Junior Exhibition of 1872 offered by the Senate of Owens College in Manchester. The Exhibition provided free tuition for three sessions.[15]

There was satisfaction in studying and being rewarded at school, but the other side of the medal was fatigue and depression. In April of 1873, for example, he went on a long walking trip through North Wales, on a visit to Mr. Wood, who had bought a house in Colwyn Bay. It was a glorious excursion through a beautiful countryside, and the letter to Mrs. Gissing which describes the trip is full of self-confidence and good spirits, as though the writer felt powerful enough to scale mountains! [16] But in a letter written within the same period, to a school friend named Bowes, Gissing mentions the walking trip only in a postscript and emphasizes instead his loneliness and misery at school: ". . . there is no other, no, to the shame of the school be it said, not one other, who would intelligently appreciate what I know you would." [17] It is true, of course, that boys of this age often search for a boon companion, but already the polarity in Gissing's temperament is clear — exhilaration followed by depression, gregariousness followed by scorn of the herd. Above all, he had a precocious ability to make these feelings verbal. The vocabulary and phrasing of the letters of his school days are not those of the average youth, and in the surviving fragments of his "creative writing" during schooldays — the "fair Emelye" passage of his short story and the brief scene of "King Richard I," sensitivity to literary associations is manifest. And in two short poems credited to the period at Alderley Edge, "On a Dead Primrose Plucked in Early Spring" and "The Sky at Sunset," [18] his quicksilver reaction to beautiful things, touched with awareness of mutability and death, is painfully apparent.

He carried his precocity, his quick changes of mood, and his prizes to Manchester, a huge city to a fifteen-year old from a small town. Owens was a new college, founded in 1852 with the pious hope expressed by the principal, A. J. Scott, in a speech to the business men of Manchester, that it would turn out bigger and better citizens of Manchester.[19] Gissing, at least, it turned out — literally — and he in turn anatomized the college and himself in *Born in Exile* of 1892. Owens College was later incorporated as the Victoria University of Manchester, but in Gissing's youth it would have been useful principally as a jumping-off place for the great universities of Oxford, Cambridge, and London. In fact Gissing matriculated with high honors at the University of London in June of 1874. Although Owens had its strongest reputation in the sciences, for the new municipal red-brick colleges were already more interested in the laboratory than in literature, Gissing interested himself largely in languages and literature, and at the end of the first session won Professor Ward's English Poem prize for his poem "Ravenna" (the crises of ancient cultures already fascinated him) and a prize and exhibition in Classics. In 1875 he took first place in Latin and English in the examination for honors following the Intermediate B.A. He also won a Shakespeare scholarship. It was an impressive academic record and augured well for the future of the young man from Wakefield.

There was gratification, of course, from such honors, but the deepest emotional needs of the boy remained unsatisfied. He might well compose prize-winning poems on heroic moments in history, but in his daily life there was little opportunity for heroism, or even for commonplace dignity, and he was painfully aware of the hiatus between his literary phantasies of Rome and Ravenna and the everyday sordid reality of manufacturing Manchester. He lived in a boarding house, with a pittance for spending money. Nothing seemed further removed than the delights of old, the walking trips in the country, the poems on a dead primrose or a sunset. Indeed it must frequently have been difficult to see a sunset through the smoke of a bustling Midlands city.

There was one phantasy which would not fade, however, even in Manchester — "fair Emelye" or ideal love. This time the young woman of Gissing's choice possessed not only such qualities as youth, comeliness, and dependency upon a knight who would protect her, but the most compelling attraction of all — beautiful, injured innocence. She was Marianne Helen Harrison, "Nell," only seventeen when George Gissing met her. She had already turned to prostitution as a livelihood, and she became thereafter her benefactor's mistress, in 1879 his wife, and, finally, his tormentor.

The scandal in which Gissing became involved in Manchester

is certainly the most sordid, as well as the most pitiful, in a life that had more than the usual share of sordid encounters. Several decades after Gissing's student days, another pupil at Manchester lamented, in an alumni publication, that in Gissing's day a program for the social needs of the student had been ignored by the college.[20] There is indeed no indication that the college cared a fig what happened to her precocious students after they left the lecture hall, but there is also no indication that such a student as Gissing would have participated in any organized community life. He made few friends at Owens, one of them Morley Roberts, who remains today the principal source, although not altogether an accurate one, for information on this crucial period in Gissing's life. One day, according to Roberts' book of reminiscences, in which Gissing figures under a pseudonym,[21] George, or "Henry Maitland," announced that he had fallen in love with Nell. According to Roberts, he was not to be dissuaded from the attachment and indeed began to "reclaim" the girl by giving her a sewing machine so that she could abandon her former trade.

Clearly he viewed himself as the savior of a girl victimized by society rather than by a single villain — a more modern concept than his earlier adolescent one but just as heavily laden with emotion. He must have felt frustrated that the material thing the girl needed most — money — was the thing he could least provide. A series of thefts began in the men's locker room at the college, detectives were assigned to the case, and George Gissing was the student who was finally apprehended and then dismissed from the college.[22]

It was the very last fate that a superficial prediction would have named for an earnest young scholar, a conscientious son, a fervent paterfamilias. Suddenly, for the sake of a young girl he had known for only a short time, he threw away honor and academic prowess, the most secure way of advancement available to a boy without wealth or family name. Why, his family and friends must have shuddered, had he committed such an act?

It would be too simple to see in this calamity the first example, of the many available, of Gissing's capacity for self-destruction, the act of a novice studying for the role of Empedocles. It is true that Gissing showed a terrible urge to punish himself in many crises in his life, for he never quite decided whether he was more sinned against than sinning; but on this occasion several impulses fused to make a positive act of defiance of bourgeois society, executed with premeditation and followed by regret for the contingent suffering of his family, but by no feeling of personal guilt. First of all, Gissing was not seeking to destroy himself: he considered himself Nell's champion and continued his relationship with her throughout the ordeal and throughout the subsequent exile in America. Secondly, the fact that the thefts were executed in a series suggests premeditation rather than a sudden urge to immolation of self. Above all, young Gissing's scorn for the community at large, which had its roots deep in the environment of Wakefield, must have left little room for guilt in the usual sense of the word, over transgressing "the law." What was the law to him but a manifestation of the self-interest of those wealthier than he who exploited such innocents as Nell? He felt no awe before such people, felt indeed his own intellectual superiority, though he winced at his shabbiness. Years later, in writing about Dostoevski and young Raskolnikov, Gissing would comment that to the average Englishman, with his simple-minded view of caveats, the twists and turnings of the mind of the Russian intellectual were incomprehensible;[23] perhaps Gissing remembered that he himself had been prey, at the age of eighteen, to terrible casuistry, and that he too had felt misunderstood by his judges. It must surely have seemed to him, in the arrogant days of his adolescence, justifiable to steal from a society he did not respect for the sake of the maiden society had wronged, since doubtless he viewed prostitution in the manner of most idealists, as a trade foisted upon the helpless by a debauched plutocracy. (It occurred to him some years later, when Nell had returned to her old haunts and habits, that constitutional factors were also involved.) According to this reasoning, transgression of the law could be excused. The only cause for remorse would be the possible humiliation of the family in Wakefield, but doubtless their reaction was considered less important than "a higher cause." Indeed, according to his own logic, apprehension by police power would be accidental — irrelevant, actually, to the moral issue. The catalyst, of course, for the whole process was the strong sexual feeling that he was experiencing for the first terrible time.

But if Gissing was able to rationalize his conduct, Owens College and his own mother could not readily do so. The one dismissed him, after giving him a certificate testifying to courses studied, and the other was in a stronger position than ever as judge. For years Mrs. Gissing was the source of her son's ambivalent feelings toward women, and only toward the end of his life did he break the tie he hated yet preserved. Indeed, a modern critic maintains that Gissing's novels are weakened by his often extreme views of women — an absurdly sentimental overevaluation or rabid hatred.[24]

Mrs. Gissing and Nell never overcame their mutual hostility. When Nell, as Gissing's wife, asked to be remembered to brother Algernon, Gissing added sadly in a postscript that he wished his mother were included in the good wishes.[25] For his mother kept herself and her daughters resolutely away from the girl whom she blamed for the ruin of her son's fortunes; indeed, even in 1879, Ellen and Margaret had still been told nothing of Nell.[26] When, in 1884, Nell, sick and irresponsible, was altogether estranged from him, Gissing was so confused about his mother that he believed himself unable to give a reliable opinion of her.

"I was rather struck with some remarks Mrs. Gaussen made about Mother's portrait the other day, in looking over my album. She said it was a strikingly handsome face, and extraordinarily full of character. I amazed her by explaining that I was really quite unable to say whether the character was in reality there or not; so utterly a stranger, on reflection, do I find my own mother to be to me. A curious state of things." [27]

What he was really turning over in his mind was whether the "character" in his mother's face was expressive of superb moral caliber or mere pettifogging; or, by extension, whether he ought to feel guilty before a righteous judge, or whether he was entitled to dismiss that judge as a fussy termagant whose views, therefore, need no longer be feared. He finally made the latter diagnosis, but he did not experience heady release from his former guilt and fear until 1888, when Nell died. It must be emphasized that at the time of his "crime" in Manchester he did not wince in his soul before his mother. It was only after Nell disappointed him again and again, sinking deeper into the slough each year, that his self-confidence ebbed away and it seemed by default that his mother was the victor, she who had such a simple and rigid moral code. But when Nell finally died Gissing felt a surging relief (characteristically he felt guilty at first over the sense of relief!) not only from her but from his mother, for the two women were intimately related in his emotions. Being rid of the reminder of his shame, Nell, he was now able to rid himself of the judge of his shame, his mother. At last he wrote about her not as an awesome enigma, but as she probably was, an obsessive woman plagued by the peccadillos of her neighbors. It was in 1888 during a visit to his brother and sister-in-law in Worcestershire that George finally found words to express his new realization of the contrast between his mother's character and his own. He wrote to his sister:

"Never do I hear a word in Worcestershire about household concerns; never is a meal discussed; never is the servant referred to in our conversation. Everything of that nature *comes to pass* merely; it is not wearisomely laboured over. . . Now *is* it worth sacrificing this human progress and peace for the sake of making sure that there is nothing in the kitchen that might not be

better? . . . No, but then, of course, the inhabitants of a house
must unite in recognizing that the mind is of more account than
the body. Mother would grant you that hypothetically, but we
know sadly enough that her paradise is in precisely the opposite
direction. It is a sad, sad thing that anyone should be rendered
incapable of spiritual activity by ceaseless regard for kitchen-ware
and the back-door steps." [28]

Not only did his changed view of his mother permit more self-
confidence in his relations with women, but, more important, it
encouraged a Flaubertian, balanced presentation of female characters in later novels rather than a naïve dichotomy of angels
and succubi.

In 1876, however, Gissing was not yet forced to make a house
cleaning of his values; instead he took the comparatively easy way
out of an impasse — exile. Rather than remain in England he set
out for the United States, without ceasing, however, to correspond
with Nell, who saved his letters until her death.

Doubtless expressions of guilt and depression were deleted
from the letters printed in 1927 from the manuscripts of fifty
years earlier; nevertheless the tone that remains — most of the
letters of this period are long, even after editing — is surprisingly
cheerful, and seems to corroborate the theory that Gissing's feelings of guilt at this stage in his life were not nearly so strong as a
naïve censor might imagine. The flavor of the letters is that of a
bold adventure in the new world, in which the adventurer finds
a new and fresh vista almost daily. He filled his letters with "We
say" and "We do," as if he had already identified his fortunes with
those of the new country. He was footloose and eager, contemplated a trip cross-country to California, set out from Boston to
Chicago with the proverbial sixpence to last him all his life. Like
an incredulous child he marveled over the "giant" railway coaches
in the new country, and praised the abundance and variety in the
American diet as well as the abundance and variety of inventions,

including the telephone.[29] He settled for a time in a boarding house in Boston, on Bartlett Street, and determined to storm the world of publishing. In October of 1876 he described as his "principal friend," Mr. Lloyd Garrison, who knew the editor of the *Atlantic Monthly*, "one of our best periodicals." [30] He haunted the Boston Public Library, thus beginning the habit of sojourns in libraries that lasted a life long, and kept busy studying German. He considered quite seriously remaining in the New World, probably in Boston. It was the promised land for the intellectual, where "everybody" knew how to read and write, where "every" town had a free public library. (The libraries in England at this time were notoriously neither free nor public!) "Altogether Boston is a splendid place. I should be very sorry ever to leave it for good." [31]

It was necessary, of course, to earn money; so in mid-winter Gissing accepted the post of teacher of languages in the Waltham High School and agreed to teach French, German, and English for a salary of eight hundred dollars a year. He was surprised and delighted with the informality of relations between pupils and teacher: "The perfect order that prevails and the respect with which the masters are treated is delightful. I never saw anything like it in England." [32]

He was not content, however, with a life which, if secure, was soon dull. In January of 1877 he daydreamed idly about reported ice floes at Niagara; a few months later he gazed upon the very falls about which he had dreamed, and felt urged to suicide. But before he passed through the countryside of Niagara he had stayed for a time in Chicago. He had arrived there in March, and was soon on the brink of starvation.[33] Desperately he sought work from the editor of the Chicago *Tribune*, and with the bravado best summoned by a hungry man, agreed to submit short stories as yet unwritten. On March 10 the first story appeared, earnest and clumsy and sensational, called "The Sins of the Fathers." Altogether eleven stories belong to the days in Chicago, and these have been reprinted in *Brownie* and in *Sins of the Fathers and Other Tales*. For mawkishness, melodrama, and jargon they cannot be surpassed. In "RIP" there is the sudden death of a young bride; in "Gretchen" a trite artist-and-model situation. Vulgarisms are frequent: "a tolerably good-looking girl," "Brownie's uncle hated his neighbor like poison," "Hark! Was that the echo only of the scream?" However, although the stories were trash, they proved three things to the young author: that he could write marketable fiction; that the most popular situations for stories were "strong" ones; and that his strongest characters were the oppressed and the underprivileged. Already the theme of money — how to get it and how to keep it — had become a central theme in his writing.

The eighteen dollars that Gissing is alleged to have received for each story supported him meagerly in Chicago and sent him on his way to New York via Troy, where a newspaper had reprinted "The Sins of the Fathers." He hoped to receive a commission and further assignments, but instead he used up his last dollar and munched peanuts to keep from starving. Luckily, however, in July his description of the Farne Islands — the first in his long career of travel books — appeared in *Appleton's Journal,* with a payment of $45 for the author.[34]

New York was Gissing's next stop, but he stayed for only a month, and, much less optimistic than when he had set out, he returned to Massachusetts. This time he became a photographer's assistant (not a plumber, as the legend relates), canvassing New England towns from Massachusetts to Maine.[35] His boyhood skill in painting and sketching now earned him his bread as he made dismal lists of the hair-and-eye coloring of the burghers of New England, presumably so that he could "touch up" the portraits. Later, in his novels, he would be punctilious about the flare of a nostril, the glint in an eye; perhaps he was first compelled to notice such details on his tour of the New England hinterland. In any case it was a new kind of reading for a bookish young man.

After going so far afield as Portland, Maine, Gissing returned to Boston in September and was back in Liverpool on October 3, 1877. Like Henry James, who was traveling in luxury while young Gissing traveled steerage, he was fleeing the Americans, after a year of deepening disillusionment. The experiment in repatriation had lasted a year. Behind Gissing were his few friends — Lloyd Garrison, whose death he was deeply to regret,[36] and two old ladies in Boston, who would send, as late as 1897, a gift to his infant son.[37] With him, ever-present anxiety, was the memory of his American debt, the clothing and beloved books left behind as "security:"[38] He was not able, until three years later, to finish paying back the money he owed; altogether he was so oppressed by the thought of penury that he had nightmares about the "moving mountains of water" of Niagara,[39] and in his first published novel, in which the protagonist also learns disillusionment and despair in the new world, the end is suicide in the great falls.[40]

The hated American debt was, nevertheless, the lesser of the two hatreds that living in America had engendered. The deeper, the incurable one, came as Gissing realized that egalitarianism and high degree of literacy, the two aspects of American life that he had most admired, were not as prevalent as he had believed. He had become soured over American politics as early as January of 1877, after the election of Mr. Hayes, Republican, as President:

"You know the election for president was held last year, and no decision has yet been arrived at as to who is elected. There has been so much corruption in the South . . . where the whites oppress the black voters terribly, that the returns sent from the several States cannot at all be relied upon. Congress is at present considering a special bill for the counting of the votes for President and we hope it will pass and things be arranged amicably."[41]

This was a single sour observation; soon Gissing's diary, in which he aired his cynicism more openly than he dared in his letters home, was crammed with other marks of cynicism, written in elegant, spidery handwriting. He borrowed from great critics; from De Tocqueville he quoted, "Je ne pense pas qu'il y ait de pays dans le monde où, proportion gardé avec la population, il se trouve aussi peu d'ignorants et moins de savants qu'en Amérique." It was an epitome of Gissing's own view of egalitarianism! He noted near De Tocqueville's remark one of his own, "How the vulgar live under the tyranny of names. If you ask them to explain some process, etc. they think they do enough if they give you the *name* of it, and think you stupid if you do not understand." This was the other side of the medal, the scorn for the technocracy that formerly he had marveled over. Feeling misanthropy welling inside him, he tried to find guidance in the great rules of fine men, listing in his diary exhortations to integrity; from Goethe "Nur das Gesetz kann uns die Freiheit geben"; from Hegel, "The heritage a great man leaves the world is to force it to explain him"; from Marcus Aurelius and from Milton words of self-consecration to make the best use of innate powers. Like so many sensitive and intelligent men of the nineteenth century who felt overwhelmed by the sudden affluence of demos, Gissing was preoccupied with the duty of the gifted man in a world of mediocrity. He was never to desert this theme, but to return time and again to it, his great monomania.

Concern over the nature of greatness was not Gissing's sole preoccupation, as manifest in the diary never reprinted; he was also concerned over the love of man for woman, as well he might be, for that relationship had already determined the course of his life. As might be expected, he found the epigrams of French writers on this subject nearest to his own orientation. The couplet he copies from De Musset is a long way, in every sense, from Palamon and Arcite: "Aimer est le grand point; qu'importe la maîtresse? Qu'importe le flacon pour ce qu'on ait l'ivresse?" Near De Musset there bristle the words of Rousseau: "Tant il est vrai ce qui nous attache le plus aux femmes est moins la débauche qu'un certain agrément de vivre auprès d'elles!" Nevertheless, as a lorn testament to the hold that the concept of true love still had upon his emotions, there is a quotation from George Sand: "Il n'est qu'un bonheur au monde, c'est l'amour; tout le reste n'est rien, et il faut l'accepter par vertu." Never again would George Gissing be able to write a story like the juvenile "My Clerical Rival."

The degree of sophistication revealed in Gissing's selection of quotations from others is not at all matched by his sketches for stories of his own, also jotted down in the diary. Indeed these outlines seem startlingly immature, all the more because they jostle the urbanities of De Tocqueville and De Musset. Of the several sketches, the three following are representative.

Ugly, despised, and miserable man has trances in which he seems to possess love and treasure. Sees a girl who resembles something seen in a dream. Pursues her and her scorn kills him.

Woman secretly marries a wealthy man. He finds out from his friends that her sister is a fallen woman. He breaks with his wife, then discovers that the sister has reformed and holds an honorable position.

Young enthusiastic man marries and is deceived by his wife. Loses all faith in women and becomes —. Woman of the town falls in love with him and reclaims him.

Clearly the sketches are the rationalizing, whether consciously done or not, of Gissing's disastrous experiences in Manchester. It is significant that one girl resembles "something seen in a dream," just as Gissing's dream always surpassed the real woman; that a "woman of the town" reclaims a man, just as, Gissing liked to imagine, Nell's love would reclaim him; that redemption of men occurs after all seems hopeless, although scorn by the loved one can kill the lover. Guilt, inadequacy, redemption, sublimation mingle wildly in the tormented mind of a very young man.

Home again in England in the chill autumn of 1877, Gissing

found it difficult to rationalize the fact that there was a shambles behind him and no clear path ahead. He could not return to Wakefield, for after the events in Manchester and the freedom in America he could never live there on the old terms. London beckoned, as it always did to the desperate and dispossessed, and Gissing responded. He would receive a legacy of about three hundred pounds when he reached the age of twenty-one;[42] this vision he kept before him when he felt most discouraged. Meanwhile two ways of earning money suggested themselves to a man without a university degree, but with university training: he could be a tutor or a clerk. Fortified by his success in Waltham, Gissing decided to do tutoring, and to write when he had spare time. The experience of selling his stories in Chicago had made him hopeful that he could impress publishers in London. He might even be able to earn enough money to support Nell in London, after a year's separation from her. If only "body and brain" would hold strong, he confided to his brother, in the struggle for existence in London.[43]

Chapter 3

POVERTY AND DISGRACE

Today in the British Welfare State "workhouse" has be-
come a quaint word. The passerby with his cradle-to-the-grave
insurance scarcely notices the sullen brick fronts of the buildings
provided by the Poor Laws as the last resort of the poverty-
stricken. But to George Gissing, newly resident in London, a so-
journ in the workhouse was in the foreseeable future, whenever
his health or his drive failed. He was never to forget the early
years in London, and even in the comparatively secure years just
before his death, he made bitter jest of joining his old neighbors
of bygone days in that teeming boarding-house, the workhouse.[1]
Of course he had some capital, which entitled him to the rank of
the genteel poor, or, as he himself termed them, the "ignobly
decent"; however, he preferred to set aside the sum for "special"
uses (he was to pay the cost of publication of his first novel with
the sum), and to live on the income from the investment, ten
pounds a year, supplemented by money from tutoring.

Ten pounds a year, plus a pound a week from three students,[2]
was hardly a sufficient income to provide a good standard
of living. Gissing went from one shabby lodging to the next,
most of them in the Tottenham Court Road district, and began his experiments on how cheaply the human body could
be sustained. Like the hoary anecdote of the farmer who
boasted of his horse's relish for sawdust, until the animal cheated
him by dying just when the experiment seemed most a success,
Gissing's account of his diet wavers between humor and pathos.
He was ever recounting to his brother Algernon his newest dis-

covery of the most for the least: one of these was a meal of Egyptian split lentils boiled with an onion, which would sate two people for only twopence ha'penny.

He had to plan for two people, for Nell had come to live with him in London. They did not marry until October of 1879,[3] when both were living at 38 Edward Street. Nell was then twenty, her husband twenty-one. (Gissing's family declare in their volume of letters and explanations that the marriage took place in 1877.) [4] Nell was on cordial terms with Gissing's brother Algernon, but could scarcely endure her mother-in-law; to the young girls in Wakefield she was unknown, or so Gissing's mother believed.[5] Tormented by almost continuous ailments — neuralgia, erysipelas, finally tuberculosis — Nell made some attempt to manage the tiny household. She sent recipes to her brother-in-law, went to work occasionally when straits were desperate, and tried to defy seasickness when her husband decided to take her out in a small launch near Hastings![6] In 1882 she was so ill that she had to be hospitalized for tuberculosis.[7] But neither poor health nor poverty was able at first to spoil the precarious, poignant happiness. Surely Gissing, opponent that he was of ritual, would not have agreed to solemnize and legalize the relationship if there had not been, at first, a modicum of peace and contentment.

The last years of their relationship — Nell died in 1888 — were so bitter and sordid that it was easy for Gissing, and therefore easier for his biographers, to forget that there had ever been any happy moments. Certainly Nell was incapable of sharing her husband's intellectual interests, but her descendant, Carrie Mitchell in *Workers in the Dawn,* suggests how much comfort a lonely man could derive from companionship, affection, and docility. (Carrie Mitchell, too, became a termagant.) Penury haunted Gissing throughout his marriage to Nell: he worried about how he would pay for his wife's hospitalization, and for a woman to care for her after an operation on her eyes.[8] Teaching, the most secure way of earning money, was hateful to him. He begrudged

the time spent on it, and comforted himself only with the thought
that most of his pupils were, at least, docile.[9]

He had few compensations for grubby lodgings and shrill landladies and confused students, so that it was with joy that he discovered a group with whom he could identify, a mission he could
perform. His uncle had a house in Paddington and belonged to a
workingmen's club, and to these places George Gissing hastened,
not minding that he was a tutor rather than a factory-hand,
imagining that thick-soled shoes and the desire to "belong" would
be enough to promote fellowship with his uncle's proletarian
friends. The pattern was visits to Paddington and attendance at
lectures at the club during the week, lectures on radicalism and
atheism, for the most part. All the men with whom Gissing mingled at these meetings were, he fancied, "workers in the dawn";
now he had thrown off the restraints of the middle class and had
allied himself with a group suddenly aware of its strength.

The speakers whom Gissing most admired were such men as
George William Foote, president of the National Secular Society
and editor of the new and aggressive paper, *The Liberal*, and
G. G. Zerffi, a historian and refugee from Hungary, who had published *Dogma and Science* (1876) and *The Science of History*
(1879).[10] Soon he chafed at the relative passivity of listening, and
one evening in March of 1879 he himself addressed the club on
"Faith and Reason." He was enthusiastically received,[11] and the
approval whetted his appetite for more lecturing. Comparative
religion was one of the subjects that he considered for future use,
for he noted sourly that most people were smitten with the "Jingo-
ish idea" that their religion was the only true one.[12] So important
for a time did the lecture platform seem to him as a projection of
his aim to enlighten that he considered using a portion of his
small capital to rent a large hall in London and thus to reach a
larger audience.[13]

London, he decided; would be his permanent home, and he
considered buying a cheap house in Hackney or Islington.[14]

(Years later the thought of living in such places would horrify him, but in 1879 he considered them seriously.) London meant lectures and libraries and opportunities to meet the exiles of Europe, to whom he felt a strong attraction, because of their wandering, so like his own, and their radicalism. Of the many he met in London, the one he did not forget was Eduard Bertz, a clever young refugee from Germany. The two met in London (not in Jena)[15] when Bertz was twenty-six and Gissing twenty-two, and their friendship lasted for many years. (As late as 1898, Gissing considered the tie strong enough to justify a routing of his European trip through Germany, where Bertz had returned.)

Gissing soon realized that Bertz gave him the kind of companionship that was lacking in Paddington. His uncle and the Paddington proletariat had more fervor than informed intelligence, and by December of 1880 he wanted no more intimacy with them: "I am rejoiced that this Xmas there will be no necessity . . . of mingling with London relations. . . I fear they put me down for a prig, an upstart, an abominable aristocrat, but que voulez-vous? The matter is entirely intellectual."[16] It was the end of practical fraternity. Characteristically, however, Gissing found it possible to forsake his own relations who were workingmen while imagining himself a champion of the underprivileged, for in the same season that he patronized his poor relations, he announced himself a champion of the oppressed.

"I mean to bring home to people the ghastly condition . . . of our poor classes, to show the hideous injustice of our whole system of society, to give light upon the plan of altering it, and, above all, to preach an enthusiasm for just and high *ideals* in this age of unmitigated egotism and 'shop.' "[17]

Gissing found in Eduard Bertz the quality that he had wanted in friendship without being able to define it; when he finally put the need into words, it was for a friend of "European culture."[18] Morley Roberts, whom Gissing had known at Owens College and

whom he saw in London whenever Roberts made it a resting-
place, attracted him in different ways: he was fiery, he traveled
in several continents, he hunted, he had affairs, he wrote both
serious verse and advertising copy for a soap manufacturer. Roberts was, in Gissing's eyes, a splendid example of the English type,
with both the attractions and limitations of the type. Bertz, by
contrast, knew the writings of the continent, and had fled from
the tyranny of Bismarck.[19] Thus he would seem a sympathetic
figure to a young man himself a Socialist who was, if not persecuted, at least unappreciated. It was doubtless Bertz who provided Gissing with the stimulating conversation that led to two
articles on German socialism in the *Pall Mall Gazette* on September 9 and 11, 1880. Bertz lent Gissing books, listened for four days
to a reading of *Workers in the Dawn,* and gave praise generously.
Indeed the closeness of the friendship left very little time for Nell;
the hours not spent with students were spent with Bertz walking
along the Thames or arguing into the night.[20] When Bertz departed for Worthing to teach in a school for girls (a dismal experience that he could endure for only a few months) Gissing
used the experience in a chapter in his second novel, *The Unclassed.*

In the early days of the friendship it would seem that Gissing
was the dependent partner, needing advice and praise, but soon
Gissing assumed the stronger role, regarding his friend as unstable and easily wounded. In the summer of 1881 Bertz set out
for Tennessee to live in an ideal farm colony conceived by Thomas
Hughes, and if Gissing shared his friend's enthusiasm, it is curiously lacking in the letters written at that time. Nor did he seem
greatly surprised when Bertz returned crestfallen two years
later.[21] He watched, sadly, while Bertz joined the ranks of the
religious revivalists and attended meetings on salvation.[22] Finally
he shepherded a manuscript written by Bertz through the office
of Macmillan's in London, and when the novel was accepted, the
money received helped Bertz to return to Germany.[23]

Fondness persisted through the years, although Gissing knew his friend's limitations, and the two exchanged letters regularly. Gissing seems to have preferred to conceal the deteriorating relationship with his second wife, although Bertz bared his humiliating family quarrels in Germany. Clearly, although the two began their relationship as peers, they did not continue in that manner. Nevertheless Bertz served well as a publicist for Gissing's work on the Continent, and during the nineties from his haven in Potsdam, he would champion the iconoclasts at home and abroad.

If Bertz was an intimate companion in 1880, Frederic Harrison was rather a generous patron. Gissing came to the great man's attention in the fashion dreamed of by penniless young writers of first novels: Harrison read and admired *Workers in the Dawn*, Gissing's first published novel, and deigned to send the young author a letter of compliment. Gissing had already realized that he would earn no profit from the novel, for he had had to pay £125 to the diffident publisher Remington in order to have the script printed,[24] but he had hoped for some attention from the lions of London. Harrison was such a figure, and Gissing was delighted to be noticed, even though the letter Harrison sent did not give unqualified praise.

"There can be no doubt as to the power of your book. It will take rank amongst the works of great rank of these years. . . It belongs to a school of which I know nothing, and which I hold at arm's length, at least I think so. I am no critic, and very rarely read a modern romance, and I especially hate the so-called realism of Zola. But your painting of dark life seems to me as good as his, and to have a better social purpose — at least I hope so. . . I do not pretend to offer either advice or criticism, your work is far above anything I could do in that way, if I wished. And I do not wish. But I will tell you what I feel about it. . . I am not sure that the social and moral aim is sufficiently strong to justify the deliberate painting of so much brutality. . . I do not think girls ought to read it at all. But men of insight will very soon discover its power." [25]

It is the kind of letter which no other century or country could produce, mingling priggishness and honesty, pompousness and generosity.

The personality of Frederic Harrison, as his letter would suggest, was a complex one. He was a preserver of decorum, an antagonist of the prurient French, an agnostic with Christian ethics, a benefactor of the underdog. When he wrote the letter he was not yet fifty, but he had already assumed the tempting role of patriarch, for he had made all his major decisions and was not to unmake any of them, even when one of his sons became a Catholic and the other a Nietzschean rebel. He had embraced Positivism in 1862, and in 1880, when Gissing first came to his attention, was president of the English Positivist Committee, as well as (proof that the Positivists were endorsed as good "security risks") a respected barrister and former member of the Royal Commission on Trades Unions.

In effect, Harrison made Gissing his protégé for a time. He wrote letters of recommendation of Gissing's novel to influential friends, and introduced the young novelist to John Morley, who in turn suggested articles for the *Pall Mall Gazette* and the *Fortnightly*.[26] Thus it was through Harrison that Gissing's articles on Socialism saw print.

They could not have disappointed the patron, for they were well-informed and concise. They summarized the rise of Socialism in Europe, particularly in Germany, and referred to Marx, Ferdinand Lasalle, and the Socialist Yearbook recently published in Zurich. The first article was primarily a factual account of the Social Democratic party, organized in 1863, cloven by disagreements between radicals and moderates, healed in 1879, and then persecuted by Bismarck. Gissing cited too the efforts of refugees in London to circulate uncensored information: for example,

Freiheit, a Socialist paper published in London, was sent to the
continent each week under a new name, so that the authorities
would be confused in their efforts to confiscate the banned journal. The most important aspect of the article Gissing wrote, however, was his insistence that Socialism was a "science."

". . . be the views of individual agitators what they may, it must
not be forgotten that the theory of socialism rests on the purely
scientific inquiries of cultured minds. Recent German writers,
such as Marx, Dühring, Schneffle, Adolph Wagner, are neither
mere enthusiasts nor demagogues; their convictions regarding the
evils of our present economic system are the result of historical . . .
knowledge which commands respect."

"Neither mere enthusiasts nor demagogues" — this was the test
Gissing now applied to those with whom he discussed social
theory. He found the English Positivists, who regarded themselves
as the over-the-channel descendants of Condorcet, a respectable
group of thinkers, and he went regularly to their meetings after
Frederic Harrison introduced him to the members. One of those
who helped him most was Professor Edward Spencer Beesly, also
a Positivist, of the University of London, who gave him the opportunity to cover English news for *Le Messager de l'Europe,*
published quarterly in Saint Petersburg.[27] Each of Gissing's con-
tributions contained some thirty pages of news of political, social,
and literary affairs in England, and for each he received eight
pounds. The first article cost him "immense trouble" and went off
to the "Land of Nihilism" on January 17, 1881. "I have dealt very
fully," he wrote, "with the Irish question, then with the English
Agricultural depression, Fawcett's Post Office reforms, the so-
called 'crisis' in the English Church. . ."[28]

Lest Gissing's adherence to Positivism seem to contain something of sycophancy, it should be pointed out that his own interest
in the movement went back at least to 1878, before he met Harrison and Beesly. Before Positivism took hold, a loosely under-

stood Radicalism claimed his allegiance, a Radicalism defined as little more than a protest against Ritualism and the slow process of existing government in dealing with social problems. Even Radicalism, loosely defined, was, however, an improvement upon the simple and dilute hedonism which had at first seduced Gissing, so that he had written to his young brother Will that he saw no purpose in living than that "the sum of happiness should exceed the sum of misery." [29] Will, who had strong feelings of self-dedication (to be cut off cruelly by sudden death in 1880) rebuked his brother, but George remained unmoved. Positivism took an increasingly strong hold, however, for it seemed to offer a non-theological system that accounted for the great achievements of humanity as well as for the presence of the almost sub-human. Above all, it seemed to provide a scientific method of thinking and of looking at time, and Gissing was obsessed with systems and science, not trusting emotions and enthusiasm. He spoke glowingly of Auguste Comte in a letter of November 9, 1878.

". . . what universal knowledge the French philosopher Comte was possessed of. His 'Philosophie Positive' consists of a most wonderful *résumé* of all human knowledge, classed thus: Mathematics, Astronomy, Physics, Chemistry, Physiology, Social Physics. His idea is to deduce from all our positive knowledge a theory of social life, which shall in time be developed into an exact science, and free us, by due attention to its laws, from the state of social anarchy into which we are at present plunged." [30]

Today, when the Logical Positivists are receiving a large share of criticism — the return swing of the pendulum — it is difficult to imagine the powerful attraction that Positivism had for the intellectual Englishman, particularly the agnostic, of the late Victorian period. The limitations of the epistemology of Logical Positivism seem now to have been fully pointed out, above all, the relativity of values, so that a "good" man is produced literally by accident. However, the early Positivists considered their "reality" as fixed, as "given" in the same sense that the law of gravity is given, though many of them discovered, sadly, as Gissing also would do, that by the confines of their own system, all they were entitled to do was point out the relativity of values.

The clue to the popularity of Positivism is found in such letters as Gissing's promise of self-dedication, the words of a man who wants to do good without having to endorse a supernatural system.

"For, though I myself look forward to no future world where the negligences of this may be made up for, I do not on that account say, 'Let us eat and drink for tomorrow we die.' The immortality of man consists in this reflection — that not a word we utter, not a thought we think, not a battle we win, not a temptation we yield to, but has, and *must* have, influence upon those living in contact with us, and from them, like the circles spreading in a pool, extends to the whole future human race. Therefore is it of vast importance to me whether I set an example of an ignorant and foolish man, or of one bent upon using his faculties to the utmost." [31]

Gissing's earlier hedonism was bound to be short-lived, for it was counter to the accumulated pressure of the past, the emphasis upon hard work, righteousness, and winning approval. Just as his humor tended to be elephantine, so his hedonism was heavy, a kind of calculated load upon the back of a hesitant pleasure-seeker. If there had not been a doctrine like Positivism in the eighties Gissing and his cohorts would have had to invent one. But Comte had spared them the necessity, and they, in turn, exhausted two editions in English of his major work, *The Positive Philosophy*.[32] (The translation which Gissing himself used was Harriet Martineau's.) Comte was the reincarnation of Condorcet in the robes of a scientist, an irresistible combination for Englishmen. Thus Comte described himself as the herald of the third stage in philosophy — "The first being theological, the second metaphysical. . . I use the word *philosophy* in the sense in which it was employed by the ancients, and especially by Aristotle . . . that particular manner of philosophising which holds that the purpose of theories, in any class of ideas, is to coordinate facts." [33]

It was a great relief, for a time, to discuss political questions in terms of a philosophy rather than mere expediency, and Gissing's feeling of relief is patent in a letter describing a Positivist discussion of Home Rule, a problem then vexing England mightily: "The possession of land is only a sacred *trust*. No one can 'own' land like he owns his watch, for instance, seeing that land is not a human product made for the individual, but the common and indispensable basis of life." [34] Above all the theory of Comte allayed, temporarily at least, his misanthropy by means of its earnest insistence upon the perfectibility of the race. Positivists advised the study of man in history and "by the exercise of warm charity to all humankind" they foresaw a continuous progress in social life.[35] It was, curiously, both a "Religion of Humanity" and a "science of social life," and it attracted members because it tried to do the impossible.[36] Eventually Gissing found the synthesis to be an inadequate resolution of opposing facts, but for a few years he was so much an admirer of Positivism that he dated his letters according to the Positivist calendar, in which 1789, the year of the French Revolution, was the first of the new era in history.

One of the attractions of Positivism was its emphasis upon the reading of history, and Gissing devoured all volumes lent him, as well as those from libraries. He drew up, finally, an ambitious plan for reading.

"I shall go through all the great standard works on general History; *e.g.* Thirlwall's *Greece*, Arnold's and Niebuhr's *Rome*, Hallam, Guizot, Buckle, Gibbon, etc., etc., and read, by the side of this, works on Philosophy. When these *general* studies have sufficiently prepared my mind, I can proceed to the *special* investigation of those points which are particularly attractive to me, *e.g.* Church history, schemes of education, etc." [37]

Actually the special investigations, in spite of much insistence that he would read philosophy, were more interesting to him than original sources in philosophy. It is likely that he began reading Kant in 1882,[38] but he usually preferred history to philosophy and made many more references in his letters to such historians as Buckle and Lecky than to philosophers. Indeed, although he would satirize in *New Grub Street* and *In the Year of Jubilee* the purveyors of great ideas for little minds, he himself sought the popularizers, although they were of a better type — such men as Leslie Stephen and Professor John Draper.

It was Leslie Stephen who provided for Gissing the most concise statement of the position of the agnostic, and it was upon him that Gissing leaned when his family protested against agnosticism. Stephen had written, in a journal that Gissing admired, some characteristically blunt words:

"Briefly, my argument is, that theology is either a scientific theory, in which case any mode of comparing between different scientific theories is equally applicable to deciding upon this theory, and, if there be no method, we are driven to suicidal scepticism, to the negation of belief as belief; or theology must escape by retiring altogether to the metempirical world (Lewes' phrase) where it can have no relation to any scientific doctrine . . . no relation to any particular facts. . .

"This, it seems to me, is the origin of the other form into which theology develops. You still retain your invisible being, but you decline to make any specific inference from his existence. He retains a nominal existence upon the strength of a tacit agreement not to interfere with any particular event. He is gradually transformed into a transcendental or noumenal being, whose existence may be necessary to everything, but who exerts (if I may say so) no differential influence: he does not affect one series of events more than another. Whether we are bound to believe in such an entity, whether there may be some universal substance of the Spinozistic kind, is no doubt a very interesting as well as an exceedingly complex question. I only say that such a being cannot possibly interfere in any way with scientific laws, which deal with phenomena." [39]

Gissing himself, in a letter to his brother, described Christianity as "one of the thousand answers" men had devised to provide for an intelligible world, an answer that would suffice, in Gissing's opinion, only until the time of an advanced science. He believed science to be more modest than religion, hence more admirable, because it refused to dogmatize on "impossible questions" like those on the origin of life.[40] Of the many books on the subject that he studied, he cited especially Strauss's *The Old and the New Faith,* J. F. Clarke's *Ten Great Religions,* and J. W. Draper's *History of the Conflict between Science and Religion.* In addition he followed the controversies in the *Nineteenth Century* and the *Fortnightly* and the new quarterly read by agnostics and budding psychologists, called *Mind.*

Gissing's preoccupation with disestablishment (he obtained much free material from the Liberation Society, whose object was disestablishment) was neither hysterical nor histrionic; actually the struggles of freethinkers in England in the latter part of the nineteenth century are comparable in importance with those of the Puritans of earlier generations. Only in 1871 were religious tests abolished for degrees and fellowships in the Universities of Oxford and Cambridge, and only in 1869 was the evidence of freethinkers accepted by law. In 1883 George Foote, editor of the *Liberal,* would be prosecuted for blasphemy and sentenced to twelve months' hard labor in Holloway jail. But of the many battles in which atheists and agnostics were involved, the most publicized and the most bitter had Charles Bradlaugh, atheist and Republican, as the central figure. In 1880 he was returned to

Parliament from Northampton after two unsuccessful campaigns. About to be sworn in as Member of Parliament, he claimed the right to affirm rather than to take oath. Thereupon there began a struggle of six years in which all Parliament was embroiled in the question of whether Bradlaugh should be permitted to take his seat. Not until January of 1886 was he finally admitted. By and large the freethinkers of Gissing's day were not "trimmers" or appeasers; they tended to remain firm, even stubborn, upon issues that the modern, more sophisticated casuist tends to label unimportant. Gissing himself did not trouble to read Bradlaugh's paper, the *National Reformer*, [41] but he respected Bradlaugh for his lack of hypocrisy. [42]

If religion was to Gissing a special topic for investigation, foreign policy was a subject which he studied day by day, in such journals as the Manchester *Examiner*, the *Liberal*, the *Dispatch*, and the *Nineteenth Century* and *Fortnightly*. In the days of Palmerston, England had interfered freely in republican struggles on the continent, and had offered haven to the rebels. In the administration of Disraeli, however, there was a tendency to play both sides against the middle, even to the brink of war. Thus England was almost precipitated into a war with Russia, and Gissing, along with the Manchester *Examiner* and other Liberal groups who opposed war and imperialism, felt it his duty to read and remonstrate. In the Balkans suppressed nationalities, among them the Serbs, were rising against Turkey; soon Russia, who had classified the British as sympathizers with repressed nationalities, declared war on Turkey, feeling rather confident that the British would make no friendly gestures to the Turks. Britain was thus left in the uncomfortable position of endorsing a powerful advance upon Constantinople (a threat to her own status in the East) in order to live up to the reputation of partisan of oppressed groups. At this point public opinion in Britain, which had formerly been hostile to Turkey, swung against the Serbs and Russians, and the British fleet was sent to Constantinople in February of 1878. War between Russia and Britain then seemed imminent.

To Gissing the sudden veering of opinion to an unexpected quarter was additional proof of the fickle nature of the mob. They could be managed, he said bitterly, by almost any powerful group, and at the moment the powerful ones were Disraeli and the Queen.

"The Queen's speech is in the evening papers: short, but as it appears to me, not very satisfactory. 'I have taken the earliest opportunity of calling you together, and making to you the communication required by law.' Indeed! Some might have the hardihood to suggest that 'Law' required a summoning of Parliament before war had been irresponsibly rushed into. But we live in the days when the spirit of the Stuarts is commencing to stalk our island. . ."[43]

At the same time the Manchester *Examiner* was running a series of letters on "The Crown and the Constitution" ". . . in deprecation of the attempts . . . being made by my Lord Beaconsfield & Co. to aggrandize the power of the Crown at the expense of the Parliament. . ."[44]

Although Britain was able shrewdly to direct the Russo-Turkish War to a close without herself becoming a combatant (she won concessions, however!), the next years were punctuated with skirmishes throughout the empire. In 1879 there was war with Afghanistan, and with the Zulus in the Transvaal as well. Thus a series of disagreements with the Boers began, to culminate in the Boer War at the end of the century. When in 1880 Beaconsfield resigned, it was clear that party lines could no longer be held rigorously as of old: there were defections, compromises, and reservations in every quarter, and even such "grand old men" as Gladstone could no longer control the new crop of "individualists." Characteristic of the new temper in politics was Joseph Chamberlain's reservation, when he joined the cabinet in 1886, that he be permitted independence of judgment, not forced into

the party line. And John Bright, a Radical, newly in power, resigned when Britain bombarded Alexandria in July 1882. Such
men, and their minor counterparts in provincial politics, had tremendous interest for Gissing, because he, like them, was question-
ing shibboleths in every category. Although he was not to consider his novels primarily "political novels" in the sense that
Disraeli's and Kingsley's had been, Gissing realized that the man
in the locus of power, in government, was one of the most complex, and the most dangerous of creatures; and it was the zealous
study of politics, particularly in the seventies and eighties, that
eventually brought forth such "canny" novels as *Denzil Quarrier*
and *Our Friend the Charlatan.*

As news of minor bursts of violence came to his ears, Gissing
murmured, "We shall all be food for powder. . ." [45] (Mercifully he
was not to see the death of his older son in the First World War.)
He tried to get on with his writing while following the day-to-day
contests of power, but in spite of his earnest intention, he found
himself being made anxious and irritable by the news of the
politicians, and he eventually found it necessary to work single-
mindedly, obsessively, upon his fiction, or forfeit the degree of
calm necessary to produce his best work.

"The novel does not get on as well as I could wish, — in fact I
feel unequal to almost any effort just at present. The sickening
political news has a great deal to do with it, I believe. . . I used
to be strongly pro-Russian, but really there seems to be such
underhand work on that as well as the other side that one gets
disgusted. It is sickening to hear all this twaddle, however, about
'British interests,' as if it was more to our interest to kill several
thousands of Englishmen and involve half the population in ruin
and beggary than to stop for a generation or two the progress of
the Slavonic races which is ultimately inevitable! To me it appears
that all we need bother about at present is the keeping open the
Suez Canal. . ." [46]

It was difficult to endorse the optimism of the Positivists while observing the social anarchy of everyday, and gradually Gissing became disenchanted with the doctrine that had succeeded in providing comfort for three years. Thus when Carlyle died in 1881 Gissing pondered the fate of a nation when her great men were departed: "What a frightful thing would be a living generation utterly made up of mediocrities, even though the honest and well-meaning exceeded the charlatans!" [47] This thought would scarcely have occurred to an orthodox Positivist; yet at the same time Gissing was trying to convince himself that he shared their "enthusiasm for the race." By the end of 1882, the once scorned metaphysics was tempting him again, as he advised his brother to read Kant. At the same time he admitted that he was a Positivist no longer.

"The pessimistic article is finished, but I shall not even try to get it published, seeing that it has developed into nothing more nor less than an attack on Positivism. So far has my intellectual development brought me. There is little hope that the *Nineteenth* or the *Fortnightly* would accept the thing, but, if they did, I should feel uncomfortable at the thought of Harrison reading it." [48]

"Uncomfortable at the thought of Harrison" — that was all that was left of the former dedication to the doctrine of Comte. Gissing feared to offend his patron, but now and then he expressed his pessimism to Harrison, only to feel depressed afterwards, for what was at issue, he finally realized, was not only a theory of social action, but also, and this consideration was even more tender to him, a theory of art. From the beginning, from the day when Harrison had first sent the letter on *Workers in the Dawn,* the older man had insisted that only "strong social purpose," and by this he meant proselyting for the betterment of mankind, could justify the portraying in art of any "bestiality" of the human race. But as Gissing observed the struggles for power in the great world, the manifold vices of a teeming city, and the small sordid realities of his own life, he felt forced to dip his pen in acid, in spite of the disapproval of his patron.

It is too simple to pretend, of course, that Gissing sank so deeply into a mood of depression in 1882 because he could find no order in the larger world. The precipitating factor was his unhappiness in his relations with his wife, although superficially life in London had never seemed better than during the days when Frederic Harrison had offered him the opportunity to tutor his sons as well as the children of Vernon Lushington, Q.C., late Secretary to the Admiralty, an opportunity which gave Gissing both a larger income and a more varied social life, for the Harrisons were generous in their hospitality to the young man.

But the more that Gissing saw of the society that he could not enter gracefully, the more embittered he became. He went down to the country house of the Harrisons in Surrey and returned with his mind stored with rich details of architecture and decoration which he would use as local color in his fiction, and with a soul starved for such a life. Thus the new circle came to be envied instead of enjoyed, for Gissing's temperament, morose and proud, could not long endure a relationship in which he was primarily the poor tutor. He ruminated over his past migrations from one cheap lodging to another, remembered with chagrin that he had actually considered the purchase of a tiny house in a shabby London suburb. His grubby living and petty pleasure in his "capital" seemed all the more pathetic as he listened to the Harrisons' plan to tour the Mediterranean in a yacht. His only tour had been steerage to America, where he had left his books and clothing as pledge to pay his debt. A letter Gissing wrote the day after a visit to the Harrisons' country house shows how bitterly he felt the contrast.

"It is a pouring, dismal, indigestion-giving day. Yesterday, on the other hand, was in every way one of the most delightful days

I have had for a very long time. . . You can imagine what kind of a day I spent and how little agreeable it is to wake up this morning to a hideous sky, a more hideous street, and most hideous work — for I am just now in all the agonies of my Russian political article, which I loathe." [49]

What he had once enjoyed now oppressed him. He began to feel smothered by the dependency of Nell. When the Harrisons asked him in 1882 to spend the summer with them in Normandy, his heart leapt at the opportunity and he asked Algernon, a little shamefacedly, for advice.[50] Duty pressed. He remained in London. Occasional journalism, which he had once found flattering, work for the *Pall Mall Gazette* and *Le Messager de l'Europe,* he now regarded as "hack work" and he resented the time it took from his fiction. Ever present before him was the contrast between his position and that of other men of letters. Ruskin was given an especially bitter judgment.

"Well, he is, and always has been, rich and comfortable. Had he been poor, and with the necessity of struggling through a wretched existence of toil, his socialistic fervour would have, ten to one, exhibited itself in furious revolutionism instead of this calm, grave oratory. Which of the two is ultimately better, I know not. Only this, I am growing to feel, that the only thing known to us of absolute value is artistic perfection. The ravings of fanaticism — justifiable or not — pass away; but the works of the artist, work in what material he will, remain, sources of health to the world." [51]

As he became increasingly a relativist, seeing all allegiances in terms of the emotional needs of the pledge-taker rather than in terms of absolute truth, Gissing became inevitably sharp and sour and withdrew to the world of his fiction, the world in which he could best compete, since in the real world he was almost out of the race.

Unfortunately for his pride, even his fiction, the only manifestation of his self in which he saw any worth at all, was neglected
or attacked. He had completed a novel that he called *Mrs. Grundy's Enemies,* a novel which Frederic Harrison found to be ex-
actly what he had feared was latent in his protege's work — a
manifesto of the relativity of values, or, as Harrison would have
viewed it, a declaration of irresponsibility in the face of grave
social crises. The two men argued sporadically on meliorative
fiction versus naturalism, and Gissing became overwrought. He
hoped, however, that publishers would see in his dark side of
life at least a degree of versimilitude and was stunned when his
novel was rejected by Smith, Elder in September 1882 as unnecessarily offensive to conventional morality. Recovering, Gissing
sent the novel to Bentley, who was acquiring a reputation as a
publisher of daring fiction, and rejoiced when Bentley accepted
his work. He drew up a preface which was no less than a battle-
cry against the Ideal Absolute and the dogged, rigid moral pronouncements which most people made from their limited understanding of the concept.

"I shall fight these prejudices to the end, cost what it may.
Have sketched following, to be put as preface to the book:
'This book is addressed to those to whom Art is dear for its
own sake. Also to those who, possessing their own Ideal of social
and personal morality, find themselves able to allow the relativity
of all Ideals whatsoever.'" [52]

The preface served as safety valve for Gissing's boiling emotions, but it was not published, for Bentley decided, after setting
the novel in type, that *Mrs. Grundy's Enemies* posed too great
a risk. A salacious bit, like those provided by Mary Braddon and
Ouida, always helped sales, but the favorite pattern, virtue
rewarded and crime punished, had to be endorsed. Gissing,
however, would have no part of such hypocrisy, for so it seemed
to him, and as his reward, he had his latest novel relegated to a

desk drawer. It was therefore impossible to be amused when he received a letter from Bentley in 1884 which opposed the "realistic" school of fiction on the premise that it was bad to sow even "one seed" that might produce an "unhealthy crop." Remembering Bentley's reputation as a publisher of titillating fiction, Gissing scarcely found the sermon moving.[53]

There seemed no way out of the morass. Gissing's fiction was not marketable, and the time he needed for practice was scarce, stolen as it was from lessons in grammar and language. He alternated between getting as close to the Harrisons as possible, even when it meant moving halfway across London, to Warrington Place, and fleeing from them to Gower Street with the "life and bustle" that he had known from the early days in London, and which, perhaps, could compensate for the kind of living from which he seemed eternally barred.[54] But it could not compensate: Gissing wore the hair shirt by necessity, not by choice, and every fiber in him hungered after beautiful things and cultivated people. Gissing's father may have found consolation in philosophy and history, but his son was less fortunate. George Gissing tried to rationalize that on the bookshelves of his grubby room were the treasures of great men, but such consolation served him poorly when he saw the real houses of his patrons, richly furnished, and their handsomely dressed inhabitants, a constant reminder that in the present, at least, he had very little of the beauty that was his ideal.

As he considered his whole family, there seemed nothing but ignominy in store. There was the niggardly group in Paddington, who now embarrassed him and whom he rejected; most of all there were the beloved sisters and brothers in Wakefield who would inevitably suffer, he feared, from the narrowness of their environment. Indeed Margaret confided to him her own terror that they would "never be anything much," and George, although he shared the same apprehension, dared not admit it, for fear of hurting her. Instead he sent words of encouragement. Mere "healthy exertion" of the mind, he said, would enable her to become "cultured." He sympathized because household routine made it difficult for her to read and study, but he pressed upon her the urgency of a plan for self-improvement through reading. Indeed he was willing to "guarantee" that if Margaret followed his counsel for a year, she would find herself much the superior of those in her circle.[55] It was indeed a "guarantee"—of almost certain unhappiness for a girl forced to be housekeeper for her mother, in a small town of limited cultural interests. George was deeply fond of Madge, but apparently it did not occur to him that his advice might make her unhappier still, might make her more and more estranged from the community in which she had to make her way, limited as she was by her schooling and the genteel poverty of the family.

The future of his brothers was also a constant source of anxiety. His brother Will had smarted from a sense of social inferiority, and Gissing tried to comfort him.

"Poor Will has written to me in his usual depressed strain speaking of the social degradation he has to suffer in his quality of music-teacher. I have written a few consoling thoughts to him. He confirms a contempt I always entertained for the society of that district. They are horrible snobs."[56]

Since George could not muster even respect, not to speak of fondness, for most of those with whom his brothers lived, he could not avoid bitterness when he heard anecdotes about the provincial self-righteous. Thus when Algernon sent him a newspaper clipping concerning a speech of a leading citizen of the town, George replied:

"The speech somewhat astounded me. You say they were probably all half drunk,—but *in vino veritas*. . . I may honestly say that it represents a degree of general culture which I had already slightly passed beyond when I was a boy at Harrison's.

You can see at once that the man is wholly in bondage to mere
names; with him the *name* is everything . . . whatever you do,
struggle to keep off that abominable narrowness of view which
stifles provincial minds." [57]

If Gissing was concerned with a single manifestation of the
stupidity of the rank and file, that singular manifestation was
substitution of the name for the reality. In America, only a youth,
he had remarked the same phenomenon and had noted it in his
diary; now, some years later, it was still tormenting him.

Will died when he was still a very young man, but the trials
of Algernon continued, as did George's advice on how to meet
them. Algernon advertised for employment, but seldom had
congenial offers. At one time he considered founding a small
newspaper, and it was the impractical George who reminded
him of the practical chores in newspaper work, like soliciting
for advertising. Algernon read law for a time, too, was apprenticed
to a solicitor in Wakefield, and matriculated at London University. Throughout the turmoil of making decisions, George
kept Algernon supplied with reading lists, "trots," and exhortations,[58] and as late as 1887, when Algernon was living in the
Cheviot hills, George was still worrying about his brother's
financial state.[59] For his sisters the future was predictable but not
joyful — spinsterdom spent in housewifely tasks, bound to Mother,
or in an occupation — teaching — that the Gissings regarded as
tedious. Clearly his family supplied George with endless raw material for novels on the art of "getting on," together with probable
failure, as heredity and environment conspired to blunt enthusiasm. Indeed, one of the most fruitful vantage points for understanding a Gissing novel is the conflict in Victorian England
between the seemingly easy escape from the class of one's birth
and the cruel and endless rebuffs as one made this attempt.

The sense of a wasted past and a blighted future might have
been less sharp if Nell, at least, had stood fast by him, strong

and comforting when he was most depressed. She, however, was incapable of rallying flagging spirits and indeed provided the last and deepest humiliation for her husband. Once docile, she was now a shrew, complaining that they never went to the crowded "interesting" places which her commonplace, gregarious nature craved (her husband hated such places, frequenting them only for local color, not enjoyment). He, meanwhile, withdrew from her demands by doing more and more of the reading that removed him as far from her in spirit as was possible for two people under the same roof. He tried every night to spend the hours from 11 to 1:30 "reading either a Greek or a Latin author" [60] but found it increasingly difficult to concentrate, knowing that his stolen time would be preceded or followed by a quarrel.

"I am getting most frightfully nervous, indeed so completely nervous that I dread the slightest variation from my humdrum life. The door-bell ringing, even, or the postman's sudden knock puts me into palpitation and head-swimming, and I don't know what. This is very greatly the consequence, I know, of home circumstances, and I fear they will continue to work upon me." [61]

If he had been able to express his hostility, returning Nell's wrath in kind, with sharp words and accusations, he might have found some little relief from his misery. But he could not retaliate in kind: years of docile yielding to Mother at home and by letter could not readily be countermanded. Instead he endured, finding some slight release by a confidence or two in letters to his brother. How wretched so passive a state could render him is vividly portrayed in *Workers in the Dawn*, in which Carrie Mitchell, of whom Nell was the prototype, shows herself mistress of invective.

His conflicting feelings toward Nell were further complicated by her steadily deteriorating health, for it must have been an ever-present source of guilt — the resentment borne a woman marked for premature death. For several years Nell had been showing unmistakable symptoms of tuberculosis, and in 1882 she

spent some time in the House for Consumption in Marylebone.[62]
Furthermore she was probably on the way to becoming an alcoholic: at the time of her death in 1888 her husband commented
bitterly that she had spent the hard won pounds he sent her on
drink,[63] and the habit, if *Workers in the Dawn* can be trusted
for a counterpart, certainly did not become entrenched in a mere
year or two.

Whether Gissing blamed himself in part for his wife's deterioration cannot be known for a certainty, but his constant anxiety
over her health, the solemnity with which he described the
possibility of their moving from east to north London for a
"change in air" — a solemnity appropriate to a move to Davos [64]
— suggests that her poor health was the one tie that kept him
duty-bound to her until finally she rejected him.

At the age of twenty-three he sounded like an old man as
he wrote to Algernon:

"Work on well, my dear Alg, as you are doing, and rejoice that
you are young and have your liberty to walk right onwards. I,
too, am young enough yet, I suppose, but the months and the
years go, go, with never a better, but always a darker, outlook,
and perhaps the best years of all are already gone. To look back
on a wasted life must be bad, but worse still, I think, to feel the
waste actually going on, to know what *might* be, and to be
helpless." [65]

In a final paroxysm of despair, he drew up his will in the spring
of 1882.[66] His father had died in 1870, his brother Will in 1880; for
all he knew, he might well be next, enfolded as he was in disease
and marginal living.

By the summer of 1883 Gissing was becoming, in the clinical
sense of the word, "depersonalized":

"Philosophy has done all it can for me, and now scarcely interests me any more. . . The world is for me a collection of

phenomena, which are to be studied and reproduced artistically. In the midst of the most serious complications of life, I find myself suddenly possessed with a great calm, withdrawn as it were from the immediate interests of the moment, and able to regard everything as a picture. I watch and observe myself just as much as others. The impulse to regard every juncture as a 'situation' becomes stronger and stronger. In the midst of desperate misfortune I can pause to make a note for future use, and the afflictions of others are to me materials for observation. This, I rather think, is at last the final stage of my development, coming after so many and various phases. Brutal and egotistic it would be called by most people. What has that to do with me, if it is a fact?" [67]

Clearly Gissing now preferred to imagine himself as a calm, detached observer of social phenomena, with no personal stake, as it were, in the outcome; fundamentally, however, his "artistic studies" became the only avenues still open to one who had suffered more than he could endure. Rather than continue the series of defeats in establishing deep and warm relationships with people, his humiliated self chose withdrawal. Nell had disappointed him bitterly, and her conduct was, furthermore, proof that his mother had been right, that he had been a puerile fool to sacrifice so much in Manchester. The one humiliation he could stomach, but two made more than he could endure. In addition, he had failed to establish a warm understanding with Frederic Harrison: he might tutor his patron's children, but he could not pretend that Harrison's sanguine views of the social problem were anything that he could respect. Lastly, even his one warm friend, Bertz, would leave England in 1883. His sisters and his brother remained, of course, to furnish some little outlet for his repressed affection, but they were dependents, not peers, and what he most needed was someone strong to sustain and fortify his battered pride. Meanwhile, in the absence of such a person,

he withdrew from his fellows and even from nature, preferring
the painting of a landscape to the countryside itself.[68] The withdrawal was now complete, for, in days of the past, even when
most depressed, he had been able to find solace in the beauty
of nature.

The summer of 1883 marked the end of a major stage in
Gissing's life. He had come to London in 1877 with the desire
to belong, to join, and had allied himself with the proletariat. In
his domestic life his early common-law relationship with Nell
had meant for him a protest against ritualism and convention. But
by 1883 his enthusiasm for Radicalism and Positivism was dead,
and his marriage was dead as well, at least in spirit, even if,
ironically, the Established Church and the State had succeeded
in putting their seal upon it. He thereupon yielded to the trait
which his childhood experiences had already established — misanthropy, the "ruling passion" that he sought sporadically to
undermine, but which was always victorious in times of stress.

In that summer he yielded to the inevitable and became a
recluse. His wife was not living with him, his pupils were, mercifully, on holiday, and he moved himself to a new neighborhood,
Chelsea, as a physical manifestation of his desire to slough off
the old ties and the old ways. Had he had enough money to
make it possible, surely he would have removed himself much
further! In the new lodgings in Chelsea he completed *The
Unclassed*, and saw it accepted by Chapman and Hall. This novel
and *Workers in the Dawn* belong to the first period in his life,
the time of hope and then disillusionment, as he, too, became
dispossessed, "unclassed," as he preferred to say.

Chapter 4

A YOUNG MAN'S
FIRST BOOKS

Flushed by Remington's acceptance of "Workers in the Dawn" (although the author agreed to pay part of the cost of publication), Gissing declared in November 1880, "Certainly I have struck out a path for myself in fiction, for one cannot, of course, compare my methods and aims with those of Dickens." [1] In the same period Meredith, Moore, Hardy, and Henry James would express a similar sense of "newness," for a curious sea change had come over the English novel. Even the reviews were constantly startled by the strange fiction they were called upon to judge. As the *Saturday Review* remarked superciliously in a review of Meredith's *Evan Harrington*, "Who would have thought that a really very good novel could have been written on so unpromising a subject as the history of a tailor who was mistaken for a gentleman?" [2]

Strange subjects were being chosen for fiction, subjects which shook up the "public truth" [3] because clever young men, critical of the middle class from which most of them came, were filling the market with their novels and fancying themselves the destroyers of obsolete "caveats." Hardy's subtitle for the story of a seduced dairymaid became "A Pure Woman Faithfully Presented"; Gissing insisted that his *déclassée* heroine in *The Unclassed* was a sensible, likeable young woman not remarkably different from the conventional sort. George Moore protested the censorship of a "tradesman, who, though doubtless an excellent

citizen and worthy father, was scarcely competent to decide the
delicate and difficult artistic questions that authors in their struggle for new ideals might raise. . ." [4] Even Henry James, though
not concerned with such "crude" problems as these, presaged
the coming of a new concept of the novel. Of the old type he said:

"It had no air of having a theory, a conviction, a consciousness of itself behind it — of being the expression of an artistic
faith, the result of choice and comparison. I do not say it was
necessarily the worse for that; it would take much more courage
than I possess to intimate that the form of the novel, as Dickens
and Thackeray (for instance) saw it, had any taint of in-
completeness." [5]

But Mrs. Grundy took reprisals for these affronts, and Gissing
was one of her victims. *Mrs. Grundy's Enemies* was not published after being set up in print; Meredith's *The Ordeal of
Richard Feverel* was banned by Mudie's Select Library, the larg-
est lending library in London, and the arbiter of starvation or
success for new novelists; Hardy's *Tess of the D'Urbervilles*
would be bowdlerized for serial publication in the *Graphic:*
the story of Tess's baby would be expunged from the record, and
Angel Clare would be forced to transport two girls in a wheel-
barrow across a raging stream because Mrs. Grundy did not
approve of his carrying a woman in his arms! [6] The saddest
victim of Mrs. Grundy's self-righteousness would be Henry
Vizetelly, the publisher. He would be singled out in a test case
in the campaign of the National Vigilance Association against
the "corrupting" influence of translations from the French. In
May of 1888 the problem of the sale of "pernicious literature"
would be brought before the House of Commons, and Vizetelly
would be fined and imprisoned. Among the items of "pernicious
literature" that he was accused of marketing were *Madame
Bovary, Nana, The Soil* (*La Terre*), and *Piping-Hot* (*Pot-
Bouille*). [7]

The great English novelists of the generation before Gissing would have been shocked to observe a novelist warring openly with the public. True, the leonine heads were often uneasy under their crowns of decorum, and it is possible to suggest, as Mr. Edmund Wilson has done with Dickens,[8] that some of the novelists most zealous to appease were, deep inside themselves, possessed of many hostile, anti-social feelings, which were, however, converted into stories of phantasy or crime, and thus, ironically, made socially acceptable. As Mr. Wilson remarks of Dickens, "He was at once the murderer and the victim." But the later novelists, like Gissing, permitted themselves no such conversion mechanisms: instead, doggedly, they expressed their hostility openly, regardless of public criticism.

Dickens' solicitude for Mrs. Grundy shows how strong a hold the good lady sometimes had upon novelists: he changed the unhappy ending of *Great Expectations* to a happy one upon the advice of Bulwer-Lytton,[9] and cast Mr. Dick's delusions in *David Copperfield* into another form, because Forster considered them, in first draft, undignified.[10] As editor of magazines which published fiction he refused stories dealing with hereditary insanity, lest they arouse the "slumbering despair" of readers.[11] An article by Wilkie Collins was bowderlized by him because it was "sweeping and unnecessarily offensive to the middle class." [12] He always made the distinction, in short, between public and private morality: thus, in 1867, when he was asked for his opinion of Charles Reade's alleged writing for prurient tastes, he replied carefully:

"I should say that was pure to an artist might be impurely suggestive to inferior minds (of which there must necessarily be many among a large mass of readers), and that I should have called the writer's attention to the likelihood of those passages being perverted in such quarters." [13]

There has been so great an emphasis upon the egalitarianism in the thought of Dickens and other "social novelists" that it has become too easy to overlook latent signs of autocracy, the deep conviction that the mass of men are easily duped and must, therefore, like children and the feeble-minded, be kept out of harm's way.

Certainly the general public gave little manifestation of any power of discrimination between pruriency and honest opinion. In 1867, for example, the bestseller in fiction was *Lady Audley's Secret*, by Mary Braddon, a novel which contained an illegitimate child, arson, and a lover thrust down a well, but which appeased Mrs. Grundy by punishing the beautiful murderess at the end of the novel. Thus a new and crass hypocrisy had emerged among most novelists who wanted to be popular, as they titillated taste for the prurient by going as closely as possible to indelicacy and then retreating to remorse. Indeed, in Rhoda Broughton's *Red as a Rose Is She* the heroine very nearly resembles a "demi-vierge" although exhortations to virtue are frequent in the pages. Charles Reade's *A Terrible Temptation* (1871) and Wilkie Collins' *Fallen Leaves* (1879) are in much the same vein. Worst of all, none of these novelists considered himself a mere purveyor of aphrodisiacs for the below-stairs reader: he wrote for the allegedly respectable and sturdy middle class, and his novels were first published in expensive formats. It is no wonder, therefore, that the generation of Gissing and George Moore viewed most of the successful older novelists and publishers as rampant hypocrites.

It was not only the "solid" middle class but also the supposedly emancipated group who, sad to say, were unable to determine for themselves that an honest naturalism was worthy of respect. Frederic Harrison's suspicion of *Workers in the Dawn* has its counterpart in a letter of Roden Noel, a well-read, intelligent man from Trinity College in Cambridge, later to be an acquaintance of Gissing, but in his earlier years an opponent of the

"French influence," which meant, loosely, anything frank and blunt.

"There is a new story by the authoress of *The Heir of Red-clyffe* which I have read with all my old enthusiasm. . . Did you ever read *Madame Bovary?* It is a very powerful book and reminds me of it by force of contrast. It shows how the ennui of mean French domestic life drags down women, whereas Miss Yonge makes one feel how full of interest the narrowest sphere of life is." [14]

It did not occur to Noel or to most literate Englishmen that "the ennui of mean French domestic life" was not exclusively a product of France, and that it would be found in novels of Gissing and Moore and many others.

Once it is realized how great a hold conventional (or hypocritical, as Gissing would say) morality had upon publishers and the general public, it is not surprising that Gissing's first novel in the realistic manner, *Workers in the Dawn,* was summarily rejected by publishers' readers. It was "undoubtedly very ably written" but was not acceptable because of its "rationalistic tendency, and certain details of a profligate character." Today a critic would be more likely to reverse the pronouncements — declaring the novel badly written, but worth reading because of some carefully detailed scenes in the naturalistic manner and some honest, if adolescent, thinking. One of the publishers to whom Gissing submitted the manuscript declared categorically, "We do not believe in fiction being the proper vehicle for conveying doctrinal opinions, for one reason that most readers will not read them." [15] In Gissing's opinion, the criticism was "foolish," as most readers of the novel would agree, for the hero can scarcely be said to endorse any particular doctrine after running the gamut of them and finally choosing suicide! Clearly, the publisher was shilly-shallying: he wanted simply to avoid so bleak a story and any danger of offense to conventional morality.

Finally Gissing made arrangements that Remington should print *Workers in the Dawn*, with the financing provided by Gissing's small capital. The old saw is that a novel paid for by the novelist is not worth the printing, but in the case of *Workers in the Dawn* there are some redeeming features.

Gissing's early wish was to describe all London life, and in such a master plan it is possible to place *Workers in the Dawn*, although its model is Dickens, not Balzac. Dickens had attempted in several of his novels to link class with class by means of melodramatic devices—mysterious legacies, secret sins of the past, and so on. Gissing, who had read Dickens since boyhood, made a similar attempt and thus linked himself with the great old tradition of the birth-to-death novel, with picaresque flavor on the way. The tradition called for several subplots, sententious commentary by the author, and detailed descriptive passages. The plot structure Gissing chose was thus elaborate, but as a novice, he was unable to build altogether soundly. For example, Mr. Whiffle, a caricature rather like Uriah Heep, is provided with a son named Augustus, who later turns out to be the seducer of the hero's wife! This turn of affairs is as surprising to the reader as Mr. Micawber's appointment as a colonial magistrate in Australia, and even more jarring, since the mood of nostalgia and fancy is less deep in Gissing than in his master.

Several times in his desperate attempt to work through the elaborate plot, Gissing forces his principal characters into relationships and activities that are not psychologically convincing, although the basic story of the runaway orphan is credible, if trite. The Reverend Mr. Norman rescues from a London slum the orphaned child of an old friend, but the boy soon leaves his foster home and returns to London, for there is his memory of his dead father. After being exploited by a variety of Londoners, including a charlatan "blind man" in the tradition of Fagin, the boy, Arthur Golding, is befriended by a working man and later apprenticed to a printer named Tolladay. From him Golding learns philosophic Radicalism, but soon his zeal as an apostle of the proletariat is sapped by a mysterious legacy which permits him to study art and to withdraw from active life. The contrast between the active and contemplative life is made manifest on still a second front, when the hero must decide between redemption of his erring proletarian wife and meditations with a beautiful, intelligent, and wealthy young woman. Bound by marriage vows to a faithless wife, and denied an affair by the virtuous young woman, Golding finally commits suicide while still a young man, thus bringing three laborious volumes to a close.

The structure of the novel and the principal features of the plot are clearly mid-Victorian, but curiously enough, the dominant tone is modern. A comparison with Dickens' *Bleak House* of 1852 illustrates the difference. In both novels the provisions of a will bring together people from all strata in society. In both novels the authors' concern with the vices of pride and sensuality and lack of charity is grave. But where Dickens provides for retribution, with the humbling of proud Sir Leicester and the death of Lady Dedlock, Gissing permits proud Gresham to flourish and shows both the slow death by debauchery of Carrie Mitchell and the swift death of the virtuous Helen Norman. And whereas little Jo is given a deathbed speech intended to draw tears from every reader, the oppressed urchins in Gissing's book suffer in silence or in the vulgar epithets of the gutter. Gissing's method is, for most of the book, that of naturalism: "Mrs. Pole — altogether coarser and more vulgar, the nose swollen at the end and red, the mouth bestial and sullen, the eyes watery and somewhat inflamed, the chin marked by a slight growth of reddish hair." Harsh in his observation of the physical appearance of his proletarian characters, Gissing was almost as harsh in dissecting their vices. As he was to declare later in a critical study of *Bleak House* ". . . though virtue may exist in the ignorant and the poor and the debased, most assuredly the delicacies of virtue will not be found in them, and it is these delicacies on which Dickens so commonly insists." [16]

Unfortunately for the novel, the acute observation of proletarian life was not matched by honest observation of those characters with whom Gissing identified, and thus one of the major weaknesses in Gissing's work as a whole is manifest even in his first published novel — his sterilizing identification with characters to whom he is sympathetic. He insists upon presenting Helen Norman, a beautiful philanthropist, as a paragon. Her intellect is superb, although the only "proof" offered — excerpts from her diary — is more pompous than impressive. Similarly the capacity of the hero for self-deception and even mawkishness is often overlooked by the too sympathetic novelist. Perhaps the most disappointing scene in the novel, because it lacks integrity at a critical juncture, is the one in which the hero, convinced for the moment that his marriage is not binding because his wife has broken her vows, proposes to the virtuous Helen Norman that she be his mistress. She declines in a pretty and ineffectual speech and thus relieves her suitor and the author of the crucial consideration of whether Golding would have had the courage to follow his convictions. Her declination is the equivalent of a "deus ex machina" who solves a problem by leaving the hero only one course of action, and it is hardly the course that a modern writer of integrity would choose.

In addition to the sterilizing identification with sympathetic characters, the second major flaw of *Workers in the Dawn* is its didacticism. Gissing opens the story with a harangue, "Walk with me, reader, into Whitecross Street," and he goes on in the same fashion for most of the three volumes, like an officious leader of a Cook's Tour of the slums. The harangues and the frequent flippancies which suggest a young and conceited author were, many of them, removed when Gissing began to revise the first edition. The revised version was never completed, but the deletions in manuscript, indicated in Mr. Shafer's edition,[17] prove that Gissing in later life became aware of the blemishes in his early work. An example of such a defect, later removed, is the description of the rector's parish.

"The duties resulting from his position were, as may be imagined, not very arduous, and the compensation, from a purely sordid point of view — that treasure upon earth which the clergy doubtless prize merely as a type of the heavenly treasure which will one day be theirs — was far from doing discredit to the pious ancestors of the village . . ."

Happily, in revision the brash remarks of a young man who could never resist a jab at the clergy were removed.

A modern critic of Gissing, Mr. Angus Burrell, finds three recurrent, almost obsessive, themes in his novels, and these are already evident in *Workers in the Dawn:*

"First, the vicissitudes of young men with good minds and no money, their resentful attitude toward society, their eventual compromise or failure; second, either an absurdly sentimental overestimation of women or the most vindictive unjust underestimation; third, heroes exhibiting flights from sex adjustments (often very cleverly rationalized) or flights into sex relationships that are usually disastrous." [18]

Certainly Gissing was not the first to present the hero with intelligence and no money, for problems about money, how to get it and how to relate it to the "good life," became central as the middle class prospered and patronized the arts; it is Gissing's variation, however, no money, keen intelligence, and latent misanthropy, which distinguishes his heroes from the struggling young men of most mid-Victorian novels, like Pip in *Great Expectations* and Pendennis. The latter try to succeed in the world of money and power — indeed the stories are made up of their struggles — but they are not eminent for their remarkable cerebration. It is Becky Sharpe who best resembles the "hero" whom Gissing

was to establish in novel after novel, but Becky was a solitary
figure in Victorian fiction, whereas Gissing was convinced not of
the scarcity of this type of egoist, but of the huge number spewed
out by the new red brick municipal colleges each year — poor,
determined young men who could read three languages but who
would be offered only clerkships.

Mr. Robert Shafer, editor of the 1935 edition of *Workers in the
Dawn,* has been kindest to the novel, calling it honest and preoccupied with values, the manifesto of a conscientious but unhappy young man. As such a manifesto it deserves respect, for
it is no less than a chronicle of one who wanted to belong and
do good for his fellow man, but who found that his own passions
and "bad luck," what Hardy would call "crass casualty," de-
molished his plan for a good life. Just as George Gissing in real
life imagined that self-help and an earnest desire for amendment
would bring progress and happiness; so Golding in fiction had
the same dream. But as Gissing broke with philosophic radicalism
and Positivism; so, too, did Golding.

The real man, however, had the ability to learn from disappointment, whereas Golding chose suicide. In his second novel,
The Unclassed, Gissing shows that he had learned a good deal
about human beings and no longer needed characters in dichotomy in order to show his own ambivalence. Whereas Helen
Norman and Carrie Mitchell were symbols of heaven and hell
for the hero, in *The Unclassed,* the heroine, Ida Starr, is the
first of the wonderfully credible women Gissing would portray
so well, at once sensual and virtuous, worldly yet simple.

The basic plot of *The Unclassed* now sounds as trite as
"Michael's Lost Angel" and even less entertaining, but the
audacious, yet sound, conception of the character of Ida Starr
redeems the book from triteness. Ida, as a child in the opening
scene, learns from nasty schoolroom gossip that her mother is
a prostitute, and in anger and chagrin wounds her informant,

Harriet Smales. (Knowledgeable about the small ironies that make up interpersonal relationships, Gissing has the two maintain a desultory friendship through life!) Ida, in rational dislike of sweatshops which have been ruining her health, turns to prostitution. Like Shaw's Mrs. Warren in a later day, she considers herself neither a tragic nor pathetic figure because of her occupation. Indeed, she scarcely "considers" herself at all; she would rather dote upon household tasks, and in such small scenes the essence of her character is revealed. Gissing had learned, after his first novel, that diaries and monologues of self-explanation are not needed, are not even desirable, to establish a character.

Of course, it would not be a characteristic Gissing novel if there were not a young man with whom Gissing identified himself uncritically, and in so doing, spared himself the pain of insight into himself. Osmond Waymark is the young man, and it is his lot to fall in love with Ida Starr. (Gissing was perennially interested in the spectacle of the supposedly self-disciplined man who succumbs to woman.) He is obsessed, like his creator, with the need to rid himself and other men of the conventions which stand in the way of self-knowledge, but he is anxious and fearful that his motives are not truly altruistic; once again the Gissing hallmark—the "good" man who becomes less and less sure that he can resist temptation. Thus, after persuading Ida that self-respect and the back-breaking drudgery of the sweatshop are preferable to the comparative comfort of prostitution, Waymark finds that his own desire for the girl is aroused. A Dickens hero, or Thackeray's Pendennis in such an impasse, would have married the girl or would have been rescued by his family. (Memorable is the scene in *Pendennis* in which Pen's incipient seduction of Fanny is interrupted by his mother's knock on the door!) But Gissing heroes are always conscientious even if they are confused, and they make labored examinations of conscience rather than yield to an obvious course of action. Waymark, convinced finally that his feeling for Ida is not "pure," stops seeing her in order to remove temptation.

If Waymark were merely puerile in his thinking about purity, he could not be taken seriously; instead, fortunately, Gissing shapes the problem so that Waymark's discovery of concupiscence in himself, a sin he had formerly castigated in society and had not observed in himself, brings to him true agony of spirit. To him marriage with Ida would be merely the legalizing of his desire, which he vaguely feels is "wrong," no better than the desire of men who have sought her in the street.

It is at this juncture that Gissing and Waymark show themselves both to be confused. The confusion is permissible for Waymark, a man unaware that sexual feeling in itself is neither pure nor impure, and that the nature of the companionship and the degree of kindness and honesty are the relevant tests; but Gissing, who should supposedly have control over his fictional creature and should remain, in a sense, above and beyond Waymark's personal confusion, cannot so easily be excused. Once again Gissing has felt a paralyzing identification with his hero and so has not viewed him altogether honestly: it does not occur to him that Waymark's renunciation of Ida could be, and probably is, his own fear of sexual feeling, no matter who the object. Like Angel Clare in Hardy's novel, Waymark never questions his own assumption that an innocent maiden is the closest approximation, for the secularist, of a guardian angel. Thus, for a time, after rejecting Ida, he chooses Maud Enderby, a hysterical girl whose lack of passion he confuses with purity.

Although, therefore, there seem to be grounds for suspecting Gissing of avoiding a basic problem in the characterization of Waymark (as in himself), the novel is an improvement upon *Workers in the Dawn*. There are fewer intrusions by the author in his own person — fewer digressions — although Waymark is always tempted to be a monologuist. Gissing became aware of the wordiness and removed the worst blemishes from the edition of 1895.[19] The preface to this edition suggests a new ability to criticize himself, an ability that he certainly did not possess in the seventies.

"Nowadays, the theme and its presentment will, at worst, be 'matter for a flying smile.' It will be recognised as the work of a very young man, who dealt in a romantic spirit with the gloomier facts of life. Revising this early effort, the author has been glad to run his pen through superfluous pages, and to obliterate certain traces of the Impertinent Ego. But the narrative remains as it was, and should be read as narrative pure and simple."

It was not necessary to delete anything before chapter 3, for the opening pages of *The Unclassed,* unlike those of *Workers in the Dawn,* are in the dramatic, not the didactic, manner. Chapter 3, however, belongs to the "wastebasket" school, now defunct, in which the antecedents of all principal characters are given in one chapter, regardless of the interruption in the continuity of the story. In the revised version, however, Gissing removed about one third of the story of Ida Starr's family, as well as such naïve remarks that Ida's mother had turned to prostitution because her health was fragile. (In the revised account he says simply that Mrs. Starr was badly in debt to her landlady and had to get as much money as possible as quickly as possible.) But the revisions which best illustrate the contrast between Gissing's wry good sense of the nineties and the curdled audacity of an earlier decade are those describing a religious conversion and the choice of a surname by Ida's mother.

1884 "She herself (Ida's mother) took the name of Starr, that being the name she would have borne, had Ida's father dealt honestly with her. Poor thing, she had hard, hard problems before her. . ."

1895 "She herself took the name of Starr from a page of fiction."

Although *The Unclassed* may be a young man's book, it is not
on that account childish. The *Athenaeum* and the *Academy*, two
respected literary journals of the day, found the novel interesting,
but recommended to the author "self-repression" and "an attentive
study of the structural elements of fiction," [20] criticism which cannot be surpassed for going to the core of Gissing's problems as a
writer. They judged as "hardly within the range of probability . . .
a long-continued platonic attachment between a normal young
man — even of aesthetic tastes — and a London prostitute." The
novel was "in the manner of Zola and his disciples" but it was not,
in their opinion, "prurient." The manner of the Naturalist school,
according to the reviewers' definition, was "to give sufficient
prominence to the shadows of life to produce a picture of powerful effect." [21]

After publishing two novels dealing with *déclassé* people and
life of the streets and slums, Gissing was to write two with a
background in "gracious living" — *Isabel Clarendon*, rarest of all
of Gissing's novels and most worthy of reprinting, and *A Life's
Morning*. After these, in turn, came a self-assured return to the
nether world in a trio of fine novels — *Demos, Thyrza*, and *The
Nether World*. Once again Gissing would taste, and then spurn,
the life of the fashionable world, to return to the haunts of the
dispossessed, where he alternately punished and exalted himself.

Chapter 5

BETWEEN TWO WORLDS

The fall of 1882 and the following year were characterized by indecision and fear in both personal and professional relationships. Although Gissing had privately broken with Positivism, he avoided an obvious rupture for fear that Frederic Harrison would withdraw his friendship and his patronage. As it turned out, the fear proved to be groundless, for Harrison was too kind to dismiss a friend for being a cynic. The tutoring of the Harrison children continued. The sorest experience of 1883 by far was the publisher Bentley's procrastination over the publication date of *Mrs. Grundy's Enemies,* for which he had paid £50;[1] delays went on through the hot summer that Gissing spent in Oakley Crescent, Chelsea. Meanwhile the disappointed novelist read Landor's belles-lettres for escape, encouraged his brother Algernon who wanted to found a local newspaper, and comforted his sister Margaret, who was engaged as a governess in Wales, and who, like her brother, was fearful of being patronized. To her he gave sensible words of advice which he was seldom able to follow himself.

"You remind me, do you know, in what you say of these matters, of Charlotte Bronte. She had that same shrinking from people who might be supposed to look down upon her, and the same half-defiant withdrawing into herself. I myself understand it also. Still, I repeat: there can be no doubt that that person commands most respect who stands simply on his or her dignity as a human being, and, though pretending nothing, disguises and yields nothing. In very deed, this is what is meant by 'good breeding'. . . Simplicity is everything." [2]

For Madge, too, he tried to clarify his scepticism, for she was clearly worried over the state of his soul.

"Taking for granted my powers of sense, I am quite justified in pursuing scientific discoveries, and saying that I can *prove* their truth; but I mean no more than that I can prove this *in relation to my own attributes*. . . In very deed, I can prove absolutely, nothing whatever. Am surrounded by infinite darkness, and live my little life by the light of such poor tapers as the sun, moon and stars. But I earnestly beg of you to understand that this position is compatible with the extremest reverence. . . All I can say is that I am so constituted that I *cannot* put faith in the light you hold to me; it appears to me an artificial reflection of man's hopes. My position with regard to the universe is that of Carlyle in the wonderful chapter of 'Sartor' called 'Natural Supernaturalism.'" [3]

Reverence and wonder were all that Gissing could concede before Margaret's orthodoxy, and quite often wonder was replaced by despair. The despair is reflected in a mediocre little poem of six lines, "Hope in Vain," which he composed and saw published in Bentley's *Temple Bar*.

> *Alas, alas, that it all was a dream.*
> *Only a dream that you were mine!*
> *And that one hour, with its golden gleam,*
> *Floated past like a rose on the stream,*
> *Tells me that never an hour shall shine*
> *Never, for ever, to make you mine.*

(Bentley also accepted a short story, "Letty Coe," which he stored in a desk drawer for some six years until Gissing's name had became more popular.) [4] The most irritating thing about Bentley was that publication was always every day but today.

By the middle of 1883 it would have been clear to an impartial observer, although not to Gissing himself, that the attachments he had formed were affording him a cross section of a class society which might well give him raw material for fiction, but which were nurturing in him the already strong tendency to split personality. It was as if he lived in a world of compartments, each compartment quite discrete, with his role that of ticket-collector, entering and leaving in lonely doing of his duty, never staying for long in any one place.

A random look at Gissing's activities during the summer of 1883 corroborates the theory that he was wandering lonely between two worlds: he was spending time again with Bertz, who had returned penniless in June from his chastening experiment in ideal living in Tennessee;[5] he was visiting the Harrisons at their beautiful, old country house near Woking;[6] he was treading the corridors of the Royal Academy to admire the portraits of the Lushington girls whom he had tutored;[7] and, projecting his own problems, he was following avidly the controversy concerning George Foote, the journalist he had heard lecture in years gone by, who was now being prosecuted for blasphemy. He had a poor opinion of Mr. Justice North's opinion on the Foote case, and implied that the revered gentleman belonged back in medieval times.[8] Buffeted by so many conflicting kinds of experience, Gissing must have felt dazzled and exhausted. Foote was a brash atheist (he was being prosecuted for "comic" illustrations of the Bible!); Harrison was a gentlemanly Rationalist; Margaret a self-conscious Anglican smarting at her role of governess; Bertz a disenchanted Socialist and, now, a religious revivalist. Nell, Gissing's own wife, was nothing at all. He had scarcely succeeded in allying himself with any one group; each of his friends and relations would have felt uncomfortable with the others, and no one made any attempt to build or cross bridges.

Because he had never had anyone stray for his sake between the two worlds, he was moved and delighted when the fashionable Mrs. Gaussen, whose acquaintance he made in 1884, included his brother and sister in her invitations and even deigned to visit him in his shabby lodgings. The friendship progressed rapidly, and because it enabled Gissing to see much of a world that previously he had only glimpsed, it was one of his most valuable experiences. True, the Harrisons had invited him to dinner and had permitted their sons to venture as pupils under his roof, but they had not been intimate with him: he visited on their terms and only when he was invited. Mrs. Gaussen, by contrast, gave advice on clothing and lodgings, gave generous invitations, and lingered with Gissing over his album of family photographs.

It was in August of 1884 that he first went down to the country house of David Gaussen, Broughton Hall, in Lechlade, Gloucestershire. Before the visit he was rather complaisant in describing the trip before him: ". . . I am getting to like the atmosphere of cultured families; I study the people, and they are of use." [9] After the visit, however, his obnoxious posturing was quite undone by the graciousness of Mrs. Gaussen, who, shortly after his return to London, sent him a bouquet from her garden. By September she informed him that she hoped to take a house in London for a year; by October she had obtained the house and had already so overcome Gissing's taciturnity that he invited her to look at his photograph album, that secret record of a past he sought to hide from most people.[10] Because the Harrison boys sat for the Saint Paul's School examination in September, Gissing was able to accept in their place as pupil Mrs. Gaussen's son, who was then thirteen. The lad came in mid-afternoon and departed at eight in the evening, and Gissing became fond of him, and fonder still of the mother who seemed the loveliest and most gracious woman he had ever known.

Limited though his experiences with fashionable life had been, he was now sought after, through the graces of Mrs. Gaussen, for supper parties, tennis parties, all kinds of parties. "I used to suffer from loneliness; now the difficulty is to get any time at all to myself." [11] He filled his letters with compliments for Mrs. Gaussen and described his adventures. Until now he had had an unreal conception of men and women of leisure, as *Workers in the Dawn* makes clear, with its "stagey" presentation of the well-to-do as artists and philanthropists who talk stiffly in drawing rooms. The ideal woman, too, in his novels had been limited to intellectual philanthropists like Helen Norman or young proletarians who worked with their hands. Mrs. Gaussen now suggested an entirely new set of standards: pitch and modulation of voice, exquisiteness of dress, the easy graciousness so different from professional philanthropy. She was the kind of woman who was to appear in *Isabel Clarendon,* Gissing's fine novel of the country house, and, more subtly, in many later novels. She was a woman not concerned, strictly speaking, with values, but with texture. Her loveliness and her glitter came not from her own labors in the vineyard, but from those of others, and in these labors she was only casually interested.

When Gissing met her, Mrs. Gaussen appeared to be in her middle thirties; she was in fact almost ten years older. She had had an exciting background: reared in India, married when very young, she told tales that held Gissing spellbound. Her husband enjoyed hunting and sport and was often in Ireland, away from his family, leaving the charming women, Mrs. Gaussen and her daughter Ella, to their own resources. Pretty Ella Gaussen had been presented at Court and enjoyed gay pageantry, including an impersonation (for the benefit of Gissing) of the languid Mrs. William Morris, who lived not very far from Broughton Hall.[12] Altogether the Gaussens drew out Gissing as no one had troubled to do before, although it was to Mrs. Gaussen that he paid chief homage. To her he exhibited his album of photographs;[13] with her he discussed his brother's visit to London;[14] because of her he became acutely aware of the drabness of his lodgings and eventually rented the most expensive "flat" he had known.[15]

It was especially comforting to have the friendship of Mrs.
Gaussen at a time when his novels were either under attack by
friends and family, or being rejected by self-righteous publishers.
Gissing had given up hope of seeing *Mrs. Grundy's Enemies* in
print, but he was not prepared for a sermon from Bentley as a
final fillip! The publisher sent him a long letter opposing the
"realistic" school of fiction, and exhorting him to avoid sowing
"one seed" that "shd. bring up an unhealthy crop." [16] Gissing found
the sermon unwelcome from a man who published such sensational novelists as Rhoda Broughton and Mrs. Wood, and as
usual he chafed at submission to Mrs. Grundy. He was forced
to admit that "moral indignation" was not "marketable." [17] He
yearned for the continent where his kind of fiction would scarcely
have seemed licentious and advised his brother to become
acquainted with Balzac, Turgenev, and Dumas.[18]

Frederic Harrison, like Algernon Gissing, could not be persuaded to approve *The Unclassed* when it was printed in 1884.

"I too have my ideals of art and social reform. . . And it so
happens that my ideals involve war to the knife with those which
are professed by the hero of the *Unclassed*. I have known something of social revolt in many forms, and have had not a little
sympathy with very many of its champions. I can feel it for
almost anyone of the positive forms of social good. That of Waymark is to me mere moral dynamite." [19]

Gissing's unrest was reflected in his changing of lodgings,
although the new ones seldom differed remarkably from the old.
He moved restlessly from place to place before, in the autumn
of 1884, he chose a two-room flat in the northwest of London
near Regent's Park, pretentiously called Cornwall Residences.
He went into the new lodgings in November and signed a three
year lease which he later renewed. He was to remain in Cornwall
Residences for six years in all, a longer time than he had ever
spent before at any one address. Here he began work on *The*

Lady of Knightswell, renamed *Isabel Clarendon,* which dealt with the new life to which Mrs. Gaussen had introduced him. The story he found difficult, probably because it dealt with "respectable society." [20]

He was reminded brutally, however, that some persons did not consider him fit for respectable society — by an article in *Punch* on January 2, 1885, containing invective as savage as any of the age of Pope, and worthy, as Gissing remarked, of the editor of *Gaiety Burlesques,* Burnand. Even Gissing's name was ridiculed, "Humbly we own that we never heard his name before, though it seems suggestive of a kind of gutteral German embrace performed by the nationaliser of the land." To Gissing, hypersensitive as he was, such cruel playing with the pronunciation of his name must have seemed unendurable.

The provocation for the bold attack by *Punch* was an open letter that Gissing had written to the *Pall Mall Gazette,* intended as a rebuttal to George Moore's article, "A New Censorship of Literature." It was part of Gissing's temperament to reply to the world at large, or at least to the literate ones of the world, in letters to newspapers and periodicals; never, however, was battle joined in the fashion employed by *Punch.*

To the honest critic there would seem little justification for the attack on Gissing, for his letter had been reasonable in tone, although scarcely complimentary to the average novelist of the day.

"English novels are miserable stuff for a very miserable reason, simply because English novelists fear to do their best lest they should damage their popularity, and consequently their income. One of the most painful confessions in literature is that contained in the preface to 'Pendennis,' where Thackeray admits that 'since the author of "Tom Jones" was buried no writer of fiction among us has been permitted to depict to his utmost power a man,' on penalty, be it understood, of a temporary diminution of receipts.

If this be not a tradesman's attitude, what is? Let novelists be true to their artistic conscience, and the public taste will come round. In that day there will be no complaint of the circulating libraries. It is a hard thing to say, but Thackeray, when he knowingly wrote below the demands of his art to conciliate Mrs. Grundy, betrayed his trust; and the same thing is being done by our living novelists everyday." [21]

Gissing's intention was primarily to lay responsibility for timorousness upon novelists themselves, and thus to refute George Moore's contention that the circulating libraries were to blame. Gissing felt that the libraries were merely the scapegoat, and that the true source of stagnation in the ideas in fiction was in the artist who did not follow his private conception of truth. His letter was, therefore, an exhortation to writers to preserve their independence in spite of the veerings of taste. Nevertheless, *Punch* chose to interpret Gissing's remarks as a defense of prurient literature and as an unwarranted attack upon Thackeray.

"O ye demigods and little Gissings. . . Not all the waters of Gissingen can do much for anybody who openly prays that the public taste may 'come round' again to the open coarseness of 'Tom Jones,' the vice of an age as much as our age has its own, which Thackeray, one of the cleanest-minded writers who ever lived, points out in that same preface to 'Pendennis' to be happily out of date. All the world knows what that preface meant, save and except Gissing, who thinks that Thackeray's artistic conscience suggested Dirt, and his art demanded it, but that he was afraid of losing money by it. . . We regret that Gissing cannot get the reading he likes . . . and we do not wholly love Mrs. Grundy. But we like her taste in books better than Gissing's. We will do all we can to help you to your desired celebrity, Gissing, though we care not to be gissing who can have brought you up. Praised be the gods for thy foulness, Gissing, but also, that, as we fondly hope, there are not very many like thee."

Not only is the taste of the article in *Punch* execrable, but also the antitheses — "clean-minded" versus "Dirt" — are almost simple-minded. Thackeray's letters make clear that Gissing's point was well made; that Thackeray for the sake of popularity and prosperity chose to act as his own censor. It may be added, however, that Gissing assumed too readily that Thackeray was fundamentally at war with his readers, an assumption which is merely a projection of Gissing's own dilemma. It is true that Thackeray wanted to make large sums of money, but his values in general were much like those of his public, including belief in God, free choice, and the virtues of humility and repentance. Thirty years after Thackeray, Gissing could not accept the values that had comforted Dickens, Thackeray, and the great Victorians of an earlier generation.

The attack in *Punch* made Gissing irate and caused his opinion of contemporary fiction in England, already low, to sink to its nadir. He ridiculed Trollope, excusing him only because "his photographing of the society of provincial towns is really so life-like. . . The dreary, commonplace twaddling talk is reproduced so that you almost *hear* the creatures." [22] The only living English novelist for whom Gissing had only praise was George Meredith, whose work seemed yearly to improve. He found it "incomprehensible" that Meredith should be so little known and declared his work far superior to George Eliot and Thackeray.[23] (Gissing was one of the small circle which at the moment was reading *Diana of the Crossways* as it appeared serially in the *Fortnightly*.) But the exception that Meredith represented was small comfort as Gissing surveyed the publishers' lists — "such mountains of literature" and most of it disappointing. Needless to say, his last resource was to persuade himself that his own talent was exceptional and that his devotion to work would eventually bring him success.[24]

The year 1885 was busy and nervewracking. Gissing was at work upon *Isabel Clarendon* and *Emily Hood* (to be published as *A Life's Morning* in 1888) but was beginning to doubt that he was wise in treating life of the manor and country-house as a subject for fiction: he was, after all, an interloper in those places. Actually the doubt was intensified by George Meredith, acting as reader for Chapman and Hall, who advised a return to "low-life scenes" and even predicted a "foremost place in fiction" for the young novelist if he chose his terrain and his local color carefully. Gissing's brother Algernon considered Meredith's advice a hobble upon George's talents, but Gissing was worried about his own competence and defended Meredith's intent.

"You misunderstand Meredith. He merely urges me to keep to low life, which is of course open to any man, though certainly it is difficult to treat it with the amazing laws which govern literature in England. Alas, alas, if one had been born a Frenchman! They alone understand the dignity and the claims of art." [25]

Ultimately Gissing heeded Meredith's advice, for when he finished the two "manor" books, he outlined a story to be called *Demos*, which would return to scenes of low life although it would avoid material "distasteful" to Mrs. Grundy. Gissing described his intention as "rather a savage satire" on the "aims and capacities" of the proletariat.[26]

"Savage" is the word to describe Gissing's dominant mood for most of the year 1885. Now the reason for his attending Socialist meetings in London was not the sympathy of days gone by, but a thirst for "copy" for his proletarian novel. He felt absolutely no nostalgia for the days when he had sat enthralled, in spite of stuffy lecture halls, listening to the speakers' promise of emancipation from superstition and poverty. His development had been from brother's brother, to brother's keeper, to brother's satirist, and his capacity for sympathy with meliorist groups had dwindled and died. He was now interested in Socialism as practiced by the fastidious, because the anomaly furnished him with good raw material for character study, and he watched greedily, now and then with horror, the development of the career of William Morris, the poet, who was hailed into court occasionally for his Socialist activities. Morris had provided a shed of sorts next to Kelmscott House, which was used as a meeting place of the Hammersmith branch of Socialists,[27] and it was in the fall of 1885 that the London police broke up a meeting of Socialists in the East End and Morris was ordered to court for assaulting a policeman. Gissing was shocked when he heard about the incident.

"Think of William Morris being hauled into the box for assaulting a policeman! And the magistrate said to him: 'What are you?' — Great Heavens! Morris answered: 'I am an artist and man of letters, I believe tolerably well-known throughout Europe.' . . . But, alas, what the devil is such a man doing in that galley? It is painful to me beyond expression. Why cannot he write poetry in the shade? He will inevitably coarsen himself in the company of ruffians.

"Keep apart, keep apart, and preserve one's soul alive — that is the teaching for the day. It is ill to have been born in these times, but one can make a world within the world." [28]

The mood of withdrawal, of "keep apart," was upon him with a vengeance, but he had by now rejected not only the "ruffians" but also the leisured class to which Mrs. Gaussen had introduced him. Those who had once seemed intelligent and winsome now were disappointing, even shams. The discovery was a painful one, for the leisured class had held a deep fascination, representing the dream of a boy who had been denied the luxuries of life. Indeed, even in the novels set in the nether world, the man with whom Gissing identifies is seldom a proletarian, but rather a person of the upper or middle class, with a good education, as fastidious and complex a creature as the author. Similarly, the woman with whom Gissing is in sympathy is not the typical one of her class, but the exception. Nevertheless, in spite of his former dreams, Gissing now felt obliged to admit that the people of Mrs.

Gaussen's group fell short of his expectations. Their interests were frivolous, their talk largely "small talk." As Gissing confided to his sister, if the weather were not available as a subject for conversation, he wondered how people would manage. He admitted readily his own difficulty in speaking society "nonsense." [29]

Although he was beginning to find his acquaintances deficient in the qualities he prized, he had mixed feelings about withdrawing from their company. Although he enjoyed the music at the home of the Misses Levy and of the Grahames, whose son Walter he tutored, he continued to feel uncomfortable. The discomfort was probably compounded of envy and virtue unrewarded: Gissing felt himself intellectually the superior of most men, and yet he was always the dependent guest, never the host. The obvious alternative, to decline invitations, was not an easy course, for his self-reliance was not sufficiently developed. Insistent about his intellectual merits, secretly he feared that people did not take him seriously. Thus when the Harrisons extended an invitation to dinner through their son Bernard rather than in the formal manner, Gissing felt hurt and decided to wear formal dress to dinner (although he could not afford the expense) as an oblique reminder to the Harrisons to treat him with care.[30] In spite of his guise of iconoclast, he sought rigidly to observe protocol in relationships in which he felt ill at ease. When feeling vindictive, he could laugh at the ridiculous aspects of the ritual of drawing rooms, but when he suspected that the ritual was suspended because no one thought him worth the bother, he became overwrought.

It was impossible for him to be casual or to breathe easily. Every social situation contained a trap, and he feared his inadequacy before the test; consequently, because he took so seriously what other men yawned over, he was exhausted after each encounter. He read Sue and Murger on the "vie de bohème," [31] but he never enjoyed that life and would gladly have exchanged it for a life replete with comfortable things. He was almost obsessive in his instructions to his sister Ellen about proper dress for a party at the Gaussens, and his first concern when invitations were extended was suitable apparel. No lady about to be presented ever received more detailed instructions than Ellen on morning, afternoon, and evening dress. Even luggage was included under the directive: it was to be encased in brown holland.[32] "By their gloves shall ye know them" was one of Gissing's formulas, although he enjoyed the phantasy of himself as iconoclast in every detail.

Exhaustion from petty encounters, the "lack of social nerve," as one critic has called it,[33] constituted a serious weakness in Gissing. It put him at the mercy of landladies and tradesmen and shrews, who always exacted their pound of flesh from him. It even placed him at the gentle mercy of Mrs. Gaussen, whose invitations first fell upon him like welcome rain, then pelted him incessantly. For once again he was worried by passing time, fearful that he would never have the prestige he craved unless he turned out one novel after the next in rapid succession. Surely one of them would have a great success.

Teaching was still disliked because it used up most days from breakfast until evening, time which Gissing would have preferred to spend in writing; nevertheless, he was conscientious in his tutoring, for his students did well in matriculation, and their families wrote letters of recommendation. Conscientiousness was possible, but not warmth, and Gissing often confided his frustrations to a letter. He had occasional favorite pupils: Bernard Harrison, for example, accompanied him in his explorations of Lambeth, for raw material to be used in *The Nether World*.[34]

An output of three novels in a year would seem to most writers an enviable record, but Gissing found no satisfaction in his accomplishment because he could not convince publishers that his work was readibly marketable. He craved reassurance from these men of business, although he had a poor opinion of the taste of most of them, and reassurance he could not get. Bentley had procrastinated for two years over the publication of *Mrs. Grundy's*

Enemies and had then relegated it to limbo; James Payn, reader for Smith, Elder, after giving promises of possible publication of *Emily Hood* in the *Cornhill* in 1885, actually issued the novel three years later. No wonder that Gissing felt only loathing, no elation, for the novels that were published long after the zeal for publication had disappeared.

On every side he saw only futility. In the larger world, war threatened, as the Russians thrust themselves aggressively into the Middle East, and the English, or too many of them for Gissing's liking, pretended they could not see what was going on.

"Why do not the bishops, priests, and deacons make their voices heard at such a juncture as this? No, they are silent, and to me, such silence is incomprehensible. If it is not part of their duty to interfere against barbarism, then what *are* they expected to do? Can you not understand the bitterness with which one regards their inactivity?" [35]

During one of his frequent depressions he considered emigration to America, trying to imagine himself, like Bertz, in the role of farmer.[36] At another juncture, tired of working so hard on novels that no one was eager to publish, he confided that he was in a poor position to bargain. He had quite given up, he said, the hope of a normal family life, because he felt a horror of being confined by the demand of any close attachment. "I fail to understand how an author does anything at all who has the claims of a family and is expected to go into society." [37]

Having denied himself most of the normal preoccupations of living, Gissing had to work obsessively, turning himself into a machine that spewed forth so many novels a year. Luckily, in 1886, just when he was on the verge of blackest despair, there came a turn for the better in his fortunes. A novel of his turned out to be extraordinarily well-timed, coinciding with the mood of the general reader, the middle-class man who was shaken over the news of riots in Trafalgar Square, as the East Enders and

South Enders, protesting the high cost of living, stormed the West End and looted the shops. The middle-class man shuddered, remembering his father's anecdotes of anarchy and Chartist riots in the thirties and forties, and wondering whether demos was amuck again. Avidly he sought the novels and articles which dealt with the denizens of Cockneydom, just as he sought in an epidemic information on the wild strange microbes. In the midst of the turmoil Gissing wrote:

"We have been in a state of riot and threatened revolution here of late. . . For myself, it is rather a good thing than otherwise, for I am writing a book that deals with Socialism, and it may prove more interesting on account of the attention that is being drawn to the subject." [38]

The prediction was borne out. Instead of having to peddle his manuscript from one firm to the next, in his usual fashion, Gissing was able immediately to place the script with Smith, Elder. Between March, when the novel was published, and May, over 500 copies were sold.[39] No such sale had ever been known to Gissing; he had achieved both a *succès d'estime* and a modest profit, and he had the satisfaction of knowing that a large part of England was guessing which prominent statesman had written the novel, published anonymously. Not since the days of Mrs. Gaskell and Disraeli had a political novel caused greater stir, and the anonymous author of *Demos* breathed deep with satisfaction, feeling perhaps like young Coningsby.

Flushed by the prompt acceptance of *Demos* by Smith, Elder, Gissing set out for Paris. It was his first visit and his joy was almost insupportable. The final fillip was the acceptance of *Isabel Clarendon* by Chapman. With pleasurable self-consciousness he registered at the Hotel Cujas in Paris as a man of letters.

He heard Louise Michel (known as *la vièrge rouge*) speak on the role of women in humanity, and perhaps stored the speech in memory for use in *The Odd Women*. He ruminated on the his-

torical past, as he was to do more eloquently on future trips to
the continent, and at the dusty, sunlit Place de la Bastille "mused
over the things that quiet place has seen." [40] But even as he paced
the corridors of the Louvre, admiring the treasures ranged there,
anxiety pricked him, urging him to return to London for first-hand
news of the reception of *Demos*. He yielded to the urging and
returned to London, there to taste anew his triumph. The publisher Smith invited him to dinner (the delighted guest recalled
that Smith had played host to the Brontës in similar circumstances
and phantasied about joining the ranks of the great).[41] Meanwhile requests were coming from the Continent for rights of foreign translation, Tauchnitz seeking the German-reading market
and Fanny Le Breton seeking permission to do a French translation.

Convinced now that Meredith's advice that he return to scenes
of "low life" had been completely sound, Gissing determined to
follow the success of *Demos* with other novels in the same setting.
He was scrupulous about providing authentic background for his
characters, and even rented a room in Lambeth from which he
could make sorties in search of local color. He visited a "lunatic
asylum," a hat factory, and a die-cutter's establishment, and
prowled about on Bank Holidays. "There is always much matter
to be picked up on such days";[42] the matter, of course, comprised
the variations of vulgarity which demos exhibited on its days of
leisure.

Gissing accepted the praises which even staid readers gave to
his novel, like John Morley's on the purple passages in *Demos*:
"One page, that describing the East End graveyard — contains a
passage which is one of the most beautiful in modern literature.
And there is genius throughout." [43] But he knew inside himself
that he was on the road to naturalism, eager to explore the fester-
ing places that John Morley and Frederic Harrison thought it best
not to discuss. He declared flatly to his brother that the writers

he found most valuable were French and Russian, that he was little in accord with English points of view, and conceded that he could not hope to be popular in England except among the most perceptive and adventurous readers.[44]

In spite of his ambitious hopes, Gissing soon found that his imagination was running dry. He made several false beginnings on novels, and felt almost paralyzed after each attempt. Finally, "driven . . . by sheer breakdown" he departed in September of 1886 for Eastbourne on the Sussex coast. He intended to stop at Brighton on the way, but found the place "impossible . . . a more hideous and vulgar seaside town the mind of man has not conceived." [45] He had always detested vulgarity of any sort, but now, during an acute depression, it almost maddened him. He recovered enough energy, however, to write a portion of *Thyrza* and in December he submitted Volume I to James Payn at Smith, Elder. But Payn decided that the book lacked "go" (how Gissing must have winced at the jargon) and although he did not reject the novel he declared emphatically that it would not do for serial publication in the *Cornhill*.[46] Gissing was crestfallen, for he had long wanted to make his name known among the large number of people who read serial fiction, and he threatened to leave Smith, Elder and give his new book to Bentley, who had published *The Unclassed*. The threat was not carried out, however, and Gissing remained with Smith because he had a reputation for "keeping up circulation." [47]

Now that he had a few pounds between himself and the next week's bills he found it increasingly difficult to stay in London for any length of time. In January of 1887 he went down again to Eastbourne, breathing the crisp, cold air, walking twenty miles daily, and searching for some cheer. The mournful faces of the townspeople, however, did not encourage a visitor to feel gay, and Gissing, having escaped, so he had thought, from the unrest in London, saw it manifest again in the hinterland.

"Everybody is out of work here. Processions of a couple of hundred men daily tramping silently and in miserable order. Wherever I go, I am stopped by decent men on the road who beg. And now the fishermen tell me there is absolutely no fish on the coast! I should think the Corn-law years cannot have been much worse." [48]

It was the sort of vacation that could have turned into a lament for things past, but luckily, from the ranks of rural laborers Gissing was able to find one man who restored his faith for a time: the man was Stephen Blackmore, a shepherd from the Downs, a "wonderful man" in Gissing's opinion, who studied Sir John Lubbock, the geologist, in his spare moments, and who read the tracts of the International Scientific Series. [49] Gissing had little but scorn for the worker who read "How to" books in his free time in the hope of obtaining a more skilled job and higher wages, but he approved Blackmore's preoccupation because there was about it a "disinterested" quality that had nothing to do with forcing a few more shillings from an employer. Clearly Gissing's views on the exercise of the mind tended to be humanistic and aristocratic.

In April of 1887 Gissing's novel *Thyrza* was published, and once again publication was followed by invitations to dinner. Having tasted the triumphs attendant upon *Demos*, Gissing could now be indifferent to such invitations, and he gave declinations regularly. Presumably, too, his relationship with the Gaussens had been broken, for in 1887 he refers sadly to his solitude and to the pain caused him by conversation with light-hearted people. Yet during the zenith of his friendship with Mrs. Gaussen he had flourished under lightheartedness and had almost forgotten the dour past. All he could say in May 1887 was: "I cannot get to know the kind of people who would suit me, so I must be content to be alone." [50]

It was the old feeling of misanthropy again, which sat upon him heavily at regular intervals, particularly when he was deprived for long periods of feminine companionship. It was not until three years later that Gissing admitted openly, brokenly, in his diary, his tremendous need to love and be loved, but now he tried to tell himself that his mood of melancholy arose largely from the view of the mediocrity of the mass of those about him. His own solitary, unloved life prompted him to damn the comfortable routine of his neighbors, and he spent lonely sedentary days contrasting the era in which he lived with glorious eras of the past, times in which, he must have phantasied, he would have been happier because he would have been better appreciated. To his sister Ellen he wrote:

"I am spending this week over a dialogue of Plato. Next time I have a holiday, I shall read some Plato to you — especially the speech of Socrates at his trial. It is one of the most inspiring things I have discovered in the world's literature.

"I often think of that story of Lady Jane Grey sitting on a summer's morning reading Plato. A strange thing that it has taken these centuries to get back — to begin to get back to the ideal of woman's education which the Elizabethans had. And who has time nowadays to read Plato? Perhaps fifty people in the United Kingdom — if so many." [51]

Working hard at his study of Greek, he now declared himself to have "as tolerable a command of Greek as anyone who is not a professed scholar." [52] He interrupted his studies occasionally with a faint word of praise for someone in the world about him, someone like Mrs. Woods, daughter of the Dean of Westminster, who had just published a novel which in Gissing's opinion was "more remarkable in its way than anything since the Brontës. It is called A Village Tragedy." [53] On the whole, however, he had few kind words for anything about him.

He suffered through the summer of 1887 like a man in a nightmare, rousing himself occasionally to note, in a strange, detached way, the steady sale of *Thyrza*. Mudie's Lending Library, which could so successfully ruin new novels by neglecting or criticizing them — witness the fate of *Richard Feverel* and *A Mummer's Wife* — had ordered 60 copies in advance and reordered 25. But, as Gissing noted bitterly, "Over against this put the fact that he had just taken 2,000 of Rider Haggard's new book." [54] He knew that his name was gradually becoming known (in July the *Pall Mall Gazette* had an article entitled "George Gissing as a Novelist") but his honesty forced him to admit that most of the little written about him was "poor stuff." [55]

A dismal autumn was a little lightened by the reappearance of Morley Roberts, who enjoyed playing the role of Ishmael. He had been a classmate of Gissing during the troubled days at Owens College, had enjoyed Gissing's confidence, but since the years in Manchester he had wandered in faraway places, in western Canada and Rhodesia, stopping in London between adventures. Like Eduard Bertz, who had departed for Germany, he was restless — Gissing was always attracted to the wanderer — but Roberts was fierce where Bertz was febrile. Bertz collapsed into tears when his plans were frustrated; Roberts ranted and banged on a table. Bertz took cold in garrets and became a hypochondriac; Roberts pretended to a noisy bohemianism and jovially turned out advertising for a middle-class firm he privately despised. Roberts, too, had ambitions as a writer and had succeeded in having some short stories accepted by the *Cornhill*, and Gissing was not a little envious, since no work by himself had yet appeared there. Nevertheless he regarded himself as more experienced than Roberts in the art of fiction and remonstrated with him for choosing "morbid" subjects for his fiction.[56]

The part that Morley Roberts played in Gissing's life is not easily appraised, since Roberts had in him a quality of ebullience which makes some of his "intimate" revelations of Gissing suspect. When *The Private Life of Henry Maitland*, a disguised biography of Gissing written after the latter's death, first appeared, many a reader wondered how much in the book was "fact" and how much the rather fulsome phantasy of Roberts. In recent years, however, since the diaries and letters of Gissing have come to light, it has appeared that Roberts, while grievously in error on many details, was closely in touch with the main events in his friend's life. Not the least of these was the sordid death of Gissing's wife in 1888 in circumstances which burned themselves on the novelist's memory, which were echoed in many a novel and short story, and which, not least of all, drove an already insecure and guilt-ridden man almost into frenzy.

The new year, 1888, had begun badly. Gissing was suffering from headache, bad weather, anything at all, and could write nothing that satisfied him. In one of the sudden impulsive decisions that were characteristic of him, he dashed off to his brother's home in Worcestershire, acting a few moments after the thought occurred to him. A few weeks in the country persuaded him that he would be able to work again, that his "breakdown" was only temporary, and he returned to London. But on Tuesday, February 7, he used strong language in his diary, "Two days of blank misery, incapable of working, feeling almost ready for suicide." Of all the diaries which Gissing left, none contains the record of more wretched moments than that of 1888. He was deprived of the normal emotional releases, yet legally contracted to a woman living in sorry debauchery in Lambeth. He must often, deep in his heart, have wished her dead, and one dreary day in February saw the fulfillment of his guilty hope.

He went down to Eastbourne again on February 13, with three checks in his pocket which must have comforted him but little — £50 from Smith for *A Life's Morning*, £15 from Frederic Harrison for coaching Bernard for a special examination, and £38 from Mr. Grahame for tutoring his son Walter. In his depressed state, Gissing must have felt unhappier still in reflecting that the money for tutoring, a trade he disliked, exceeded the sum received for a novel into which he had poured all his imagination; but he had almost become resigned to receiving recognition for the qualities which he valued least in himself. He felt sufficiently depressed to ask Morley Roberts to come down for a few days and spread some good cheer.[57] Roberts complied, and soon the two were hiking long miles together along the coast in the cold air, and once again Gissing pretended that his malaise had been nothing fundamental.

Then, on the last day of February, a telegram arrived from London — a telegram from Nell's landlady, stating that her lodger was dead. Gissing wired Roberts, who had returned to London, to stand by, and Roberts was at the door of Cornwall Residences when Gissing arrived distraught from Eastbourne. The next morning the two set out for Nell's lodging house in Lambeth. It was a bitterly cold day, and Gissing wondered nervously whether the telegram might not have been, after all, merely a ruse to lure him to Lambeth where Nell would again upbraid him and ask for more money. To reassure himself he asked Roberts to proceed alone and confirm the facts, while he paced up and down in the cold outside Waterloo Station, awaiting Roberts' return with the news that Nell indeed was dead.

It is not too much to say that Gissing "memorized" the room in which his wife lay dead, as he memorized a page from one of his dearly loved classics: the sense impressions etched themselves in his memory just as the smell of camphor and the sparkle of the water in the aquarium had hidden themselves in the memories of his boyhood before his father's death. Although he preferred to think of himself as a man of ideas, a theoretician, in the central episodes of his life he was the personification of an eye and an ear, recording like a terror-smitten child the phenomena with which his senses were bombarded. Thus, when in his novels he is most open and receptive to these sense impressions and least zealous in "explaining" them, he is most convincing and most artistic.

The house itself was a shabby, miserable place. The landlady was friendly and tearless, and anticipated with undisguised pleasure the approaching funeral, for which she would be decked in new mourning clothes, paid for by the widower as was the custom in such circumstances. This kind of delight in the trappings of funerals seemed to Gissing nothing short of barbarous, but he gave the woman her shillings, decided not to attend the funeral, and proceeded to store his disgust in memory until it should be exhibited in his next novel, *The Nether World.*

It was the room in which Nell lay, however, that most stirred in him mingled feelings of compassion and repulsion, for manifest were both his wife's earnestness to reclaim herself, and the wretched proof that she had failed. On the one hand was a pawnshop ticket for her wedding ring, but carefully preserved in a drawer were all the letters her husband had written to her, even from the days in America, proof to her no doubt in moments of remorse, that once a man had given up honor and career for her sake. There was, too, an old photograph of her husband and, strewn about, cards like those carried by people who "take the pledge."

On the walls cheap engravings, among them a Madonna, stared icily at the drab bed with its gray, threadbare linen. A bizarre figure under the Madonna lay Nell herself, who had changed for the worst. Like a Flaubert, Gissing noted with fascinated horror that only her fine white teeth remained amidst the ravages of disease and dissoluteness upon her body. This was *Workers in the Dawn* dramatized: eight years ago he had predicted in fiction the reality before his eyes. Yet, looking at Nell for the last time, he could not admit to himself that he had been responsible in any way for her downfall. Instead he railed against "the social order," that perennial solace for one's own misery.

". . . In nothing am I to blame; I did my utmost. . . Fate was too strong. But as I stood beside that bed, I felt that my life

henceforth had a firmer purpose. Henceforth I never cease to
bear testimony against the accursed social order that brings
about things of this kind." [58]

His rage against society served as a powerful goad in producing another novel. He had yearned for some stimulus which
should prod his flagging imagination, and now he had one such
as he had not dreamed of: for five tumultuous months, from
March until July, he worked at *The Nether World,* in a fever of
energy and fury.

Always after it appeared that he had purged himself of his
scorn of the proletariat and his own self-pity by writing the novel,
there came again moments of despair to plague him and to
remind him that he had not really achieved a true purgation.
When he kept busy, falling into bed exhausted, the daily round
was endurable, but all too often came the days when he could
not work, the nights when he could not sleep ". . . in agony of
loneliness . . . on the verge of madness. This life I *cannot* live
much longer; it is hideous." [59] Released from the wretched
contract of marriage, he felt little comfort, aware only of wasted
years behind him, wasted ones before him unless he made some
basic decisions about his emotional life.

He does not seem to have understood at this point all the
sources of his difficulties; indeed, a second unhappy marriage
was to succeed the first before he set about satisfying his needs
in the most adequate manner. All that he recognized after Nell's
death was that he needed companionship and someone to manage
his household. An affair, apparently, was not adequate: for a
man so devoted to matters of the intellect, Gissing was singularly
interested in the pettinesses of housekeeping — from competence
of servants to the details of the dustbin. On the one hand he
demanded the "ideal" woman, the woman he had sought to
describe in the characters of Isabel Clarendon, Helen Norman,
even Thyrza. On the other hand, his income was small, and he

would have to find a woman willing to be manageress of humble lodgings.

Certainly he never realized that the model for his ambiguous relationship with Nell, and now his confused ideas about a second marriage partner, was the marriage of his own parents. Thomas Gissing had been a studious man, concerned over the opinions of his neighbors, scornful of those of lesser intellectual attainments than his; yet he had married a plain woman of domestic interests, who, as her son observed, was more concerned with the backstairs than with things of the mind. Just as George condemned his mother for her lack of intellectual interests but sent his love to her in every letter, so he vacillated in his relationship with Nell, enjoying her affection and easy domesticity, hostile when she yawned over matters that interested him. Thus, when Nell died, he felt both exhilarated and depressed, the inevitable consequence of unrecognized mixed feelings.

To comfort himself, Gissing determined to fall in love again, a kind of homeopathy in which he partook again of the poison that had almost killed him. Two months after Nell's death he was brooding passionately over another woman; two years later, on a summer's day, he fell violently and mutely in love (on one day's acquaintance) with a friend of his sister in Wakefield; yet in the very autumn following the fanciful love of the summer he met and married, after a courtship of only four months, still another young woman, so like his mother in some ways that, had Gissing been a fatalist, he would have said the gods were laughing at him cruelly.

Although a self-avowed iconoclast, like the heroes in his novels, Gissing in 1888 was still the slave to an imperfect understanding of his emotional needs and the solutions he might best effect; and, like the heroes in his novels, too often he blamed "society" for the errors in judgment, the stupidities of an imperfectly educated young man with too little knowledge of self. However, as he learned more about his motives and the labyrinthine tracts of his unconscious desires, he would have a larger sense of what constituted "the social problem." And with such knowledge there would come, too, a mature "psychological novel," the forerunner of the more skilled specimens of the twentieth century, in which "society" is no longer the whipping boy for one's own self-deceptions.

Chapter 6

NOVELS OF MANOR
AND OF SLUMS

"Isabel Clarendon" was an essay in a new setting. In 1884
Gissing abandoned the tenements and went to the country house,
forgot the women of the demi-monde and dreamed of those in
fashionable and secure places. A new vista had opened to him
when Frederic Harrison, and, above all, Mrs. Gaussen, befriended
him, and he could not but be dazzled. Country houses redolent
of luxury and ancient deeds of valor now lay open to him, and
he noted every detail with the hungry accuracy of the starved
man who thinks this may be his last meal. True, in the gray day-
light hours back in London he recognized that there were crudities
in this panorama! The finest parts of Broughton Hall, Mrs.
Gaussen's country house, had long ago been pulled down, he
noted;[1] and the Frederic Harrisons merely rented, not owned, the
lovely house in Surrey. Perhaps they too, in a sense, were
déclassé in comparison with the aristocracy which had the wealth
and prestige of centuries. But most of the time Gissing was
enchanted with the new scene, not critical. The lyrical descriptions
in *Isabel Clarendon* testify to the eagerness and the reverence
with which he welcomed the glimpses of a life he had never
known, the kind of life his parents would have liked to live.

If Gissing had needed the model of another literary man wooed
by the charms of gentle living, he could have found it in Meredith. The two men had much in common, above all the sensitive,
almost excessive concern for the manners of a class to which

they were strangers, but to which they hoped to be admitted. Meredith had fared better, in more practical ways, than Gissing. Born in the lower middle class, the grandson of a tailor (recall the wounded pride of Evan Harrington in similar circumstances), he was introduced to the fashionable world of Thomas Love Peacock and married his patron's daughter. He thrilled to the glitter of the new society, but kept at his side the sharp sword of common sense with which all the glitter could be dashed to bits. To Gissing, Meredith was the greatest living novelist in England, one who bore fancied resemblances to himself. He met Meredith in 1884, visited Box Hill from time to time, and corresponded with him even during the years of self-imposed exile in France.

Like Evan Harrington, Bernard Kingcote in Gissing's novel falls in love with a woman whose social position is superior to his. Like Evan he feels that his pride will not permit patronage, even if the patronage comes in the kindest and most loving way. Unlike Evan's, his financial position is not restored by a benevolent old man who resembles Dickens' guardian angels. Instead, Kingcote retreats from Isabel and her world and opens a stationer's shop by means of which he will support a widowed sister. By the end of the novel it is clear that Gissing's novel is much more "realistic" than Meredith's. Both Evan and Kingcote are self-conscious, but Kingcote has ennui as well. Evan, even in his saddest mood, believes that he will be rescued from tailordom; Kingcote denies "the will to live" because he knows that the odds, the probability, are against him. He has a sister—just as Gissing had and the Victorians produced in abundance—weak, pretty, poor, indecisive after marriage and widowhood and too many children.

Some of the Meredith "tricks" of style are found in Gissing's novel—the "imps of the air" who, Meredith fancied, observed and mocked the foolishness of vain human beings. There is a sardonic view of education, in the Meredith manner, as the source of "robust young Britons." But most important of the awarenesses that Meredith's work foisted upon Gissing — coming, of course, only after he had been smitten by the experience in real life of Mrs. Gaussen — was the new conception of the womanly woman.

Isabel Clarendon, the lady of the manor, would have made a gracious neighbor of Fielding's Amelia, or Jane Austen's heroines, or Thackeray's Mrs. Pendennis. She belongs to the great tradition of the English gentlewoman, wherein "lady" is not merely a matter of title, but a matter of character. She is kind and gentle without being weak, a proper successor to the original "Lady of Knightswell" after whom her estate is named, the lady for whose love a valiant knight once fought and died. (Kingcote is his foil, with some irony.) As her sharp-tongued ward remarks, "Men — all men — see her so differently." Differently, of course, from the way women see her. Her womanliness, the latent sexuality which is implicit in her lazy grace and unhurried efficiency, make a captive of Kingcote in a very short time. Her emotions are simple and direct; confronted with Kingcote's gloomy face, she does not comfort him but asks instead, "Why should you so have forgotten the habit of cheerfulness?" She enjoys the intrigues and posturings of society, but is not sullied by them.

"She was, as Lady Kent had seen, born for society; it was her element; it brought out all that was best and loveliest in her; it made her a complete being. Society could not give her more than it was in her to produce, but on the other hand, it planted not one seed of alien evil."

Isabel is a "complete being" incapable of rancor despite past years of a marriage that was incomplete; her widowhood is an opportunity for new love and she believes Kingcote to be the man. But he is incomplete, gloomy, sensitive. He is "explained" by Gissing in the first chapter and in the last chapter the explanation still holds true:

"Things which most men accept as the everyday rules of the
world were to Kingcote among the worst evils of existence; the
most ordinary transactions with uneducated and (as he held)
presumably uncivilised persons at all times made him uncomfortable."

Kingcote realizes that his introspective habits have almost
crippled him in his human relations and he gives bitter counsel
for someone else. "Let the mind take care of itself. . . Occupy
him with vigorous bodily pursuits; keep the mind from turning
inwards; save him from reflection." He must make two decisions
which concern Isabel: whether a poor man should marry a woman
of wealth and social position; next (when the woman loses both
because of the malign will left by her dead husband) whether
he should permit her, who can so easily remarry wealth and
prestige, to live grubbily as his wife. In his previous novels
Gissing had manipulated the plot so that his heroes were spared
the problem of carrying out their decisions. Thus, in *Workers in
the Dawn,* Helen refuses to be the hero's mistress, and thus
Golding is permitted both the luxury of "immoral" feelings and
the retention of his idealized vision of "pure" Helen. Similarly,
in *The Unclassed,* Ida Starr is provided by the author with a
legacy which solves her problems and her lover's. It is a curious
irony that despite all the "realism" of the two first novels in their
proletarian setting, the moral realism is less evident than it is
in the "romantic" atmosphere of *Isabel Clarendon.* This is only
another way of saying, of course, that *psychological* realism must
be present or "realism" is only a bag of tricks.

The author spares Kingcote in no way: if Isabel rich furnishes
a conflict, so does Isabel poor. "Few men surpassed Bernard
Kingcote in ingenious refinement of self-torture." In spite of his
wish to be just he remains weak, and Gissing comments, "If a
man have not strength, love alone will not suffice to bind a
woman to him; she will pardon brutality, but weakness inspires

her with fear." Much as he loves Isabel, Kingcote withdraws, supposedly because of his concern for her welfare. But Isabel interprets his decision as the result of fear and inability to face reality, and eventually she agrees to marry another man.

The audacity of the basic conflict in the novel (there are others as well) is striking even today, and it was even more striking at the end of the last century. Throughout Victorian fiction self-denial and self-sacrifice had been deemed virtues. Suddenly a novel appeared which suggested that these "virtues" are sometimes no more than the rationalizations of confused and fearful people. It is Isabel who holds the reader's sympathy, Isabel who prefers a full relationship with a poor husband to a fervid correspondence from an ivory tower. True, Gissing finally bestows upon Kingcote a serious reason for celibacy: he must support a recently widowed sister. But Kingcote seizes upon the new excuse only after he has delayed for other reasons. A "ménage à trois" — his sister, his wife and himself — would be "suburban," and a subsidy from Isabel would offend his pride. He thus denies love because he can endure it only when the context is ideal. The man to whom Isabel turns for companionship is less intense than Kingcote, but also less exhausting.

Thomas Seccombe observed that in *Isabel Clarendon* Gissing "began really to write." [2] Certainly in this novel there is greater dexterity in the choice of situations which indicate character. In the very first chapter Kingcote, hiking along a country road, comes to a fork, and must choose between the old, weed-invaded byway, and the brash, straight, new road. He chooses the tortuous path and at the end of it comes upon the house of the Lady of Knightswell. There is also a skilled use of flashback in Book I, chapter 7, when the years are rolled back to the arrival of Isabel's young ward, who begins as a child to nourish an increasingly intense dislike of her guardian. Several of the characters are well-drawn, and succinctly, without the long descriptions of the earlier novels. Ada Warren — a "woman of character" as Gissing calls her, is the first of the clever, sharp-tongued, love-starved women he was to study in so many novels; and Vincent Lacour is the first of the half-educated, amoral, handsome young egoists who find that their "love" can vary with a bank balance.

There are, of course, some weaknesses in technique that were overcome only years later. Thus in chapter 2 the reader's curiosity about the Lady of Knightswell, which has been aroused by conversations between Kingcote and the rector of the village, is quite destroyed when the author steps in with a signed, sealed, and delivered history of Isabel's past. His remark on Isabel's late husband is intolerable: "For this gentleman's qualifications see above."

The *Athenaeum* considered the novel "stronger in conception than in execution" and was annoyed with "sundry improbable incidents." [3] (In each of Gissing's first seven novels a will and legacy are involved, with rather confusing ramifications.) The *Academy* was more enthusiastic: *Isabel Clarendon* was "above all things a mature book" and was compared with "the practice of Henry James by leaving nearly all the threads of the story hanging loose at the end of the last volume." [4] Thus Gissing's intention was executed. He had wanted the ending to be "as unromantic as could be. Several threads are left to hang loose; for even so it is in real life; you cannot gather up and round off each person's story." [5] The *Academy* concluded with a recommendation of the book "to that cultivated class of readers who seek in fiction what Mr. Matthew Arnold says is to be found in good poetry — a 'criticism of life.'"

A Life's Morning, although not published until 1888, was written after *Isabel Clarendon* and belongs to the same manner. When Gissing saw it unravel in serial installments in the *Cornhill* Magazine from January to June of 1888 he was embarrassed by it, and yearned to see the last installment and the disappearance of the story from print. His own reaction is an insufficient test of the strength of the novel, nevertheless, for no novel pleased him once another was in the process of being written. The book was reviewed cordially: "Except for a tendency to wordiness and an occasional heaviness of touch, *A Life's Morning* is excellent as regards incident and characterization. Mr. Gissing understands the value of contrast; his characters do not remain stationary." [6] Perhaps the review was excessively cordial, for the book survives largely because of the clever use of contrast and some fine, credible scenes of provincial life. All Gissing's fine irony, which he had used with Kingcote, appeared to desert him as he prostrated himself before Wilfrid Athel.

The story opens with the return of the young man from Oxford to his father's house in Surrey. By the end of chapter 3 he has fallen in love with Emily Hood, the governess in the family. The chapter entitled "Lyrical" is the one in which the pair fall in love, and it seems patterned after the scene of young love in Meredith's *The Ordeal of Richard Feverel*. But where Meredith's touch is light, Gissing's is heavy. The nature setting, intended to complement young love, is forced, theatrical.

"'May I tell you the plan which I have made in the night?' he said, as they stood on a spot of smooth turf netted with sunlight."

During the love scene Emily is to the hero "the goddess that made herself woman for his sake." But to the reader, Emily's common-sense replies to a rather overcome young man suggest a sensible, poised young woman of not quite the kind Gissing intended. Had he wished an ironic contrast to a lover's hyperbole, like Meredith's in *The Egoist*, surely he would not have tried to make the scene lyrical. The reader can only conclude that in having Emily sound like Jane Austen, and Wilfrid like a caricature, Gissing failed to provide unified tone. If only Gissing had realized that Wilfrid was no demigod, the scene would have been worthy of Meredith.

Emily Hood is far more interesting than her lover. Like Isabel she loves directly and unequivocally, but she lacks the older woman's self-sufficiency and poise. Harrassed by a "seedy" dependent family in the Midlands, she can scarcely believe that a prosperous and happy marriage will be hers. Her fears are confirmed, and after some small peculations by her father, and the improper advances of her father's employer, who uses the father as a tool to secure the daughter, she finds it necessary to reject Wilfrid Athel, without, however, giving him any explanation. The sustained silence which causes Wilfrid to believe that Emily loves another man is the most serious improbability in the novel. Surely a girl like Emily, with a keen sense of justice, would have confided to her lover her reason for postponing the marriage. The furtiveness, although designed to protect Wilfrid's good name, is contrary to the conception of Emily's character which has been established. Wilfrid turns to politics, Emily to frenzied mortification of the flesh. At the end of the novel, for no reason except the insistence of the publisher upon a happy ending, the two are reunited after years of separation.

If Wilfrid's success in politics is just as incredible as Mr. Micawber's as a colonial magistrate in Australia, Emily's family and their activities are altogether convincing. The chapters which show Emily in Yorkshire with her parents are among the best in the book. The drab mill town is an appropriate setting for the drab little man, Emily's father, whose self-possession can be shaken by the loss of his hat. No "stagey" larks are needed in *these* chapters; the details are "natural" and yet they have symbolic significance. Thus Mr. Hood is no more than a scarecrow: when he loses the garments that make him look like a man, he is exposed to the cruel wind of ostracism and dies from exposure.

Mr. Dagworthy, Hood's employer, who wants to possess the best woman in town just as he owns the best of everything else in it, is a sturdy contrast to Wilfrid Athel, and in his intransigent passion may be compared with Bradley Headstone in *Our Mutual*

Friend. He knows that Emily fears and dislikes him, but her very fastidiousness titillates his appetite. In his attempt to force her to marry him he uses blackmail and is indirectly responsible for the suicide of her father. In contrast to his credibility there are Wilfrid and his cousin Beatrice Redwing, who belong in one of the lesser novels of George Moore, peopled by garrulous opera stars. Although Dagworthy's vehement speeches often continue for a full page, the cadences ring true; Wilfrid's rhapsodies are usually hollow:

" 'My fair wise one!' he murmured, gazing rapturously at her. 'Oh, Emily, think what our life will be! Shall we not drain the world of its wisdom, youth, and its delight? Hand in hand, one heart, one brain —what shall escape us? It was you I needed to give completeness to my thought and desire.' "

After much more in the same manner, the reader is tempted to agree with Meredith's advice that Gissing return to the nether world, in which he is less likely to confuse Oxonian breeding with Ouida's guide to the manners of young gentlemen. *Isabel Clarendon* is well-organized and authentic, but *A Life's Morning* is only half-convincing; perhaps Gissing better understood the feelings of a courtier for a lady than those of a young patron for a poor governess. He had been rather a Kingcote; he had never been a Wilfrid. He would return to Emily's world in *The Odd Women,* six years later, but in that investigation he would be more dispassionate, and Wilfrid would disappear.

Although *A Life's Morning* was postponed by publishers from year to year, *Demos* was snatched hungrily by Smith, Elder and published in the winter of 1886 while all England was gossiping over the riots in Trafalgar Square. As the publisher had foreseen, the brisk sale was due to the curiosity of the middle class about the habits and appetites of the lower. The "proletarian novel" — the novel with characters and scenes drawn from the working class — had waxed and waned: had waxed in the forties and fifties with Mrs. Gaskell and Dickens, Kingley and Disraeli; waned; then would wax again in the nineties when Israel Zangwill would write *Children of the Ghetto,* and William Morris, *A Child of the Jago,* and Somerset Maugham, just beginning his career, *Liza of Lambeth.* But in the eighties the proletarian novel was only beginning its upward climb, and George Gissing and Walter Besant were the chief contenders.

All the reviewers agreed that the author of *Demos* (who remained anonymous) had an intimate knowledge of the working man, but one of the most discerning readers was Frederic Harrison, who recognized the "aristocratic tone" of the novel.[7] For Gissing was no longer a partisan of the working class, and was interested, in fact, in only the most unusual specimens it had to offer. Richard Mutimer, the hero of *Demos,* far exceeds the bulk of his class in ambition and intelligence, just as Thyrza is far superior to the working girls who surround her. Only in *The Nether World* are the characters "average" enough to win for Gissing a valid comparison with Zola. As Gissing says bluntly of Richard Mutimer,

"Richard represented — too favourably to make him anything but an exception — the best qualities his class can show. He was the English artisan as we find him on rare occasions, the issue of a good strain which has managed to produce a sufficiency of food for two or three generations."

Richard's survival in a grubby part of London has been that of the fittest; equally sturdy, although less intelligent, is his sister, the "Princess." But if Richard finds the most gratification of his ego as a leader of working class men, the Princess finds hers in the adoration of sporting men. Richard's younger brother lacks both drive and robust health, as though the "good strain" of the Mutimers had exhausted itself after producing the other children. He has the quality of a ferret, and survives by guile alone.

By means of still another freak will, Richard falls heir to a factory and a fortune. He seizes the opportunity to prove that he is a leader of men on a large scale and to reward the workers, with whom he identifies, with a greater share in the profits.

"He thought, poor fellow! that he could rise . . . and thunder forth his indignant eloquence as he did in Commonwealth Hall and elsewhere; he imagined a conscience-stricken House, he dreamed of passionate debates on a Bill which really had the good of the people for its sole object. Such Bill would of course bear *his* name. . ."

Not only does Richard have a fantastic notion of the impact he will make upon the world, but also he fancies that only the most fastidious gentlewoman within his acquaintance will suit him as wife. He rather resembles Dagworthy in *A Life's Morning* in his desire to own a well-bred wife as he would own a well-bred mare, but his desire is more heady than Dagworthy's because he has come from nothing to power, whereas Dagworthy has been for a long time an important figure in the community. Richard chooses Adela Waltham, whose family is, after the Eldons, the most respected in the town, and "falls in love" with her in the uncommon interpretation of the "falling" which Gissing was one of the first Victorian novelists to emphasize. Adela's coolness fans his ambition for the unattainable, which in him is closely related to sexual passion, and indeed, intensifies it. In order to marry Adela, he forsakes the girl of his own class who, nevertheless, remains more loyal to him than his wife.

Gissing considered Adela "delightful" and regretted that "few people seem to understand and appreciate her."[8] He intended her to be a "sympathetic" character despite, possibly because of, her eventual desertion of her ambitious husband. But the many readers who found Adela quite the reverse of Gissing's intention had ample justification, for once again, because of his hostility to the self-assured, semi-literate represented by Richard

Mutimer, Gissing gave too ready homage to their opposites. Hubert Eldon, the well-reared foil to Richard, is treated much like Adela, and one feels that Gissing has deceived himself about these two. He says of Adela after her marriage,

"The high-hearted one! She would have died rather than let her mother perceive that her marriage was less than happy. To the end she would speak the words 'My husband' when it was necessary to speak at all, with the confidence of a woman who knows no other safeguard against the ills of life. . ."

Yet Adela's motives in marrying Richard scarcely justify the epithet "noble-hearted." Her mother considers her passive: the daughter will marry because her mother wants her to do so. "The dear child has, I believe, no will apart from her desire to please me. Her instincts are so beautifully submissive." But the "dear child," the "high-hearted one," is actually persuaded into marriage by a vision of her power as the wife of the most important man in the community; furthermore she wishes to punish Hubert Eldon for his past defections. In spite of these motives, she manages to think of herself as a martyr, and Gissing unfortunately assents in the self-deception by insisting that she is grossly treated.

The view of Hubert Eldon is similarly muddled. On the one hand, "Hubert could not remember a time when he had not been in love. The objects of his devotion had succeeded each other rapidly, but each in her turn was the perfect woman." Nevertheless, each of these adventures, Gissing would have the reader believe, was glorious. "He had lived through a glorious madness as unlike the vulgar oat-sowing of the average young man of wealth as the latest valse on a street organ is unlike the passionate dream of Chopin." Aside from Gissing's insistence, there is no proof either of Eldon's ability or his fastidiousness. His love for Adela is less like a "passionate dream of Chopin" than a narcissistic experiment of a bored young man in the Midlands. Fortunately, Hubert Eldon and Adela are not central in the novel, and the brilliance of Gissing's larger aim shines out in spite of them. He intended the novel to be "rather a savage satire on working class aims and capacities," and that it was. It was also a satire of another class, although he had not intended this — the class of leisured egoists who drifted about the continent in search of the "passionate dream of Chopin."

The rise and fall of Richard Mutimer is prepared every step of the way. Every mood is shown — his triumph when Adela consents to marry him; his delight when the butler (laughing up his sleeve) calls him "Sir,"; his horror when he loses his fortune; his hatred of his own class when he is brought to bay by a mob whose money he has invested unwisely. Gissing is careful to show Mutimer from many points of view and among the most effective are the "little" scenes, like the one in a tavern, where the bartender, aware of Richard's sudden fortune, calls him "Sir" and urges him to buy a whiskey. Afterwards he confides to a friend, "Wouldn't 'ave 'had it but for the 'Sir'. . . Never used to when he come 'ere unless I stood it!" The most effective of the "big" scenes is the one at the end of the novel when Richard is pursued and trapped by those whom he had dedicated his life to help. Deserted by all but the dull girl whom *he* had deserted, he says in despair,

"They'll break the door through. If they do, the devils are as likely to kill you as me . . . listen to them, that's the People that is! I deserve killing, fool that I am, if only for the lying good I've said of them."

In some respects the novel comes as close as is possible to being a modern tragedy. [9] The oracle of a secularized, capitalist society is a legal document which causes a reversal from bad to good fortune, and then from good to bad again. The chorus is now a Midlands minister. But Richard, at least, shows himself great in "recognition" of his mistakes and in suffering. Alone and dying, he realizes at last that he is a peccant individual and not only an inviolate part of "demos."

Thyrza is the only one of Gissing's three fine proletarian novels which is gentle in tone. It was written soon after *Demos,* with a wish to take advantage of the success of the earlier book. Perhaps the "savage satire" of *Demos* had exhausted temporarily Gissing's hostile feelings, just as its intricate plot had exhausted his ingenuity. Whatever the reasons, *Thyrza* appeared without savagery or intricacy before a cordial public. The *Athenaeum* declared, "In power and pathetic treatment the novel is above the average." [10] Thomas Seccombe has called it Gissing's "first really notable and artistic book." [11] Thyrza herself, who moves luminously through the book and holds it together as the plot cannot do, is "designed in the school of Dickens . . . almost . . . a pastel after some more highly finished work by Daudet." [12] The comparison is excellent. Gissing had been reading Daudet, relishing his kindness and largeheartedness. (Even the gloom of Daudet, as modern critics have remarked, is a "fake" gloom; he is much more interested in the wetness of water and the rosiness of cheeks.) Most of the characters in *Thyrza* are touched kindly, without either condescension or sentimentality. By this time Gissing had learned completely the art of striking the keynote immediately: thus Gilbert Grail, whom Thyrza is to marry, is introduced during one of his regular visits to Westminster Abbey, an uncommon place for the leisure-time activities of a hardpressed workingman. Immediately Grail's reflective, gentle character is suggested. For Thyrza too, from the moment she sings in one of the "friendly leads" in Lambeth, her ruling passion is established. Her heart is on her sleeve, and she is aware of it without being "precious." At the beginning of the story she says, "I think I should die if I hadn't someone to love me." And if at the end of the novel she does not die from a broken heart (Gissing is too clinical for that!), she dies from a heart ailment.

All of Thyrza's compatriots on Paradise Street — although the street in Lambeth is hardly paradise — are credible beings. Bunce, a bitter atheist who scorns charity and regards religion and private philanthropy as the opiate of the people, is a foil to Gilbert Grail. Like him is Luke Ackroyd, a less intelligent variant of Richard Mutimer in *Demos:* he is the worker who attends "How to" lectures in the evening and abhors all but the practical. Most of the women in the novel are interested neither in "How to" lectures nor anything remotely resembling an idea. When they accompany Gilbert Grail to libraries and galleries, they marvel less at the wonder of art than at the wonder of Gilbert wasting his time.

The credibility of these women of the working class, busy with their workshop gossip and their next door neighbors, gives the lie to the criticism that Gissing always projected on to the nether world his own discontent at having to live grubbily. Gissing knew well enough that a legacy of £250 was no fortune, but he knew that for Totty Nancarrow the sum was tremendous; therefore he takes seriously her concern over it. And no scene in *Thyrza* is more moving than the one in which old Mr. Boddy, Thyrza's grandfather, is given a new overcoat to replace the threadbare one. Dickens would have squeezed innumerable tears from the scene, and so does Gissing. Yet the characters have more awareness than those in Dickens: the girls cannot afford the gift, and the old man knows it; and he cannot afford to feel sorry for himself, and they know it. Thus the bathos that mars similar scenes in Dickens is completely lacking.

There are three classes of people in the novel. At the base are the masses of the nether world; in the middle are the "sports," the rare products of the class who possess superior intelligence and sensitivity; at the apex is Walter Egremont, the idealist, who sees as a factory owner the opportunity to make Paradise Street live up to its name.

He offers neither soup kitchens, nor coöperative ownership,

nor a Radical program. He does open a free library and gives an evening course in English Literature. (Gissing clearly is in sympathy with Egremont but has acquired enough objectivity to note that Egremont's lectures are unintelligible to most of his listeners.) Egremont meets Thyrza and falls swiftly in love with her, although she is betrothed to Gilbert Grail, the workingman whom Egremont most respects. Torn by the conflict between love and loyalty and painfully aware that Thyrza returns his love, Egremont departs from Thyrza's life and travels across the Atlantic, much like Angel Clare in *Tess of the D'Urbervilles*. Unfortunately for the characterization of Egremont, however, his decision is not wholly his own, for he is urged by a meddling *dea ex machina,* Mrs. Ormonde, whom Gissing thinks admirable. She insists that Thyrza is a great, though untrained, artist – and that her talent can best be developed in a state of celibacy. Mrs. Ormonde acts as patroness, Egremont leaves for America, and Thyrza languishes and dies.

Although Gissing was angered by the opinion of James Payn, reader for Smith, Elder, the criticism seems just. Payn declared that the novel ought not to be published in the *Cornhill* magazine, and criticized the large amount of "preachment" and the "priggish" quality of Egremont.[13] Egremont with a conflict between love and duty is an interesting character, but as a passive listener to Mrs. Ormonde's patter about Thyrza's "art" he is not convincing. As Payn said, too, the scenes with local color in the slums were the most effective. However, they are rivaled in merit by those in which Victor Dalmaine appears. He is the new junior statesman, differing from the Tory tradition of gentleman-statesman, the Liberal tradition of barrister-statesman, and the Radical experiment of proletarian-statesman.

"His education had not been liberal; he saw that it made no difference, and wisely pursued the bent of his positive mind where another man might have wasted his time in the attempt to gain culture. He saw that his was the age of the practical. Let who would be an idealist, the practical man in the end got all that was worth having."

And Dalmaine sets about getting "all that was worth having." Included in his list is Paula Tyrrell, although she has a habit of saying "clever" things, intolerable for the wife of a politician! Like Petruchio in the taming of his shrew he tames his clever wife quickly, and in a short time she plays a contented second fiddle. Her father knows what kind of man Dalmaine is but does not resent him.

"Look at Dalmaine. How much do you think he cares for the factory-hands he's always talking about? But he'll do them many a good turn; he'll make many a life easier; and just because it's his business to do so, because it's the way of advancing himself."

Dalmaine is the winner and takes all, and Egremont, the idealist, loses everything. He recognizes at last that his school for enlightenment is not practical, and that he had not the courage to take the love of Thyrza while it was possible. At the end of the book he proposes to Annabel Newthorpe, knowing very well that this is second best. She knows it too. They are climbing a mountain and Annabel refuses to go to the summit (once Gissing discovered symbolism, he rather pounced on it!). She says coolly to Egremont,

"I can tell you what I know to be the truth, that you missed the great opportunity of your life when you abandoned Thyrza. Her love would have made of you what mine never could, even though she herself had been taken from you very soon. I can tell you the mere truth, you see. Dare you still ask for me?"

Egremont replied,

"I don't ask, Annabel. I have your hand and I keep it."

It is regrettable that in so good a novel the important an-

tagonism between Dalmaine and Egremont should be left un-
developed, whereas chapters are wasted upon Mrs. Ormonde,
who seizes more and more words as the novel progresses. Only
the return of sensible Annabel saves the end of the novel from
crumbling.

The Nether World, published in 1888, atones for the lack of
unity in *Thyrza.* There is surprising order amidst a disorder
redolent of Hobbes, for in the nether world there are only force
and matter and anarchy as each character pursues his own self-
interest in blind collision with others. It should be remembered
that Gissing began the novel after the death of his wife, with
the sordid details of that plebeian life burned into his mind.
Writing the novel was indeed a catharsis. Savagery and pessimism
were poured into the book. There is not a single character from
an ideal "outside" world, and therefore there is not a single
example of the author's duping himself as he had so often done.
For this reason, and for the reasons of unity and slashing realism,
the novel must rank as one of Gissing's best.

It is as though his whole perspective had changed; it is like
Alice in Wonderland's discovery that the Red Queen is, after
all, only a cat — except that Gissing remembers that a cat is
related to a tiger. The benevolent patron of *Workers in the Dawn*
has dwindled into a fussy old man with a religious mania that
his granddaughter should save the world at the expense of her
own happiness — this despite the fact that she has neither the
intelligence nor the drive to accomplish the purpose. At first Mr.
Snowden is a sturdy and heart-warming figure as he stumps
about Clerkenwell Green in search of his long lost granddaughter. But several years later Jane has become merely the
instrument of his frenzied philanthropy, and he emerges as a
man who will sacrifice human beings for the sake of a vague
idea. Jane herself is a Helen Norman off the pedestal. To please
her grandfather she works in a soup kitchen, but she soon learns
that the beneficiaries take advantage of her timidity. The scenes

in the soup kitchen sometimes verge upon farce, like those with Mrs. Jellyby in *Bleak House*, but Jane herself is never ridiculous.

The dominant figure in the novel is not Jane Snowden, however, but Clem Peckover, cruel, lively virago. She spears young Jane, maid of all work at the Peckovers, with the same gusto that she uses in spearing the sausages for her supper. Her marriage, dictated like all her activities by sheer selfishness, ends in the discovery that her husband has outdone her in deception. The man who really attracts her wears the new badge that Gissing had discovered — the white collar. Hewett and Clem singly are savage enough, but in conjunction, like the planets of old, their influence is indeed baleful. In chapter 12, "Io Saturnalia!", they appear together at the Crystal Palace on a Bank Holiday, a day that Gissing hated. It is also Hewett's wedding day, and he can think of no more suitable place to take his young bride than the noisiest, most crowded place in London. "Pennyloaf," his wife, is a degenerated Penelope, in name and in character, and her waiting for her erring husband has in it only the pathos of a suffering animal. But, for that matter, all the people in *The Nether World* are little more than struggling animals, even Sidney Kirkwood, who had hoped to rise above that world, but who sinks back because of a confused loyalty that binds him to his lachrymose wife.

In his manipulation of "mass" scenes, Gissing comes close to Zola's method, as the reviewers agreed: there is the funeral in chapter 5 (a civilized orgy), the scene in the Crystal Palace, and the tracking down of Bob Hewett by the police. Above all, any scene in which Clem figures is vivid and detailed.

"Clem laughed heartily, then finished her beer in a long, enjoyable pull. Her appetite was satisfied; the last trace of oleaginous matter had disappeared from her plate, and now she toyed with little pieces of bread lightly dipped into the mustard-pot . . . at sixteen she had all her charms in apparent maturity, and they were of the coarsely magnificent order. Her forehead was low and of great width; her nose was well shapen, and had large sensual apertures; her cruel lips may be seen on certain fine antique busts."

Unfortunately, the coarse sensuality of Clem is a trifle bowdlerized since, as Gissing realized bitterly, English readers rejected realism in sexual matters. Thus, as in *Demos,* the strong sexual feelings are merely hinted at.

Less ambitious than *Demos,* for it has no character as complex as Richard Mutimer, *The Nether World* is more dexterous and more consistent: the author sees clearly all he surveys and rationalizes for no one. By the time of the publication of *The Nether World,* the last of Gissing's trio of proletarian novels, it was clear that a new and important author had entered the field of novels of the "didactic and speculative class." Such was the opinion of as testy a critic as Gladstone, who, as he himself confessed, did not usually read fiction. Gladstone lamented, however, that the word "sin" in Gissing's novels "had never been . . . a word of mighty import." [14]

It was a sharp observation from a man who had been reared on the grand old Victorian novelists who had had a deep and abiding sense of sin as well as sympathy. Little Em'ly, Jasper in *Edwin Drood,* and even Pendennis, in spite of their weaknesses, acted with a realization of right and wrong and deserved punishment after transgressions, but Gissing's creatures, many of them, seem to behave only as their constitutions and their early environment have forced them to behave. Thus Gissing's use of authentic detail in sketching the haunts of his proletarians was no mere surface brushwork in a picture essentially romantic in conception, and his work, therefore, was altogether different from that of Walter Besant and others beginning to exploit the nether world for local color. It was left, however, for Miss Edith Sichel to point up the contrast in an article in *Murray's Maga-*

zine for April, 1888. She contrasted Besant's work (*All Sorts and Conditions of Men* and *The Children of Gibeon*) with Gissing's *Thyrza* and concluded:

"Being himself, as far as his books reveal him, devoid of any conviction, even the conviction of doubt, he fails to give us any solution, or to offer us either the guidance or the comfort which he lacks himself. We feel more inclined to try and comfort him than to receive any explanation of life from him. . . Mr. Gissing writes us a realistic jeremiad, whilst Mr. Besant gives us a Bowdlerized Whitechapel — a family edition of the East End."

Gissing's work continued to be a "realistic jeremiad," but by 1889 and *The Emancipated* his clinical method had come to be applied to another class, the middle class. He was no longer interested in the nether world, was rather jaded after exploring it so intensely, and the death of his first wife had freed him from the most powerful tie that bound him to it. Thus, in June of 1888 he attended a lecture on Socialism at the Bermondsey Gladstone Club for no purpose except satire: he had finished with his former enthusiasm for the theory of Socialism. He attended, as he bluntly declared, to reassure himself that "prejudice alone" was not responsible for the scorn he felt for such people. All the speakers save one he found disappointing.[15]

He wanted now to analyze the class that had spewed him forth, and thus, eventually, to see his kind more honestly. For years he had been spinning grotesque stories of the waif who suddenly is given the opportunity to have his heart's desire, only to have "fate" thwart the fulfillment. Now, gradually, he began to be aware of his overweening capacity for rationalization, began to realize that he had ennobled his heroes in order to spare himself the pain of acknowledging their limitations. *The Nether World* showed how cruelly his mind could analyze while his heart protested, but most of the wriggling human beings were outside the environment that had produced Gissing himself, and toward which he felt far more hostility than even the nether world roused in him. Now, in the bitter years of self-analysis after 1888, he created character after character in search of the truth about himself. In the earlier novels no one except for Isabel Clarendon, perhaps, may be said to have much knowledge of self, but in the later novels, each man is upon the rack. Now Gissing would consider self-conscious men who knew their own measure, and he would discover, with sadness, that the truth does not necessarily make men free.

As a period to *The Nether World,* the book as well as the environment, he set out for France and Italy. The tour marks the end of a major stage in Gissing's life, for never again, except in a hastily done short story, would he write in the old manner. He had written out his life and Nell's, and she was dead.

Chapter 7

MARRIAGE
AND MISANTHROPY

The heady feeling of release that came after Nell's death was translated into impulsive trips to the continent and a new kind of reading. Where formerly Gissing had limited his traveling to a fortnight in Paris, now he threw caution to the winds and traveled extensively, with a male friend, with his sisters, by himself; the context did not matter: he knew only that he found peace in putting as much distance as possible between himself and the "prison" that London now represented. His reading, too, reflected his wish to dissociate himself from the ties of community living and from the "causes" that had once been dear to him. Gone was his interest in tracts on atheism and the Disestablishment of the English Church, banished were the tracts on Socialism and Communism. Just as his wandering feet trod strange soils and spurned the clay of England, so his mind was stimulated by the ideas and art of the continent and rejected the comparatively unsophisticated preoccupations of such typical Englishmen as Frederic Harrison. When he was forced by business matters to remain in London, he sought solace in Trubner's bookstore, where he bought the new antiseptic writings of foreign authors.

What Gissing was seeking in his reading was philosophy in a new key. Academic philosophy had ceased to interest him, just as political theory had ceased to do, and now he turned his attention to a comparatively new study, Comparative Psychology.

Instead of accepting a priori statements about the nature of man, he went to the studies of animal intelligence, consulted deterministic biographies of men he thought representative of the age.

Even in Gissing's early work, it is true, there had been a strong suggestion of determinism, in spite of the occasional election by the protagonist of action theoretically opposed to former conditioning; but the view of determinism was that of a young man better able to say, "The world is against me," than "My own inadequacies are thus and so." Now Gissing was to study, in the works of others, and to translate the conclusions into his own work, the area of "unconscious choice," the terrifying concept aired by such literary critics as Paul Bourget in France and by such scientists as George Romanes. The formidable conclusion reached by these men was that many actions allegedly the result of free choice are, in fact, the results of physiological and emotional states.

Romanes' book, *Animal Intelligence,* which Gissing lists in his diary [1] was much more than the usual Victorian collection of anecdotes about clever animals. It was intended not to make a lady smile at the antics of a lap dog, but to make thoughtful men wonder if, after all, *homo sapiens* possesses free will any more than do the lower animals. Romanes' thesis was stated in the opening chapter:

"Whenever we see a living organism apparently exerting intentional choice, we might infer that it is a conscious choice, and therefore that the organism has a mind. But further reflection shows us that this is just what we cannot do; for although it is true that there is no mind without the power of conscious choice, it is not true that all apparent choice is due to mind."

Romanes did not dare to deny free will, but he did attempt to narrow the area over which "mind" alone exerted authority.

In Paul Bourget's work, particularly in *Essais de psychologie contemporaine,* Gissing found the same clinical method applied, but this time to men rather than lower animals. Bourget declared categorically, ". . . il n'y a ni maladie ni santé de l'âme, il n'y a que les états psychologiques au point de vue de l'observateur sans métaphysique." [2] Probably because Gissing gave assent to this pronouncement, his later fiction breathes no condemnation of human behavior; it attempts rather to understand the action in terms of the crucial experiences of the past. Gissing in fiction, like Bourget in biography, would supplement the great trio in criticism, "race, milieu, moment," with physical constitution and the trauma of childhood. And Gissing's dispassionate studies would, in turn, be flailed by English reviewers who wanted a stern father to tell them what was right and wrong about characters in novels as in life.

Romanes and Bourget might provide a theory of clinical psychology, but Gissing studied as well the practice of the French Naturalists and the Russians. In 1888 he first read the journal of the Goncourt brothers and made a characteristically "Gissingish" observation: "The personality of these men is repugnant to me, & much of the journal loathesome, but I read the book with extreme interest. In their writings I can feel no kind of interest." [3] Clearly it was not easy for him to mingle, even on the pages of a book, with the very men whom honest curiosity forced him to study. He also read Maupassant's *Pierre et Jean,* the first of Maupassant's books that he had seen.[4] Tolstoy he admired (*Polikonchka* and *Une tourmente de neige*), but not so much as Turgenev and Dostoevski. *Crime et Châtiment* was a "marvelous" book.[5] *Väter und Söhne* was "a stronger book than *Die Neue Generation.* Bazarov a wonderfully drawn character . . . typical nihilist. It is the purely negative mind, common enough now-a-days in men of thought." [6] Gissing also read Ibsen, for he refers to "Nora" but he confided no comment on the lady to his diary.[7]

The great names of the continent are well known today to the literate, but in the England of Gissing's time the ignorance of contemporary achievements in fiction was abysmal. Indeed most of the English novelists either followed the rather archaic conventions of the "social protest" school (Walter Besant fancied himself daring while novelists of the continent would have chuckled over him), or, worse still, they turned out endless, nondescript "romances," as most Europeans viewed them. Gissing could not avoid, therefore, a growing contempt for most contemporary British novelists. He found the mind of George Moore "crude," [8] and, by 1889, George Eliot's work "heavy," and the style in *Daniel Deronda* "monstrous." He conceded Eliot's intellectual gifts, but decided that these alone were not sufficient in a work of art.[9] He had indeed traveled a long way in literary criticism and was well past the day when "intellectual power" was his sole criterion for fiction.

Side by side with the books of the moderns lay the works of Theocritus and Aristophanes, and Gissing read them all, often dreaming of an idyll of his own in a Mediterranean setting. The dream became reality. The force that made the dream come true (and when he decided to travel he was not in a very much better financial state than he had been in former days), was an ever-increasing fear of death: he might die, and soon, from the disease that Nell had had. So obsessed did he become with the symptoms of tuberculosis that he never coughed without putting a finger to his mouth to test for the telltale scarlet.[10]

He had known as early as 1880 that Nell was suffering from tuberculosis, and yet he had managed to avoid preoccupation with the contagion of the disease and the probability of his own illness. When in those days he felt depressed, the cause was not fear of illness, but repressed anger over the small vexations that took time away from writing. Why then did he wait until his wife's death to behave like a man soon to die, anticipating the scarlet symptom before it appeared? Certainly his health in 1888 was not worse than it had been. It would seem therefore that his sense of the imminence of death was the result of feeling of guilt, not necessarily on a conscious level. True, he had insisted at his wife's bedside that "in no way" had he been at fault (and to the bystander, Gissing does seem more sinned against than sinning in the relationship), but the years of quarrels, of shame at being an unsuccessful novelist, must often have seemed proof of his inadequacy as a husband. Furthermore, although he felt such relief after Nell's death that he was spurred on to write, the alternate depression and exhilaration that followed thereafter suggest that the death had not brought with it a true purgation of his feelings. Curiously enough, he was more conscious of loneliness after the death of the wife from whom he had been separated for years: he was seeing little of former friends and was left haunted by a sense of passing time. Such feelings prompted him to decide in September, half a year after Nell's death, to make the long-desired pilgrimage to the classical past, as far away as possible from the painful memories of the recent present.

It was characteristic, however, that he should be unable to proceed alone on his journey: in his mind's eye he was the solitary pilgrim, motivated by an intensely personal love of the historical past; in fact, as he was to admit sadly, in occasional flashes of insight, he was dependent during the day-to-day round of life upon human companionship, even when it was of a mediocre kind. Thus he departed for the continent with a friend from Chelsea named Plitt, a garrulous egoist of the very kind scored in Gissing novels. Plitt borrowed money, cheated when dividing the day's expenses, and, worst of all, considered himself an authority on objects of art, when indeed, if Gissing can be believed, his taste was poor and his knowledge scanty. Although Gissing noted with growing concern the venality of his former friend, he did not have the courage to confront the man with his lies, nor to express hostility with any openness. With Plitt, as with most people, including his wives, Gissing did not dare to be honest; instead he confided his woes to his diary and yielded "not out of affection, most surely, but mere cowardice."

"Strange that I, all whose joys and sorrows come from excess of individuality, should be remarkable among men for my yield-ingness to everyone and anyone in daily affairs. . . It must be a sign of extreme weakness and it makes me the slave of men." [11]

He was still the somber lad from Yorkshire who did not dare to admit openly his own conflicting emotions, and the only release when the tension was too great to be endured was in flight. Paris, the city that he had so enjoyed on his short and solitary visit, no longer delighted him, though dutifully he made the rounds with Plitt of the Louvre and Notre Dame. By the end of October he could no longer endure the relationship, and Paris as part of it, and thereupon he set out for Marseilles and Italy, leaving Plitt behind him with a bribe of money.

Alone, he visited Naples and Capri in November and at the end of the month was in Rome. He was ravished by the sight of the ruins, disgusted with the modern city. He shivered a little at the sight and sound of a male soprano,[12] as he shivered at most sexual anomalies while he studied them with fascination. Indeed, he would have liked to rid the streets of Rome of most human beings, the better to savor the past.

"Then, there are the indescribable Italian tints on the Alban and the Sabine hills, but to see them you must climb to some high place; the streets of modern Rome are monotonous and wearisome to an incredible degree, and there is absolutely no picturesqueness in the common life of the people." [13]

So he fled the modern city and reveled instead in the Colosseum.

His reaction to the ruins of a magnificent and frightening culture was intensely personal. When he saw the palaces of the Palatine, it was not as an antiquarian of the nineteenth century, but as a subject of a Roman ruler. He was indeed so seduced in imagination that, while standing in an ancient judgment hall, he felt, sharply, the same emotions evoked in him when he was judged by his contemporaries. It was as if absolutism stirred with the very dust, and Gissing, sensitive throughout his life to tyranny in any form (and secretly attracted, as well as hostile, to it), tingled with the sensation.

"In one of the palaces on the Palatine you see what used to be the judgment hall of the Emperors. It is a vast space with a semi-circular tribunal at one end, where the Emperor sat. There are a few scraps of the variegated marble floor remaining and even a little bit of a beautiful marble trellis that divided the tribunal from the hall. Stand there, and think of the poor creatures who have trembled on that spot of ground, in face of Caesar Augustus! At one moment I burst out laughing, at another I felt miserable and uncomfortable." [14]

It was the ability to project his own seething emotions on to the visual objects of history that would later be manifest in *Veranilda*, Gissing's unfinished historical novel, and *The Emancipated*, the first novel in a modern setting to make use of Gissing's trip through Italy. Like *Roderick Hudson*, Henry James's rich and too-ambitious novel, Gissing's showed the mingling of pain and delight as his own *idées fixes* gained depth from the visual stimulation from the past.

But a day of magnificent empathy always ended with anger and repugnance for the present, particularly for the special weaknesses of the tourist.

"Every day I am more surprised at the vulgar character of the mass of English people one sees here. It is monstrous that such people should be able to come, when those who could make a good use of it cannot. Oh, the idiotic remarks that are always falling on my ears." [15]

The Latin people were regarded by him, however, with a little more sympathy than the British, because of their suavity and easy good cheer. He did not delude himself, of course, that the smile was witness of an open heart, but he preferred the mask as more pleasant than open boorishness.

"You may say all you will about these virtues of which I speak being merely on the surface. It is very true, but I had rather have an Italian who cheats you with a pleasant smile and poetical phraseology than an Englishman who cheats you none the less under the guise of bluff and brutal independence. . . I like the Italians greatly better than the French — at all events than the Parisians. The former have been sneered at for their age-long submission to tyrants, but the explanation of it lies in their suave passiveness, a virtue which recommends itself to me far more than the spasmodic melodramatism of French history." [16]

Clearly he had traveled a long way from the family Puritanism.

To see the ruins was to feel a surge of excitement, but to experience the discomforts of travel and the dampness of December and January was enough to make him think of warm fires at home. He was only thirty-one, but sometimes he wrote like a very old man: "For it is no use — wherever I am, I am enjoying nothing if the weather is cold. At once I lose all interest and shiver and shrink and feel wretched." Most of all, although he repressed the thought most of the time, he resented being forced to travel on a pittance; indeed, his first day in Venice, January 29, was almost ruined for him by envy, as he contrasted Ruskin's leisurely studies of Venice with his own hurried visit. Bitterly he remarked that Ruskin always addressed himself to "rich people." He never quite forgave Ruskin his prosperity.

By the first of March he was back in London, determined to work hard, convinced that six months abroad must have provided a needed change of scene and consequently an impetus to get on with writing. Meanwhile *Demos* was being translated

into German and French, and Gissing felt that the time had
come for him to follow up the earlier successes. But it was easier
to break vows than to keep them, and time and again he threw
down his pen as the words came out jumbled and confused. His
head ached furiously for the first time since he had left England
in the autumn,[17] and when he could endure the migraine no
longer he deserted London and went to Wakefield for a few
days with his family. In March and again in May he permitted
the family to pamper him, and in between the visits he worked
at *The Emancipated*.

During the months of 1889 life in London was made a trifle
more pleasant by companionship with the men of the "Quad-
rilateral." [18] In the group were Morley Roberts, temporarily
sojourning in London, Alfred Hartley, the painter, and W. H.
Hudson, whom Gissing had met in Hartley's lodgings in March.
Gissing was the fourth. All four were more ambitious than
successful, and long evenings were passed amidst diatribes against
the Philistines. To Gissing, belonging to the group was important not only because it provided a respite from lonely evenings, but, more important, because it provided him with intimate
knowledge of clever young men which he would put to use,
often with satiric purpose, in such novels as *New Grub Street*
and even the late *Will Warburton*. But Quadrilaterals of young
men usually turn into couples in summer weather, and Gissing
soon found himself deserted. He turned, however, to his sister
Madge and, having finished his manuscript in August and
placed it with Bentley, set out for Guernsey with her. Once again
he was happy, as a passive and pretty young woman listened
to the things that so few people, he mourned, appreciated.

But he could not remain long with his sister, and in September he
was back in London, dreaming of the blue of the Mediterranean.
Still his dreams encompassed more than the Mediterranean: he
was, he finally admitted, starved for companionship. He called
upon Edith Sichel, the aggressive career woman who had written

so favorable a review of his work the year before, whom he had seen only once, and was overwhelmed to realize that she was beautiful as well as intelligent. He returned from the visit with confused feelings and with a bitter recollection of a handsomely decorated apartment, the kind of lodging as far removed from his limited means as possible.[19] It had become almost more than he could bear, that the women to whom he was most attracted, such women as Mrs. Gaussen and Edith Sichel, should be so far beyond his reach. As early as 1884 he had plumbed the misery attendant upon such a contrast in *Isabel Clarendon,* had, indeed, said all that could be said about poor young men with the temerity to fall in love with beautiful and wealthy women. Now, five years later, he was still smarting from the realization that his means were little, his future insecure. He could scarcely endure waiting in London while the proof sheets of *The Emancipated* were slowly corrected. Flight once again was all that he could turn to, and on November 11 he set out for Sicily and Greece via Marseilles.

The journey took him through the straits of Messina, past Sicily and the Ionian Sea into Greece. There, preparing deliberately to be thrilled, he proceeded to the Areopagus, but again he was stunned by the contrast between the glory of the past and the grotesquerie, the sordidness, of the present.

"In the innermost recess of the great cleft among the rocks found the Eumenides' Well. . . The whole place is a vast public ordure-ground, in reality, one would think, a centre of pest."[20]

At night he read Aristophanes, and in the day marveled at the Athenian plain and "the rugged Hymettus, where the famous bees still make their honey, as in the classic days." There were few statues to see; they had "long ago been distributed over Europe."[21]

In January of 1890 he was in Naples with an English friend, Harvey Shortridge,[22] who had an Italian wife. Together they explored "Old Naples — the most wonderful and fearful place in Europe."

"One day we went out to Pozzuoli, Baiae, Cape Misenum, and lastly to Cumae, the first Greek settlement in Italy, now a desolate shore, with the hill on which stood the Acropolis, but scarcely a ruin left. Hard by is a great wood of evergreen oaks, where there are many wild boars. For impressiveness, the scene comes after Paestum, I think." [23]

Gissing was so strongly impressed by Southern Italy that he told his brother he might settle in Salerno. But the day for the expatriation had not yet come. There was "bread money" to be made first.

On February 27 he was back in London, but still unable to write he decided to take his sisters on a trip to Paris. The whole year had been spent in running away, but Gissing still did not acknowledge what he was running away from, and what he could do to spare himself the need of constant pilgrimages — no matter the place so long as the scene changed each day. He complained bitterly of the "mill-grinding business, this, of book after book." [24] Just as a few weeks before he had contemplated transplanting himself to Salerno, so in the spring he considered spending the rest of his life in Germany, where Eduard Bertz was flourishing. "Everything points to the likelihood of my practically leaving England for a long time. London is too solitary for me. . ." [25] Yet when Miss Sichel invited him to visit her, he refused.[26] He wanted either to feel at ease in English society, as he could not hope to do, or join Continental society in the role of an English man of letters making a tour of Europe. No compromise was possible for him any longer, although occasionally he met the Harrisons or heard from the Gaussens in Ireland.

By April 1 *The Emancipated* was in print, and Gissing's sister Ellen, among other readers, was horrified at its "satiric vein." To her criticism he replied,

"But no, you will not like my future books. I have been waiting until my position with the publishers enabled me to write with more freedom. Even you must recognize that hypocrisy in literature, however mild, is not admirable. My part is with the men and women who are clearing the ground of systems that have had their day and have crumbled into obstructive ruin." [27]

He assured his sister that the object of his onslaught was "'formalism,' an obstinate belief in things that were disproved by sheer arithmetic long ago, which even such an old fashioned book as Newman's 'Phases of Faith' . . . rendered forever untenable."

There were "strained relations" in the family because Ellen continued to believe that she had furnished the model for Miriam, the narrow Puritan. But Gissing assured his sister that she would be almost "broad-minded" if she were less concerned with forms,[28] and with the ironic compliment Ellen permitted herself to be soothed, and went off to Paris with her brother after all.

Upon their return to England all three set out for Wakefield, where Gissing remained for about three months. Once he had not been able to live with his family; now he sought Wakefield as an escape from living alone. His diary for the time is studded with the word "misery." He was disheartened further when he learned that only 412 copies of *Thyrza* had been sold, and that the publishers considered the copyright worth only ten pounds to them! [29] To add to his distress, he discovered in himself a capacity which he had succeeded in overlooking — the capacity to fall violently in love on very short acquaintance. Thus one day in summer during the visit to Wakefield he was introduced to a friend of his sister — a girl with a beautiful voice, the quality which Gissing so prized in women. He confided in his diary, "I am in love with her, & there's an end on it." [30] It *was* the end. He left for London shortly thereafter.

In his diary for September 16 he finally put into words the drive behind all his flights over England and the Continent. "Feel like a madman at times. I know that I shall never do any more good work until I am married." [31] Life was an agony! "Am on the very verge of despair, & suffering more than ever in my whole life. My brain seems powerless, dried up." [32]

The recognition of his need was at last made explicit. Not for him was the casual liaison of other men. He wanted not only the normal sexual relationship, but companionship, the easy domesticity that so many took for granted, but that had long been denied him. Despite his idealization of such a woman as Isabel Clarendon, who never set foot in the clutter of the kitchen, he now admitted that he had been happy, or at least content, in the days when Nell had cooked his meals, tended his lodgings, and listened with bland lack of comprehension to his monologues on art and literary criticism. Thus when Gissing said he needed a wife, confiding the need to his diary, he was not merely using a euphemism, although a too sophisticated critic might infer the possibility. He was a little weary of the life of a nomad: he suffered from chill, he suffered from indigestion, and had a keen practical sense, keener even than that of the Philistine, of the advantages of home and hearth. If any testament of the needs of a weary bachelor is wanted as proof of Gissing's realistic awareness, such a testament is found in *The Whirlpool*, one of the most realistic novels ever written of the marital relationship. He might dream of Ella Gaussen or Edith Sichel, but he knew that his limited means and social status made marriage with such a woman highly improbable. In a novel, an Isabel Clarendon might propose marriage to a poor young man, but, in reality, an Isabel Clarendon was merely "a good friend," or, at the most, one who condescended to a brief affair with an "artist" for the sake of a new titillation, relief from the prosperous but rather dull living of every day. In any case the relationship could not compare with marriage, the day-to-day comforts which Gissing needed to work regularly and steadily. If he was selfish about his needs, he was also honest. The desire of the moth for the flame he left for Shelley: he was an English Realist, after all!

According to the rather fulsome passage in Morley Roberts' "biography," Gissing found his new bride-to-be simply by rushing into the London night and returning with a young woman,[33] but more to be trusted than Roberts' proclivity for exaggeration is Gissing's simple notation of a visit to a coffee shop on Oxford Street and eventually the initials "E. U." for Edith Underwood.[34] It is quite likely that his search was a deliberate one; the initials follow too closely the words of yearning after marriage to be coincidental. Nevertheless, the exposure of himself to situations in which he might meet a suitable young woman is not the same thing as mad running in the streets.

Edith's initials are first noted on September 24, and soon thereafter things are noted that Gissing had for a long time ceased to regard, like the beauty of the moonlight. A month later he confided to his sister that he would probably marry before the end of the year.

Had Gissing been seeking a foil to Isabel Clarendon, he could have found a no more startling one than Edith. No cards bearing the engraved words "At Home" (sent by Edith Sichel) were needed when he called upon his Edith. He knew her for three weeks before her father could be persuaded to greet the suitor who spent evenings regularly in the flat in Camden Square. She, in turn, came unselfconsciously to his lodgings and spent the evenings with him. Sometimes he read poetry to her, poems like "The May Queen" and "The Pied Piper of Hamelin," which he thought she might understand because of the story-like quality. As for Edith herself, with her "extreme quietness and docility," she probably listened with some patience and more bewilderment, thinking that men of letters were doubtless different from her father, sculptor of the working-class, according to a letter from Gissing to Algernon[35] (but more likely, an everyday craftsman).

Thus the old pattern was being reëstablished: a full day of writing, and then a passive, affectionate girl when he turned from the desk. In November Gissing met Edith's father who greeted him laconically. In December he finished his new novel, and the speed and comparative ease of composition, after months of migraine and delay, convinced him that he had found the solution to the former "block." Occasionally he felt depressed and fearful of being ostracized because of his return to the haunts of former years: "I suppose I shall never again sit at a civilized table."[36] It was characteristic of him seldom to adopt a line of action without remorse: having cut himself deliberately from the fashionable world, he feared that it would forget him! Nevertheless, moods of depression were few, and the decision of marriage was finally arrived at when Smith, Elder accepted *New Grub Street* at the turn of the year. Gissing secured Edith's consent (she was later to waver and then to yield) and set out for Exeter in search of a house to rent. He had determined to quit London, or at least to make it a place to visit. He found lodgings, and immediately and characteristically took a dislike to the landlord. Then he returned to London, where he and Edith were married on February 25, 1891, in Saint Pancras parish. On the day that the couple set out for Exeter there appeared in *The Times* the bridegroom's letter on accent in Greek verse.

The interest roused by *New Grub Street* augured well for the prosperity of the couple. The *Illustrated London News* devoted a whole column to the novel, the *Daily News* mentioned it in a leader, and Andrew Lang made himself a target, but also brought new readers for the book, by declaring that Gissing had exaggerated the sufferings of the writers of Grub Street.[37] Controversy raged, and the pages of *The Author* dedicated to letters-to-the-editor were filled with letters from unknown aspirants on Grub Street testifying to the truth of Gissing's description of their plight. But Lang insisted, "In real life, the melancholy hero of Mr. Gissing would have had a devoted wife who believed in her husband's genius; but to give him such a wife would not be Realism. . ."

Whatever wives Mr. Lang had in mind to prove his contention, Gissing's Edith was not one of them, although at first life in Exeter went smoothly enough. Gissing was working productively, busily, with *Godwin Peak* (later rechristened *Born in Exile*) ready to submit in July, the second of two novels written in less than a year. The publisher Bentley, shrewd as he was, took advantage of the publicity attendant upon *New Grub Street* to issue a short story that had been filed away for years. It seemed that there was finally a market.

But Gissing's name, if it was upon many lips, was not upon many bank checks, as he commented bitterly in his diary. In spite of the success of *New Grub Street* he found himself unable to afford such small luxuries as a subscription to the library. Indeed he barely managed to meet routine household expenses. The state of things was in his eyes "monstrously" unfair.[38] He must certainly have felt scathing contempt for Andrew Lang's contention that Grub Street was, after all, not a bad place! To make matters worse, Smith, Elder were cool when Gissing asked £250 for *Godwin Peak*. James Payn, whose fondness for sour grapes was well-known, declared that, in spite of all the free publicity, *New Grub Street* had failed financially.[39] In desperate need of ready money, Gissing agreed to sell the new novel for only £150, if it could be done immediately. Yet this was not the limit of his humiliation, for Payn refused to be hastened and returned the manuscript with the sour comment that Gissing's pessimism was responsible for his failure! Stung once too often by Payn, Gissing wrote to C. F. Watts, the literary agent, asking £200 for the manuscript. Watts was not immediately successful: Chatto and Windus hesitated, Longmans declined, until only Bentley seemed possible.

Gissing began to be alarmed, with only £27 left in cash and a baby expected in December.[40]

Domestic life soon became Micawber-like, but devoid of the one quality making it endurable — humor, and indeed humor is more usual by retrospect than by prospect. The Gissing family deserted Prospect Park with relief after disagreements with the landlord that had left Gissing enraged and shaken but prompted him to consider writing a book of short stories which would bear witness to the misery of living in lodgings.[41] With relief they settled in an eight-room house, with a rent of almost twenty pounds a year, in St. Leonard's Terrace. Here they remained, with intermittent holidays at Clevedon and Weymouth, until September of 1892, when Gissing became impatient to be nearer to the fine libraries of London. Lodgings were found in Brixton, where the family remained until February 1894, when the doctor advised that Gissing's young son have a change of climate. After visits to Clevedon and St. Leonard's on Sea, the family removed to Eversley in Epsom. Here Gissing remained until he left his family and England in 1897.

Moving about was disliked by Gissing, who hated packing and unpacking and the disarray of his precious books, but most disliked of all were slothful servants, wailing infants, and querulous wives. The maid of all work changed her name every week, but never her habits, for a salary of nine pounds a year was scarcely calculated to insure a superior maidservant. Furthermore, Edith had no great gift for managing either the servant or the household, and Gissing, obsessively neat like his mother before him, found his nerves becoming frayed. There were, successively — a fire, an explosion, cheating by repairmen, scenes with servants — all of them repulsive to a man who winced before disorder and loud voices. He was discovering to his sadness that his quiet and tractable Edith was really neither, and that her bewilderment with his way of life was changing to impatience and anger. The diaries of the nineties are studded with details of disorganized household routine, details later crammed, in all their disagreeable array, into such novels as *In the Year of Jubilee.*

But he could not spend his time lamenting the turn his domestic life was taking. More important before him was the task of establishing better relations with publishers to insure an adequate income. It was in 1891 that he first heard of Lawrence and Bullen, through Morley Roberts. They were among the first publishers to use the "account system" rather than outright purchase, and were very much interested in one-volume novels as cheap in format and quick in turnover. They offered Gissing 100 guineas for a short novel to be published at six shillings;[42] this, which became *Denzil Quarrier,* was finished on November 12. The 100 guineas were received on November 25, a welcome birthday present for the new baby, Walter, born on December 10. The easy placing of *Denzil Quarrier* did much to lure Gissing to the new convention of the one-volume novel, especially since *Born in Exile,* completed months before *Quarrier,* was not accepted until the beginning of 1892 by the publisher Black, who offered only £150. Watt received 10% as agent.

But after one novel there had always to be another, for Gissing had resigned himself to the prospect of modest sums for his work. He made seven false starts on a new novel, among them a story about "competition among shopkeepers." He rejected the idea finally, only to revive it years later in *Will Warburton.* But in September an idea came suddenly, and Gissing wrote the story in record time, six weeks! Once again it was Bullen who offered the most enticing terms for *The Odd Women* (a title which they hoped would prove alluring) — an advance of 100 guineas. Gissing would receive three shillings on each copy of the three-volume edition and sixpence per copy on the subsequent cheap edition of 3/6. He was also pleased with Bullen's activities in placing books overseas.[43] For example, 1500 sheets of *Denzil Quarrier* were sold to Messrs. Potherwick in Australia, and Macmillan in

America was given the right to bring out an American edition
with the English publishers to receive 10%. On the continent
Heinemann and Balestier were approached by Bullen, who also
proposed cheap editions of *Isabel Clarendon* and *The Unclassed*.
(Only the latter was actually reprinted.) Actually the number of
copies of novels by Gissing distributed in England is only a small
percentage of those printed or distributed in the rest of the world:
Bell and Company, for example, ordered for their New Colonial
Library 1200 copies of *Denzil Quarrier*, 750 copies of *The Emancipated*, and 1500 copies of *In the Year of Jubilee*, which Gissing
composed from January to April of 1894.

During 1892 Gissing had discovered that it was not necessary
to be a member of the Authors' Society in order to make use of
the Authors' Syndicate. He was becoming increasingly aware that
he, like most authors who were not phenomenal "best sellers,"
was at the mercy of the publishers. Although by now he was no
longer capable of plunging zealously into reform movements, he
watched with interest the growth of the Society of Authors.[44]
In the first year of the organization, 1884, there had been only 68
paying members; in 1892 the number had grown to 870. Cotter
Morrison and Walter Besant were important names in the group,
and Morris Colles, who in 1898 arranged for the sale of *The Town
Traveller*, was its counsel and later its president. The organization
published its own journal, *The Author*, which began publication
on May 15, 1890. Among the functions of the Authors' Syndicate,
a subcommittee, was the sale of serial rights to magazines, journals, and newspapers. (The author retained volume rights and
copyright.) In addition, the group undertook to act as American
agent, and asked no percentage from authors on any of the sales.

Partly through his new interest in the Society of Authors and
largely through his new acquaintance with Morris Colles and
Clement Shorter, editor of the *English Illustrated*, Gissing began
an invasion of the short story market. "Lou and Liz," redolent of
the days of *Thyrza*, was published in the August number, 1893.

"A Honeymoon" and "In Honour Bound," well-constructed and subacid in flavor, were written in December. Shorter also requested a serial story of 60,000 words to be published in the *Illustrated London News,* and Gissing satisfied the stipulations with *Eve's Ransom.* He was delighted to be sought after by the magazines: between January 1893 and June 1895 he received payment for fifteen short stories and sketches, one of them in *La Revue Blanche.* For the stories he received an average of 12 guineas each, and for the "London Types" requested by Jerome K. Jerome, Morris Colles thought that three guineas per sketch could be obtained.

In the same period of time he had written no fewer than eight novels, and on only two of them had he spent more than three months! Three of the group — *Denzil Quarrier, Eve's Ransom,* and *Sleeping Fires* — were short novels published in one volume. Even Smith, Elder and James Payn, who had so often been diffident, solicited him for a one-volume novel. The tables had been turned: "I never conceived it possible that they would come to me," Gissing rejoiced in his diary.[45] And on January 25, 1895, James Payn placed a complimentary paragraph about Gissing in his column in the *Illustrated London News.* Fisher, Unwin, too, was seeking the resuscitated author, offering him £150 for all rights to a story of 30,000 words to be ready by 31 March. The offer was made in January, and Gissing had *Sleeping Fires* ready by March 1. Furthermore *Eve's Ransom* was a great success. The story was run serially, and on the very day that it was published in book form, 800 copies were sold. By the end of the week 1100 copies had reached the public. *The Unclassed* was reissued, too, in 1895 in a revised edition, after the author with much difficulty removed large portions from the old edition. Bullen also bought from Black the rights to *Born in Exile,* thus collecting under a single imprint much of Gissing's early work.

With the attention of the publishers, there came the attention of the photographers, whom formerly Gissing had dreaded. In

1895 he sat for Elliott and Fry, photographers of the great men of letters of the period, and turned his sharp, aristocratic profile to the camera. Not yet forty, he was slight of figure, with a sensitive mobile face, distinguished with its deep-set eyes and fine features. The hair, chestnut and wavy, was rather long and unruly, but not so long as to conceal the well-shaped head.

In many ways the gods, in whom he did not believe, seemed to be smiling on him at last. He was certainly not a wealthy man, and never would be, but when he looked over his accounts for 1894 he saw that he had earned £453 and that his expenses had been only £239.[46] With justifiable pride at having a favorable bank balance, he wrote "bravo" in his diary.

Not the least of the pleasures of being a small literary "lion" was the ever-widening circle of acquaintances that publicity provided. In the nineties Gissing saw much of such men of letters as Hardy, Meredith, and H. G. Wells. Wells later implied that he had known Gissing intimately for many years, but in fact the two met as late as 1896 at a dinner of the Omar Khayyam Club in London.[47] Thereafter Gissing visited Wells occasionally, although he came to find his blend of mysticism and science rather irritating: "In his lecture to the Royal Institute he goes, I think, altogether too far in talking about the eternal activities of the spirit of man and defying the threats of the material outlook."[48]

Hardy, whose novels Gissing had always read critically, was also on the visiting list of the nineties. Gissing was consistent in believing him the inferior of Meredith, as a man and a novelist, and was amazed to discover that he knew less, in spite of his reputation as a commentator upon rural life, about the flowers of the field than scholarly Meredith.[49] The impact of Hardy's personality was felt most strongly one day in September 1895,[50] when Gissing was sitting at table with Hardy. His host, in the middle of conversation, seized a table knife and squashed a wasp against the flat of the blade. Hardy later talked about a pig's "pizzle" which he would use, in powerful and vulgar irony, as a means of bringing together a man and woman in one of his most stirring novels. Gissing must have felt almost nauseated by the incident and the conversation — he who could not, or would not, in most of his novels, permit his heroes the crudities that are almost commonplace in Hardy tales. With a sigh of relief he must have traveled to George Meredith at Box Hill, must have comforted himself with the thought that, in *Diana of the Crossways* and other novels, Meredith had not found it necessary to make anatomical drawings of passion. To put it bluntly, he was not at ease with Hardy, but found Meredith all he had imagined a great man of letters would be. He had the opportunity to pay personal tribute to Meredith at a dinner meeting of the Omar Khayyam Club, when he recalled the days of Meredith's duties as reader for Chapman and Hall, and the kind and perceptive criticism that had come forth.

It was Edward Clodd, however, who was primarily responsible for opening to Gissing a circle that he had secretly dreamed of entering.[51] Until the nineties he had had few men friends from fashionable life, and indeed played the role of courtier to the ladies rather than equal of the men, but with the friendship with Clodd there came house parties at Aldeburgh and acquaintance with both substantial citizens and gay and passing celebrities.[52] At Aldeburgh Gissing met George Whale, the solicitor, later his legal advisor; Grant Allen, the popular, wealthy, and vainglorious novelist; Sir Benjamin Ward Richardson; Clement Shorter, editor of the *English Illustrated News,* who asked him for short stories. If ever he had doubted it, he now realized that there was power in knowing and being known. He who had identified himself with the withdrawn and suffering Reardon in *New Grub Street* now found himself a veritable Jasper Milvain, a partaker of gossip, one who joined for the sake of advantage and amusement and vanity. True, joining the circle which formerly he had satirized was in turn part of his education, part of his eager lessons on English society of the nineteenth century. Now, instead of envy-

ing Ruskin for being rich, he found himself gossiping with wealthy
men on the whispered reasons for the failure of Ruskin's marriage. Now, too, instead of continuing his rather naïve classification
of men into solemn wise men and gay fools, he began to understand the complexities of personality which made possible a man
like Grant Allen, who wrote popular, superficial fiction (i.e. *The
Woman Who Did*) and who had also held the Chair of Professor
of Mental and Moral Philosophy at the newly-founded Government College in Spanish Town, Jamaica. Ten years before Gissing would have over-simplified such a personality; now he accepted Allen in all his rich complexity.

Most of the group at the Aldeburgh house parties were sceptics.
As Allen remarked to a critical relative,

"You say, 'You must remember that Evolution is not a philosophic system; it is only the highest *Empirical* generalisation yet
reached.' The word I have wave-lined suggests the idea that you
are on the look-out for a Cartesian or Leibnitzian 'a priori' intelligible system. For such, I at least have long ceased to look." [53]

It seemed a long time since such tenets as those of Positivism,
the "Religion of Humanity," had been acceptable. Indeed, when
in 1896 Gissing met Frederic Harrison again after a lapse of six
or seven years, it came over him with a rush that although Harrison's junior, he was far more world-weary. He had lived to see
the decline of the robust scepticism of Spencer and Morley and
Frederic Harrison, the scepticism which these men were able to
use to shake off the bonds of dogma, without sacrificing optimism
or self-confidence. It was a miracle possible only for a generation
content not to push scepticism to the ultimate, content to abide
by Christian ethics without Christian theology. Already the children of the grand old seniors had given up the struggle to en-
shrine an anomaly: young Bernard Harrison had become a convert to Catholicism, while his brother Austin, according to rumor,
was becoming a "Nietzschean Rationalist," [54] intellectually a crea-

ture whom his father could not comprehend. The stern yet generous patriarch had been unable to make his kind of compromise
acceptable to either son, and had succeeded only in forcing them
into opposite poles, the one wanting an absolute and original sin
instead of the shaky optimism of Comte, the other craving self-
knowledge and alliance with supermen. To Gissing the spectacle
was still another sign of the times.

It was Edward Clodd who probably furnished Gissing with the
model which Frederic Harrison could no longer be for him. Clodd
was a self-made man, successful in the world of banking and fi-
nance; he was also the author of a sound biography of Thomas
Henry Huxley, and possessed a live and disciplined curiosity.
Almost twenty years older than Gissing, he was still to outlive him
by a quarter of a century, dying "in the Epicurean faith" which
had for fifty years sustained him.[55] It was he who must have reminded Gissing that his early dogmatic conception of the successful man had been a little too superficial to be important; in any
case, the fine and subtle portraits of the man of action in *Will
Warburton* and *The Whirlpool* suggest that along the way of
maturing Gissing discarded his earlier, too-simple notions of the
successful man.

He was learning a great deal about man in society, now that
he had learned to substitute honest inquiry for hostility, although
he was not always happy after learning his lessons. It seemed to
him that most of those he now understood were hovering on the
edge of a whirlpool, needing reassurance, yet suspicious of it,
with the ground behind them impossible to retread, and only the
maelstrom before them. Gradually he came to feel that he himself
was spending too much time in that frenzied crowd, and sought
to retreat to the country, to safety, sanity, to his home in Epsom.
But when he got there, he discovered that it was not a haven, but
in its way another whirlpool. Edith had been feeling neglected,
and had been cherishing resentment against her husband. His
notion of the whirlpool, the wearying demands of society, was

incomprehensible to her. A Londoner born and bred, she preferred the bustle and noise, the shops and soot of London to the dull countryside of Epsom. She had married, she thought, a successful writer who would have a good income and take her to interesting places. She discovered to her disappointment that he thought her place was in the home, rather a modest home at that, with a single servant. The parties in London and Aldeburgh might have been on another planet, for all that Edith knew of them. Seldom did anyone visit the house: her husband did not like her family, and his friends did not feel at ease with her. Walter Grahame had visited in Exeter in 1893, once Morley Roberts had come, and very occasionally a sister from Wakefield, although there was little understanding, and no affection, between the Gissing sisters and Edith.[56] Gradually the relationship between husband and wife deteriorated, to the accompaniment of railing and quarreling. Not even the advent of a second son, Alfred, could mend the breaking ties.

The heroine of *In the Year of Jubilee* finally accepts the decision of her journalist-husband that she live apart from him in a tiny house in the country and there raise his child, with occasional lover-like visits from him after he assures her that no "civilized" couple should live under the same roof unless the roof covers a very large and well-staffed house. The heroine in the novel accepts her lot, but Gissing's wife did not. One of the vexations was the interference (with pious intentions) of one of those self-assured, helpful, and incredible women who are inevitably attracted to men like Gissing. Clara Collet had lectured to the London Ethical Society on "The Novels of Mr. George Gissing," and Gissing was ever the willing slave of any woman who spoke glowingly of his work. She was furthermore the daughter of Sir Mark Collet, and one of the Labour correspondents of the Board of Trade.[57] She was, in short, altogether admirable in Gissing's eyes, one of those strong, capable women he admired but never married. He received a note from her in May 1893, and by September she had so far advanced their intimacy that she was able to make an astonishing proposal, which he considered seriously and gratefully. She offered to rear, or at least supervise young Walter Gissing, if his father should ever "break down." Miss Collet must indeed have been kind, for she interceded in several tense experiences, and she was also generous with the Gissing children. (Later, too, she would be co-executor, with Algernon, in Gissing's will.) But to Gissing's wife Miss Collet's good offices could only have seemed obnoxious and meddlesome.

Gissing himself soon showed the strain of domestic discord: at night, dreams of death and illness haunted him. Memories of his dead brother Will came back to sadden him, and he dreamed of dying from cancer. Finally, one night he woke to find echoing in his mind the words, "O Rome, my country, city of the soul," [58] and, whether or not in his thirst after guidance he chose to interpret the dream as the true expression of his desire, he soon decided to spend the following winter in Italy, alone, even if his wife protested. The house was in a shambles, he could endure it no longer. He had even become anxious about his beloved son Walter: when the boy was away at a nursery or with his aunts in Wakefield, he yearned for him, but when the child was at home he often found him troublesome.[59] Nevertheless, Walter was often in his thoughts, and he bought models and toys and read him stories, as his own father had done.

It was in February of 1897 that the final dreadful scene occurred between husband and wife, complete with all the noise and railing that Gissing had always hated and had criticized so openly in his novels of the nether world. But no scene in the novels was more bitter and more sordid than the one in real life. Gissing stormed from the house, unable to endure more, and took shelter at Romney at the home of Dr. Harry Hick, a tried and good friend.[60] Later a persistent cough drove him to the doctors who in turn advised him to rest in Devon or Cornwall until June. In September he packed his belongings in Epsom, visited his sisters in Wakefield and arranged for Walter to stay with them, and on September 19 he set out for the continent. Only the year before he had finished a novel entitled *The Whirlpool,* a novel which foretold the unhappy climax of his second marriage, just as *Workers in the Dawn* had foreshadowed the miserable end of the first marriage. Henceforth, except for a few months in London and then another basic decision, he would spend the rest of his life in wandering on the continent, "emancipated" at last, but in exile and in poor health.

As he looked in retrospect at the years of his second marriage, studded with disappointments even as his first had been, it must often have seemed to him that he had learned too little and too late. He was not fit for the role of Pygmalion. He had sought to counteract the effects of the early environment of two wives, and twice he failed: Nell had remained weak and vacillating, Edith hungry for noise and bustle. He had supposed that a "simple life" conceived in ideal terms was the kind of life that most "normal" people could be encouraged to desire, but finally learned that only the complex being values the simple life. It had taken him many more years to understand himself and others in real life than to understand the people on his printed pages, and insight in the daily routine of life came with more pain than insight on the lecture platform and in the study.

He felt now that his sanity could be preserved only through complete honesty: he had to rid himself of pretense and the old shibboleths. Thus, when a saccharine article appeared on the subject of "Mr. George Gissing at Home," in which Gissing was made to express affection for the "peasants" of Italy with whom he had spent a year, the infuriated novelist sent a letter posthaste from Rome to the London *Academy,* which was printed in the issue of March 19, 1898.

"Worse . . . is the long passage you quote in conclusion, a sort of general confession. . . Every line of this is distasteful to me, and in no conversation, at any time of my life, did I so express myself. It is monstrous that one should be made to pule about one's 'little happiness,' about 'toiling millions who never see the blue sky,' about 'toil for *Weib und Kind*,' and so on."

Gissing was not so hungry for publicity to appease Mrs. Grundy as to agree to sentimental trash about himself. To him, for example, paternal feeling was one of the strongest and finest emotions possible for men, but he would not permit that feeling to be degraded by sentimental paraphrases.

He was equally blunt about his scorn for the hypothetical virtues of demos, which were being much praised in the nineties. Indeed he shared, along with Edmund Gosse, the uncomfortable duty of calling halt to the sentimental exaltation of the masses. How far journalism could go to ascribe virtues which common sense would deny is illustrated by the lachrymose accounts of the funeral of Sir Alfred Tennyson, in which the masses were alleged to have shed tears and muttered lines of Tennysonian verse to themselves. Edmund Gosse felt his gorge rising and stoutly expressed his "scepticism . . . with regard to the universal appreciation of the poet." Gosse described his attendance at the funeral and his search for ". . . horny hands dashing away the tear, seamstresses holding 'the little green volumes' to their faces to hide their agitation." But he sought in vain for corroboration of the journalists' raptures: "Entering the Abbey . . . we distinguished patience, good behaviour, cheerful and untiring inquisitiveness, a certain obvious gratitude for an incomprehensible spectacle provided by the authorities, but nothing else." [61]

Gissing read the stringent article and felt it his duty to give confirmation. (Gosse later reprinted Gissing's letter in an appendix to *Questions at Issue*.)

"Optimism has made a fancy picture of the representative working-man, ludicrous beyond expression to those who know him in his habitat; and the supremely ludicrous touch is that

which attributes to him a capacity for enjoying pure literature. . .
The custodian of a Free Library in a southern city informs me
that 'hardly once in a month' does a volume of verse pass over
his counter. . .

"What else could one have anticipated? To love poetry is a
boon of nature, most sparingly bestowed; appreciation of the
poet's art is an outcome of studious leisure. Even an honest liking
for verse . . . depends upon complex conditions of birth, breeding,
education. . . It was needless folly to pretend that, because one
or two of Tennyson's poems became largely known through popular recitation, therefore Tennyson was dear to the heart of the
people. . ."

If Gissing was stern in evaluating the "taste" of the masses, he
was also stern in his remarks on the wealthier members of English
society.

"Everywhere there are the many and the few. What of the
multitude in higher spheres? Their leisure is ample; literature lies
thick about them. It would be amusing to know how many give
one hour a month to the greater poets. . ."

A decade before, when he had become hostile to the proletariat,
he had turned, temporarily, into a "snob," but now he had become completely self-reliant, self-critical, while retaining a cool
and unprejudiced view of the several classes of English society.

By 1897 Gissing had chosen the values which would remain
until his death. He had satisfied himself that romantic idealism
was not for him, nor its stepchild, gross sentimentality. Most of
the great emotions that moved the men of his era no longer stirred him — neither rampant nationalism, love for democracy, sympathy with female suffrage, adulation of science. A few primeval
emotions still gripped him, but he was scarcely verbal about
them, except, perhaps, when speaking through such a character
in fiction as Harvey Rolfe in *The Whirlpool*; these were paternal

feeling, strong sexual attachment not necessarily connected with marriage, sensible and honest companionship. But the popular interpretation of even these emotions was not his. By 1897 he was not only a man without a country, but, more lonely still, a man without a group. To such an impasse had the critical faculty brought him.

Chapter 8

THREE LATER NOVELS

*Publishers could rely upon Gissing to choose either an abom-*inable title or an excellent one. The abominable titles began with unpronounceable proper names, like *Denzil Quarrier* and *Will Warburton.* The clever titles were tinged with irony, and one of the cleverest was *The Emancipated.*

The novel was published in 1889, after Gissing had returned from his first tour of Italy. Like Henry James, whose *Roderick Hudson* had appeared in 1876, Gissing was fascinated by the impact of the old, overripe Mediterranean culture upon Puritans from fog-bound lands. But where James's heroes and heroines are beautifully vulnerable, strangely "available" to love and pain, Gissing's young heroine is more phlegmatic and less "wonderful," to use one of James's favorite words. Miriam Baske, a widow at twenty-four, is convalescing in Naples. She intends to spend the fortune of her late and lukewarm husband on a chapel in the Midlands, and in the warm sun of Naples she surrounds herself with architects' drawings. She has come to Naples for very "sensible" reasons: the warmth is good for her, and her old friends, the Spences, are available for both companionship and chaperonage. Miriam does not realize that at times she seems a kinsman to another traveling Britisher, Mrs. Bradshaw.

"Though natural beauty made little if any appeal to her she interested herself greatly in Vesuvius, reading it as a serio-comic phenomenon which could only exist in a country inhabited by childish triflers. Her memory was storing all manner of Italian absurdities — everything being an absurdity which differed from English habit and custom — to furnish her with matter for mirthful talk when she got safely back to Manchester and civilization."

Miriam, however, views her surroundings less as "absurd" than as dangerous and unbelievably theatrical, in the same way that she looks upon her brother Reuben. (How he hates his Biblical name and the parents who bestowed it!) Reuben is wicked, ingenuous, and amoral by turns, and is, he believes, thoroughly "emancipated." Nevertheless, although they are opposites, Reuben and Miriam cannot be at cross purposes until another human being forces them into active roles vis à vis one another. Ross Mallard, a painter, and his ward, Cecily Doran, therefore enter the story in principal roles.

Mallard is the kind of man to whom Gissing was usually sympathetic — brusque, worldly-wise, yet conscientious and fastidious. He has seen as much of life as Reuben, but has not made his past an excuse for irresponsibility. Nevertheless he is not altogether elated over being guardian to Cecily during her visit to Italy, for though she is only eighteen she too is "emancipated." Sin and damnation, realities to Miriam, mean nothing to her; yet she is radiantly innocent, like Milly, perhaps, in *The Wings of the Dove*. She falls in love with Reuben amidst the ruins of Pompeii, in a scene that could have been only a lurid stage set if Gissing had not been so restrained. But the scene is convincing because there is no faked chiaroscuro, and because Reuben seems no mere rake and Cecily no mere ingenue. They agree to elope in spite of the protests that they know will be raised. So ends the first half of the novel.

It is a serious technical risk for any but the cleverest novelist to plan his story so that there are two halves and a lapse between halves, and Gissing was not yet clever enough. The reader suspects that Reuben will soon prove faithless to his wife, that Cecily will recognize the fatuity of her past notions of "emancipation,"

and that Miriam is the one who will really become emancipated.
The problem in construction is whether the novelist can sustain
interest in a slow march to nemesis, after a first part full of action
and sudden decisions. Unfortunately, the problem is not successfully met, and the only interest in the second half lies in the
passionate speeches of Reuben, who soon discloses to his wife
that immutability in love is an incomprehensible concept to him.

"'Suppose, Ciss, we all of a sudden lost everything, and we had
to go and live in a garret, and I had to get to work as a clerk at
five and twenty shillings a week. How soon should we hate the
sight of each other and the sound of each other's voices? . . . I
should behave like a ruffian.'

"'Yet we hear,' suggested Cecily, 'of wretched women remaining devoted to husbands who all but murder them now and then.'

"'You are not so foolish as to call *that* love! That is mere un-
reasoning and degraded love — the same kind of thing one may
find in a dog. . . Can my reason discover any argument why I
should not love you? I won't say that it might not some day, and
then my love would be by so much diminished.'"

From this point Cecily becomes a patient Griselda without benefit
of verse, enduring the recriminations of her husband without being verbal about them. The penalty is that her one good speech,
given her by Gissing when finally she decides to leave her husband, comes when the reader has already resigned himself to
thinking of her as one of the pathetic creatures her husband had
described.

"A tragedy can go no further than its fifth act. . . I have shed
all my tears long since, exhausted all my indignation. You can't
think what an everyday affair it has become with me. I am afraid
that means that I am in a great measure demoralized by these
experiences."

Unfortunately the reader is not shown the "demoralization" in active process. Instead the scene shifts to Mallard and Miriam, and Cecily's difficulties are reported rather than made manifest. She appears from time to time furnished with an epitome speech, just as Reuben does, but a novel, after all, should be concerned with manners and process, not résumés. *The Emancipated* is therefore one of the least satisfactory of Gissing's novels, in spite of the promising beginning; it is a mere essay upon a theme that would be developed more fruitfully in *The Whirlpool.* By that time Gissing would have learned that a novel can have more than one hero and one heroine without also scattering intensity and interest.

      *   *   *

It seems incredible that *New Grub Street* was written in the same year, 1889, as *The Emancipated,* for its technical excellence is incomparable. It is the one novel of Gissing which both his contemporaries and the "new school" critics of today have found admirable. The novel has been reprinted in the Modern Library and has been named a member of the select group in the nineteenth century which serves as link between the best fiction of the eighteenth century and the serious twentieth century tradition.[1] In 1891, however, reviewers were concerned less with the "technical competence" of the novel than with its "veracity," and Gissing's gloomy saga of Grub Street provoked a series of controversial articles and letters-to-the-editor. Andrew Lang in a leading article stated his conviction that Gissing's "realism" was unreal, that his gloomy presentation was not true of real literary life in London. Thereupon the "real" literary men replied in defense of Gissing, with many a sharp remark about the prosperous men of letters who had forgotten what penury was like. Most reviewers agreed that the "treatment and touch" in the novel were "distinctly realistic," and that it showed a "lightening of touch," that is to say, more dexterity than had been apparent in earlier novels.[2]

The plot was one for which Gissing had needed to make no tours of London or Italy in search of documentary material. It was very like his own life story, so like that for years those seeking the facts of Gissing's life have forgotten whether it was Gissing or Reardon or Whelpdale who almost starved and ate peanuts in Troy! Indeed the search for a *roman à clef* has been one of the reasons for the popularity of the novel. But though the story may be close to the facts in the life, it is "story" none the less; that is to say, Gissing does not describe the decline and fall of Eugene Reardon, a man much like himself, with any overwhelming emotion either of pity or scorn. Jasper Milvain, the foil to Reardon, receives equally good characterization, and is quite as vital as Reardon, although all Gissing's self-pity must have tempted him to make a caricature of Milvain. If Gissing understands the desperation of Reardon, he also understands the impatience of Reardon's wife, who has "contracted" to marry a "promising" writer, and will break the contract if the promise is not fulfilled. As Milvain says:

"But just understand the difference between a man like Reardon and a man like me. He is the old type of unpractical artist. . . He won't make concessions, or rather, he can't make them; he can't supply the market. I — well, you may say that at present I do nothing; but that's a great mistake, I am learning my business. Literature nowadays is a trade. Putting aside men of genius, who may succeed by mere cosmic force, your successful man of letters is your skilful tradesman. He thinks first and foremost of the realities; when kind of goods begins to go off slackly, he is ready with something new and appetizing. . . Reardon can't do that kind of thing, he's behind his age; he sells a manuscript as if he lived in Sam Johnson's Grub Street."

Jasper's shrewd cheerfulness is suggested in dialogue on the very first page of the novel (no more harangues in the opening page): he is eating his boiled egg at breakfast and recalls without discomfort that some nonentity is being hanged that day. He is pleased that *he* is not being hanged, as he remarks jocosely, but he is quite content with his egg and hopes for a small fortune before the age of thirty. By his own admission he is a "clever fellow" who "knows how to use the brains of other people."

The "clever fellow" assays Reardon with accuracy: Reardon has some self-knowledge, but he cannot change the traits of temperament which hinder him in social groups and impinge on his writing. With a little rationalizing, and some truth, Reardon blames poverty for a good deal of his failure. "My instincts are strongly social, yet I can't be at my ease in society, simply because I can't do justice to myself. Want of money makes me the inferior of the people I talk with, though I might be superior to them in most things. I am ignorant in many ways, and merely because I am poor." His books are, like himself, not readily likable. Gissing describes Reardon's novels, and there is no reason to suppose that Reardon would have disagreed with him.

"They dealt with no particular class of society (unless one makes a distinct class of people who have brains) and they lacked local colour. Their interest was almost purely psychological. It was clear that the author had no faculty for constructing a story. . . But strong characterisation was within his scope and an intellectual fervour, appetising to a small section of refined readers, marked all his best pages."

Among Reardon's few friends is Biffen who eats his supper of bread and dripping with a knife and fork because "this always makes the fare seem more substantial." The two friends spend their leisure time discussing Greek meters "as if they lived in a world where the only hunger known could be satisfied by grand or sweet cadences." But if Biffen goes for delight to the Golden Age of Athens, in his novels he turns to the brass age of his own day. He considers himself the forerunner of a new kind of novel.

"What I really aim at is an absolute realism in the sphere of

the ignobly decent. The field, as I understand it, is a new one;
I don't know any writer who has treated ordinary vulgar life with
fidelity and seriousness. Zola writes deliberate tragedies; his vilest
figures become heroic from the place they will fill in a strongly
imagined drama. I want to deal with the essentially unheroic,
with the day-to-day life of that vast majority of people who are
at the mercy of paltry circumstance. Dickens understood the possibility of such work, but his tendency to melodrama on the one
hand, and his humor on the other, prevented him from thinking
of it . . . the result will be something unutterably tedious. Precisely. This is the stamp of the ignobly decent life. If it were
anything *but* tedious it would be untrue."

(Later reviewers were to accuse Gissing of falsely projecting his
own boredom with vulgar life upon the people who daily lived
it.) Biffen is too honest to suppose that the "people" will read his
descriptions of their tedious lives.

"The working classes detest anything that tries to represent
their daily life. . . It's downright snobbishness. Dickens goes down
only with the best of them, and then solely because of his strength
in farce and his melodrama."

Biffen's "big" scene is the rescue of his manuscript, *Mr. Bailey
Grocer,* from a burning tenement. One can best appreciate Gissing's irony if one contrasts with it the probable treatment that
Dickens would have given the scene. There would be a rush to
the door of the burning building, the rescue of some helpless
human being inside, and the emergence of brave Biffen, sooty
and smiling, soon to be made a junior partner by one of the
Cheeryble brothers who happened to witness the rescue! In Gissing's version, on the other hand, Biffen leaps into the smoking
building in order to rescue his manuscript, notices the prostrate
body, dead-drunk, of the man who had started the fire, assumes
that the man is either dead or unimportant, but does not stop to

investigate. His goal is the manuscript. When he has it, he escapes onto the roof, where he narrowly misses death because his weak muscles, after years of sedentary and penurious living (as the author observes), will not support him in the crisis. When Biffen emerges at last into the street, no one will give him food or temporary shelter because he looks so begrimed!

Reardon's wife is extremely well-drawn. Although the reader feels sympathy for her husband, he cannot but pay a grudging respect to Mrs. Reardon, whose terrifying will to live will not permit her to sink into the penury and despair rapidly engulfing her husband. Romantic love has become meaningless to her:

"Best or worst, novels are all the same. Nothing but love, love, love; what silly nonsense it is! Why don't people write about the really important things of life? Some of the French novelists do; several of Balzac's for instance. I have just been reading his 'Cousin Pons,' a terrible book, but I enjoyed it ever so much because it was nothing like a love story. What rubbish is printed about love!"

It is the final ironic commentary upon her values that her husband's attempt to effect a reconciliation fails because he looks so shabby! Had Reardon been practical man enough to procure by hook or by crook a decent suit of clothes for his interview, that ridiculous trifle might have made all the difference in what was to result. "Clothes make the man" is a philosophic thesis, whether in a novel of Gissing or in *King Lear* or Swift or *Sartor Resartus*. Yet Gissing is unwilling to canonize Reardon or to damn the wife and Milvain. Although his own heart may be wrenched, he permits his characters to reveal themselves in action and dialogue in their strongest and weakest moments. *New Grub Street* is one of Gissing's best novels precisely because the characters appear to be unraveling themselves, as it were, instead of reading summaries of traits never shown in action. The realism is no mere bag of tricks; that is to say, there is more than superficial use of

local color: overwhelmingly convincing is the contrast of the will
to survive of a wife-mother and the disposition to failure of an
intelligent, sensitive, and insecure husband.

There are, of course, well-drawn characters in other novels of
Gissing; therefore the praise which has been bestowed upon *New
Grub Street* by the most fastidious critics comes by virtue of the
novelist's skilled use of counterpoint (Milvain versus Reardon)
and the hard-packed narrative. Doubtless fastidiousness about
construction is a virtue rather wasted in a critic of Gissing; nevertheless, in such a rare novel as this the critic finally comes into
his own!

         *   *   *

The Victorians were deeply interested in compromise, or, as
the seventeenth century would have said, "the character of a
trimmer." John Morley, an acquaintance of Gissing and an eminent man of letters, explored in a fine essay the very important
distinction that also obsessed Gissing — the difference between
honorable compromise and ignoble expediency. The subject was
central to the Victorian period, for were there not, on every
front, at home and abroad, evidences of good and bad compromise — from reform bills to the imbroglios in the Balkans where
Britain seemed to be playing both sides at one time.

For Gissing compromise was a personal problem as well.
Twice he had made compromises in marriage, forsaking his
dream of ideal love for "peace," by which he meant orderly
domestic arrangements and relief from sexual tension. In his
work, too, he had had to yield to publishers, on *Mrs. Grundy's
Enemies* and on a happy ending for *A Life's Morning*. It must
have seemed to him that all his life he had been making compromises — with one great irony — that he had never compromised
happily.

In *New Grub Street*, published in 1891, he had created a pair
of antagonists, Reardon and Milvain, one rigid and morbid, the
other opportunistic and cheerful. Now in *Born in Exile* he focused

his attention upon a more difficult creation, a man complex
enough to combine the qualities of both Reardon and Milvain.
Godwin Peak's egoism is not as ebullient as Milvain's, but it is
more dangerous. Furthermore Peak comes not from the world
of Grub Street journalism, where Milvains are the rule rather
than the exception, but from the world of the clergy.

Mrs. Humphrey Ward had produced a "shocking" best seller
in *Robert Elsmere,* first published in 1888, the story of a clergyman's doubts and temptations, but compared with Godwin Peak
Mrs. Ward's hero roars as gently as any sucking dove. Perhaps
Mrs. Ward's book furnished a model, but Gissing already had
several in real life — clergymen he knew in London whose thinking was so "broad" that it was often ambiguous. In his letters to
his family he noted with surprise that reservations in doctrine
did not cripple a clergyman in carrying out his practical pastoral
duties,[3] and in *Born in Exile* he created a young man who
thought that he, too, could manage the "business" of a clergyman's life without assenting to the dogma. As the *Athenaeum*
remarked when it reviewed the novel,

"The young man is scarcely a hero over whom one can become
very enthusiastic. His motives need close analysis, and the reader
who will give them that analysis under Mr. Gissing's guidance
may find his reward in a series of interesting psychological
puzzles."[4]

And another reviewer declared, "Godwin Peak neither for-
feits the reader's sympathy nor wins his admiration."[5] For Peak
was the intellectual sceptic presented in an entirely new fashion:
"Intellectual scepticism has had a fairly good turn in the novels
of the present generation. . . Hitherto, however, the religious
sceptic has been presented in a suitably heroic guise."[6] Such
was not Peak's fate.

Peak enters manhood from a red brick college in the Midlands, like Gissing's own Owens College. He enters with an

armful of prize books and honors in the classics, but hovering at the edge of his triumph like a fly at a rich feast is the thought of his draggle-tailed family and the dim prospect for worldly advancement. Musing upon "inherited tendencies" and half fearing a resemblance to his doltish brother, he leaves home with alacrity. He makes few friends, but makes use of them whenever possible. It seems to him finally that taking orders will best advance him in the world. Covertly he envies acquaintances who have the qualities he lacks: thus Malkin is explained, "The hearty extravagance of his friendliness was only possible in a man who had never been humiliated by circumstances, never restricted in his natural needs of body and mind."

Peak finally has an opportunity to visit in Exeter at the house of Martin Warricombe, a wealthy man interested in the possible reconciliation of science and theology. Secretly Peak is the author of a satire upon such vain seekings — he calls the article "The New Sophistry" — but he is able to forget the article sufficiently to astound the dinner guests in Exeter, and even himself, with his tender eloquence upon the reconciliation. But, after all, he has set out to demonstrate that "one's philosophy has nothing to do with the business of life" and his "business" is to succeed in the world of the wellborn. He admits frankly that he despises his own class! "I suppose you cannot call a man a democrat who recognizes in his heart and soul a true distinction of social classes." One of the most savage scenes in the novel is that in which Peak stands in a crowd that he hates, yearning to be with two aloof ladies who hover above the crowd.

"Here he stood, one of the multitude, of the herd; shoulder to shoulder with boors and pickpockets; and within reach of his hand reposed those two ladies, in Olympian calm, seeming unaware even of the existence of the throng. Now they exchanged a word; now they smiled to each other. How delicate was the moving of their lips! How fine must be their enunciation! . . .

They were his equals, those ladies; merely his equals. With such as they he should by right of nature associate. . . He hated the maladorous rabble who stared insolently at them and who envied their immeasurable remoteness. Of mere wealth he thought not; might he only be recognized by the gentle of birth and breeding for what he really was, and be rescued from the promiscuity of the vulgar!"

He is almost "rescued" in Exeter, when he is taken up by the Warricombes. It even seems that Sidwell Warricombe will fall in love with him. But soon nemesis comes, Peak's pretensions are unmasked, and he leaves for a manufacturing town and poverty. With his back to the wall, he is finally saved by a legacy, and hopes that Sidwell will marry him. But Gissing's heroines are seldom slaves of passion: Sidwell declines the offer, as Peak had half expected her to do. He muses afterwards,

"Well, she was not the heroine of a romance. Had he expected her to leave home and kindred — the 'little world' so infinitely dear to her — and go forth with a man deeply dishonoured. Present, his passion had dominated her: and perhaps her nerves only. But she had had time to recover from that weakness.

"A woman, like most women, of cool blood, temperate fancies. A domestic woman; the ornament of a typical English home. . .

"But neither was he cast in heroic mould. He had not the self-confidence, he had not the hot, youthful blood. A critic of life, an analyst of moods and motives, not the man who dares and acts. The only important resolve he had ever carried through was a scheme of ignoble trickery — to end in frustration."

Peak ends his life as he had begun it — in exile, with more money but with neither love nor social position. His life had been an attempt to prove that one's philosophy had nothing to do with the business of life, but the attempt had failed. Yet the implication in the novel cannot be that casuists and charlatans are doomed, for if Peak dies in wretchedness, the Reverend Chilvers, a mellifluous hypocrite, prospers. As for Sidwell herself, because she avoids decisions she belongs in limbo, not hell.

The unity of the novel lies in its emphasis upon Godwin Peak, who has no rival in interest. It is the concentration upon him which saves the book from diffuseness, for the scenes are strung together on long musings of Peak before and after action. In this day Gissing might have used stream of consciousness, for he was most interested in the inner monologues of Peak. However, his technique was not quite able to cope with stream of consciousness, and the novel remains an ambitious, not entirely successful, attempt to solve an inner puzzle, without dramatizing the puzzle in the conventional way. The reader is forced to judge Peak largely from interior monologues, although these are not deep or penetrating enough to be called true "stream-of-consciousness."

Chapter 9

REGRESSION

"Denzil Quarrier," published in 1892, the same year of Born in Exile, is the revised title of *The Radical Candidate.* Once again Gissing shows himself concerned with the egoism of a complex man, this time one as envious of his fellows as Godwin Peake, but more wicked, since he is already affluent but cannot endure the hard-won successes of others. Indeed Eustace Glazzard is one of the rarities in Gissing characterization, the thoroughly despicable man. "Vanity knows no satiety" might well be the motto under Glazzard's crest. Despite so rich a theme, however, the working-out is disappointing; more than that, the *Academy* went so far as to call the novel "commonplace." [1]

The most likely target for criticism is not the theme, but the sketchiness of the execution, for the book reads like a brief scenario: to use a much misused word, the "texture" is thin. Even the outline seems hurried and implausible. Denzil Quarrier, a man of some culture and means, is living with a woman whom he calls his wife, but who is legally (for involved and tedious reasons) the wife of a convict. Quarrier shares his secret with only one man, his old friend Eustace Glazzard, who like an Iago stores it for future use. At first Glazzard is not aware that he hates his friend, but gradually his slumbering hatred is aroused when Quarrier is chosen as the Radical candidate for Polterham, an honor which Glazzard would have liked for himself without exerting the energy to achieve it. It seems that his star is setting as Quarrier's begins to rise.

If Glazzard's feelings were those of usual envy, the denouement would be commonplace, but his hatred and his method
of revenge are intricate enough to be those of an epicure. Toward
the end of the novel his feeling is described explicitly.

"He had come to hate Quarrier. Yet with no vulgar hatred,
not with the vengeful rancour which would find delight in
annihilating its object. His feeling was consistent with a measure
of justice to Denzil's qualities, and even with a good deal of
admiration; as it originated in mortified vanity, so it might have
been replaced by the original kindness, if only some stroke of
fortune or of power had set Glazzard in his original position of
superiority. Quarrier as an ingenious young fellow looking up to
the old comrade . . . was acceptable, lovable; as a self-assertive
man, given to patronage (though perhaps unconsciously) and
succeeding in life as his friend stood still or retrograded, he
aroused dangerous emotions. Glazzard could no longer endure
his presence, hated the sound of his voice, cursed his genial
impudence."

The scheme for revenge is planned and executed beautifully.
In the midst of the campaign for election (and Gissing provides
amusing sidelights which are fiendishly accurate) Glazzard plots
with the convict husband of Lilian Quarrier, in an attempt to
discredit Quarrier and make him lose the election. Lilian, however, aware of Glazzard's hatred and fearful that her existence
will prove a continuing source of blackmail, commits suicide.
As for Glazzard, in a characteristically "Gissingish" ending, he
remains above suspicion, but with his Epicurean relish for his
friend's ruin a little spoiled because the suicide was a cruder
denouement, a less subtle one, than he would have liked. In
the melodramatic last scene Glazzard models a head of Judas,
to the admiration of his passive and wealthy bride from the
provinces. The last pages — the Judas episode — confirm for
the reader what he had already suspected, that Gissing was

composing in a hurry, that he chose the most obvious, the most
florid, means of advancing his story. The satire is often heavy-
handed, some of the characterization is "thin," and the whole
tale smacks of composition by the ticking hands of the clock.

*   *   *

The Odd Women, published in 1893, was not patently concerned with homosexuality, although doubtless the publishers
must have hoped for brisk sale of an ambiguous title. The title
actually came from an observation in statistics, that the number
of women exceeded that of men, that most of the women were
without dowry, and that their probable fate was to remain odd
women, extras, unmarried, confronted with the decision of what
to do with their odd lives. However, the tone of the book is one
of detachment; Gissing does not appear to be more than a
recorder of the plight of such women. As the *Athenaeum* remarked ". . . we have pages of something more resembling the
reporter's than the artist's touch. . . In spite of this the book
is better than merely readable; it is absorbing." [2]

The story begins with Gissing's favorite irony — the decision
made too late. "Tomorrow" Doctor Madden will take out life
insurance, but before tomorrow he is dead, leaving his daughters
penniless. Monica, Alice, and Virginia must support themselves,
but since they have no assets except a little bad schooling, they
are at a loss over how to begin. To be "companion" or teacher
seems the only recourse, for, as Gissing remarked ironically, what
is more suitable for the ignorant and frightened than to teach!
Both Alice and Virginia deteriorate in mind and body, Virginia
becoming a tippler and then an alcoholic, as Gissing catalogues
every change in the manner of Zola. Meanwhile Monica, the
youngest and prettiest, brought up "half a lady and half shop-
girl" sees marriage as the only escape from a clerkship both dull
and exhausting.

Struggling against the ignorance and the apathy of the "odd

women" is one of the most interesting women Gissing ever created. Were she merely a suffragette, she would seem, as well as the novel itself, merely quaint today. But Rhoda Nunn does not foresee the solution of the woman's problem in terms of employment and improved legislation. The emotional problems, the "intimate" problems, as the Victorians would have said, most concern her. She differs from Miss Barfoot, an older woman who has founded a secretarial school for the daughters of the genteel poor. Miss Barfoot observes, and Rhoda challenges.

"'Let us be glad if we can put a few of them in the way of living single with no more discontent than an unmarried man experiences.'

"'Surely that's an unfortunate comparison,' said Rhoda coldly. 'What man lives in celibacy?'"

But Rhoda finds it more difficult actually to work out a "modern" relationship with a man than it had seemed in theory. The man to whom she is attracted is challenged by her character of virago.

"If Rhoda were what he thought her, she enjoyed this opportunity of studying a modern male, and cared not how far he proceeded in his own investigations, sure that at any moment she could bid him fall back. The amusement was only just beginning."

The amusement ends, however, in a fashion which neither partner had predicted. Barfoot, whose original aim had been mere conquest, the act of seduction, finally wishes marriage with Rhoda, while she, who theoretically had scorned the ties of marriage and the insistence upon marital faithfulness, realizes that she can feel emotionally secure only when she is promised absolute faithfulness. In one of the most poignant scenes in a Gissing novel, both persons finally realize the difference between intellectualization and true emotional acceptance.

Unfortunately, however, the novel is a shambles in construc-

tion, despite individually moving scenes, for Gissing becomes
so overburdened by that Victorian monster, plot and double
plot, that he paralyzes his most important characters under the
weight of the plot. Were Gissing a Tolstoy describing all Russian
society in one novel and a battle of nations as well, he might be
justified in so much shifting about of his characters; unfortunately, in a story which covers only a small range in society,
such manipulations are disastrous. By the time that Monica
Widdowson and her husband have a deathbed reconciliation,
there is only one fine scene left for Rhoda and her suitor. Crestfallen, fearful of further deception, Rhoda now finds the thought
of marriage repugnant, whereas Barfoot, erstwhile iconoclast, has
decided that he wants a wife, not a mistress, after all, and a
secure, conventional place in society. It is a daring and, for the
Victorians, original, irony, but by this time the reader is exhausted from the details of a lumbering plot. The primary intention, to show the physical and social deterioration of a family,
has been lost by the wayside, thanks to the seductions of a
woman first envisioned as only a secondary character. Clearly
the novel is not a success, because it has no semblance of unity;
nevertheless in the history of English fiction it will doubtless be
recognized as an important specimen of the style of Zola on
Victorian soil.

                        *   *   *

In the Year of Jubilee was published in 1894, but it had as
the year of its action the golden anniversary of the reign of
Queen Victoria. If ever a novel began with promise, like a
cornucopia about to tumble out its treasures, this one does.
"At eight o'clock on a Sunday morning, Arthur Peachey un-
locked the front door, and quietly went forth." Behind the closed
door is the reason for the stealthy departure at an early hour:
back of the door is the mad-kitchen scene of Alice in Wonderland and the chaos of the Jellyby household in Dickens. The
house is in De Crespigny Park in Camberwell, a pretentious

suburb made for invasion by satirists like Gissing. "Epatez les bourgeois" might well be the motto for the story, which anatomizes the Peachey household, particularly the wife and her two sisters, each outdoing the other in handsomeness, shrewishness, and ill-bred conceit. Not since the days of *The Nether World* had Gissing written such sharp-edged satire. Although there are lamentable breaks in construction (as reviewers pointed out,[3] Peachey does not reënter the story for dozens of pages after he closes the front door) so fascinating are the shrews that Peachey is scarcely missed. With incisive strokes Gissing draws every vulgar manifestation of the "raw material which the mill of education is supposed to convert into middle-class ladyhood."

Contrasted with the sisters French is their friend, Nancy Lord, who like them is spoiled and aimless and half-educated, but who has a self-awareness that they will never possess. Like so many Gissing characters Nancy suffers from a paralyzed will, until in a burst of abandonment she joins the mob parading the streets of London on Jubilee night and discovers with horror that she tingles to the same sensations as the ruffians! The scene serves as foreshadowing of her yielding to primitive impulse when a crisis comes: she succumbs to Lionel Tarrant, the one man she has met whom she can neither dupe nor dominate. Then, as Hardy's Tess would do, she spends the rest of her life learning patience and caring for her child, while her husband, who marries her soon after the seduction, wanders in the Bermudas in search of a fortune. While Tarrant is off stage (and indeed Gissing does not know what to do with him for half the book) the progress is noted of Fanny French and Samuel Barmby, two young entrepreneurs in a crass new age. Barmby, who read Samuel Smiles in his day and would read Dale Carnegie in this, pays unwelcome court to Nancy, never dreaming that she is secretly married and has a child as well. Credulity is strained further by the return from America of a reformed Tarrant. He is reconciled with his wife and has the prospect of a modest career in journalism, but he decides that for him to live with his family in Suburbia would be ignominy. Tarrant's posturings occupy many a page, and the story falls to pieces. Once again Gissing has failed in construction, unable to decide on the design. The glimpses of the sisters French and Peachey, and the development of Nancy Lord are best things in the novel, but on the whole the promised riches of the first chapter are strewn in disorderly array. As for Lionel Tarrant, it was the *Athenaeum* which remarked that his "preposterous views on the married state are developed with fatiguing iteration." [4]

Chapter 10

"THE GENRE
OF NERVOUS EXHAUSTION"

As early as 1884 Gissing had described his joy at seeing how the "old three-volume tradition" was being "broken through" because of continental influence.[1] Years later in an unpublished letter to Monsieur Davray, the French critic, he remarked that like a schoolboy he "had not the time to make his work shorter," but that he looked to the future for opportunities to "cut and revise" his old novels.[2] Although such an opportunity came when Bentley published a revised edition of *The Unclassed* in 1895, there was never an opportunity for Gissing to subject all his work to such reconsideration. It is quite clear, however, that except for *New Grub Street, The Whirlpool,* and perhaps *Our Friend the Charlatan,* Gissing never made the best use of the long, three-volume novels. The tradition had been foisted upon the public by the lending libraries, which preferred to overwhelm provincial subscribers with three-volume novels, handsomely bound; and by the publishers who charged a guinea per volume for novels in such form. However, for novelists like Gissing whose imaginative powers were not those of Dickens, the three-volume novel encouraged prolixity, lack of concentration, and tedious sub-plots. Fortunately, therefore, Gissing had the opportunity in the mid-nineties to write three short one-volume novels, of about 60,000 words each. These were *The Paying Guest, Sleeping Fires,* and *Eve's Ransom.* Fortunately, too, after *Denzil Quarrier,* Gissing learned that a short novel does not have to be thin, and that if terse dialogue and symbol are used, characters lose nothing in conviction even though they are developed in shorter space.

The Paying Guest is not brilliant, but it is lively in spirit and compact in structure. To Gissing it was just a little thing dashed off quickly in order to close a contract with Cassell's Pocket Library, but it made readers chuckle and then applaud, for Mr. Gissing had never before had the reputation of humorist. *The Saturday Review* asked why this was so much more entertaining than the former novels, and answered its own question: for once Mr. Gissing had abandoned the "colourless theory of fiction" of which he had "hitherto been the ablest as Mr. George Moore is perhaps the most prominent exponent. . ." The "colourless theory," according to the reviewer, had the following characteristics: "Let your characters tell their own story, make no comment, write a novel as you would a play. So we are robbed of the personality of the author." [3] As a matter of fact, the earlier novels of Gissing had not lacked the author's personality; a point of view was evident, but it was a somber one, not the gay one of *The Paying Guest*. But this time Gissing could smile occasionally at the lower middle class instead of trouncing it.

The plot is simple, and so is characterization. The Mumfords of Sutton are having a difficult time in meeting the expenses of their pretty house, and so decide to take in a "paying guest," their euphemism for "boarder" or "lodger." Louise Derrick, an "enfant terrible" such as Daudet might have chosen, joins the household as paying guest, and proceeds to involve the formerly decorous household in her private life and that of her vulgar but rich family. Fortunately for construction, most of these people, except for Louise's mother, are kept off the stage, but are reconstructed by conversation between Mrs. Mumford and Louise. The escapades, including the courtship of bluff Mr. Cobb, who almost sets the house afire, are often farcical and always pleasant. The entertainment of the book derives primarily, however, not from strong incident, but from the merry conversation. For once Gissing reproduced the capacity for humor in his subject as well as their idiom and accent.

*　　*　　*

If *The Paying Guest* was a little thing skillfully turned out, *Sleeping Fires* was more ambitious and less successful. Nevertheless it held the attention of reviewers.

"It is a brave venture in a new style . . . the author struggles with a problem in morals, and solves it by the methods of the present generation rather than by those of the generations that lived before us. . . Mr. Gissing is sane and delicate; he may have sacrificed some of the intensities that a keener spirit would have read into such a theme as he has chosen, but he has worked out his story on straight and sensible lines." [4]

The story takes place, like *The Emancipated,* on the Mediterranean shores Gissing loved so well, and is again concerned with the regaining of the will to live. Now, however, the scene of the ancient world is interpreted as a lure away from the problems of the present. Sojourning in Athens is Edmund Langley, a man of independent though modest means who has been spending the years in quiet study and travel in the south of Europe. At forty-two he has shorn himself, except for an occasional memory, of the passionate involvements of his youth in England. But just when he thinks himself most secure there bursts in upon his quiet life a young man old enough to be his son — who is in fact his natural son — by an affair in youth. Louis Revill, although he appears for only a few pages, is thoroughly credible and thoroughly likable, with a great capacity for love, although he himself has received so little. Louis is the ward of Lady Revill, who had rejected Langley's proposal of marriage years before when she learned of the pre-marital affair he had had with another woman. In Athens the friendship between the two men, unknowing father and son, develops quickly, to the delight of the boy's tutor, who is eager to be rid of his charge.

There are poignant moments — almost all the scenes in which father and son are together, and the interview between Lady Revill and Langley in London, in which she tries desperately to maintain the icy reserve of so many years. When Louis dies, both survivors realize that their years have been wasted, but Lady Revill prefers atonement by withdrawal to reëntry into the turmoils of living. As for Langley, he determines to tear himself away from the "sorcery of Athens," from his habit of mourning ancient glory and withdrawing from the present. "The world never had such need of the Greeks as in our time. Vigour, sanity, and joy — that's their gospel. . . And lots of us who might make it a reality mourn through life. I am thinking of myself." Langley realizes that he can no longer blame "fate . . . a convenient word for all the mistakes we live to be ashamed of."

The reader has two reasons for dissatisfaction with the novel: the sudden discovery by Langley that Louis is his son strains credulity, for presumably Lady Revill has kept the secret through the years, and yet her character is not developed sufficiently to make it credible to the reader that she would be capable of such dissimulation. Secondly, her rebuff of her lover because he had once had an affair is reported rather than rendered, so that the reader cannot sympathize with the decision. The reader feels bludgeoned into acceptance of Langley's view of Lady Revill as a tragic figure, for in actuality the sketch presented of her reaches no such dimensions.

❖   ❖   ❖

Eve's Ransom is the finest of the trio of short novels, and indeed it represents Gissing's best work, along with *New Grub Street* and *The Whirlpool*. It seems unbelievable that he whose touch was so often heavy could fashion anything of such exquisite quality, but "exquisite" is fitting praise for the novel. The story is slight but not thin, the flavor subacid, the presentation terse and convincing. Gissing has managed to avoid every one of the customary pitfalls: Paris, which once would have been described stone by stone, is in this novel no more than a backdrop in quick dexterous lines for the feelings of Maurice Hilliard; and later the red brick villa in the suburbs, which would have been anatomized earlier, is delineated in a few strokes. The method is impressionism, but this is by no means a denial of a realistic point of view. Instead it is as if the essence of character and place were now sought instead of long and laborious photography. So, too, revealing rather than general actions are shown, and symbols are used. Things merely seem to "happen" rather than to be explained by the author with full antecedents. Thus when Hilliard receives an unexpected sum from a debtor of his dead father, he is simply given a choice — to husband the money or to permit himself some of the experiences that he has hoped for vaguely. In London he meets Eve Madeley and, surprising even himself, asks her to accompany him to Paris. In former years Gissing would have explained why Hilliard made the offer, would have analyzed the elements of lust, pity, and ennui in the offer; now the offer simply *happens;* the reader senses from Hilliard's tremulous behavior with waiters in restaurants, from his very gait, that something *will* happen, but the pleasure is not marred by a long and turgid explanation from Gissing in his own person. An added delight is the refusal of Eve Madeley and Hilliard to think out loud and to air their consciences freely. They are revealed by what they do, and sometimes by what they say in spite of themselves. Eve especially is the custodian of her own secret life: the reader can only surmise about her, not crawl into her swiftly turning little mind. When she marries Hilliard's best friend after her return from Paris, the reader suspects that it is because of the red brick villa "rather new, of course" just provided for her, but Eve is too self-contained ever to give the reader, or her husband or former lover, any long explanations. As for Hilliard, although at first chagrined, he commits neither suicide nor murder. It simply occurs to him one day when he is out walking in the country that he suddenly has feelings of relief rather than sorrow. There is not one false note in the book, not one lapse from a style that Maupassant or Balzac might be proud to acknowledge. Narramore is rather stiff, perhaps, and fond of dissertations, but, alas, he is only too credible.

The *Saturday Review* for April 27, 1895 gave a long review of the novel and a good description of the principal characters.

"There cannot be any question of the finished workmanship, the minute observation, the absolute truthfullness of Mr. Gissing's latest novel. Eve Madeley is a real and credible woman, fundamentally mean as is the way with his women, with a sweet intellectual face and an inherent refinement and seriousness that exhort our respect, and with just one dash of sordid romance with a married man to vary her dull life of work and parsimony. Hilliard again is a subtly studied character, a mechanical draughtsman, bored to death by his monotonous life without the energy or ability to rise or to fall tragically out of it. . ."

In the same review, entitled "The Depressed School," exception was taken to the opinion that Gissing's view of life was "absolute veracity."

"The true Realism, we hold, looks both on the happy and on the unhappy, interweaves some flash of joy or humour into its gloomiest tragedy. Weighed by that standard, Mr. Gissing falls short. . . That horror of being hard up, the fixed idea of the dismalness of middle class life, is not only the keynote of this book, but of all his books. That evil shadow lies upon all his work; it reduces it from the level of a faithful presentation of life to *genre*. It is the *genre* of nervous exhaustion. . . And yet we must needs admire it because it is so remarkably well done, and we must needs read it to its bitter end for the grim interest of it that never fails."

"The genre of nervous exhaustion," although invented by the *Saturday Review* for *Eve's Ransom,* is even more suitable for Gissing's next novel, *The Whirlpool,* published in 1897, when he had had his fill of London society and domestic discord, and had decided that his integrity could be preserved only by retreat from the "whirlpool," the maelstrom of drowning human beings clutching their vanities and delusions. The *Academy* gave the novel a warm welcome:

"A salutary and valuable investigation of grime and gray-ness in social life: a mournful, mocking strong book. . . All this told with a curious simple sincerity, with no forced or violent emphasis, leaves the reader with a kind of aching admiration or jaded enjoyment of Mr. Gissing's very notable art. Harvey Rolfe and Alma; Hugh Carnaby and Sibyl . . . no other of his books can show more brilliant characterisation. Mr. Gissing is in love with ideas and can illustrate them through flesh and blood: his work lives." [5]

The praise of characterization has been repeated in recent years, and Alma Rolfe has been compared even with Emma Bovary. "The carefulness with which Gissing has worked in the details makes Flaubert's treatment of them look patchy. Flaubert has, of course, the inestimable advantage of sharp outline, vivid color and boldly simplified plan." [6] Mr. Shafer might have added that the story of Alma Rolfe seems less a matter of a butterfly broken on a wheel: that is to say, Alma has all the weak sensuality of Emma Bovary, but more brain. She is a violinist skillful enough for drawing-room performance, and aggressive enough, if not sufficiently talented, for performance in the concert hall. Yet the novel is not merely another variation on the loves of artists; Alma's

wish to be a concert violinist is merely another way of satisfying
her overwhelming need for love and praise.

The novel opens with Harvey Rolfe at his club, not an especially
distinguished club, but then he is not a very distinguished man.
He is, however, an intelligent man, a sensible man, and the word
"honor" means a good deal to him. When he first meets Alma, she
is rather flattered by the attention of an older and "odd" sort of
person, a sort of civilized grizzly bear. She does not take him seriously as a possible marriage partner until the financial disgrace
and suicide of her father makes it clear to her that henceforth
offers of well-to-do men will be of affairs, not marriage. This is
Alma's first lesson in the relativity of morals which she had regarded as fixed: as the daughter of an important and wealthy man,
she was sought after as a wife; now she finds that men take liber-
ties because she is suddenly deprived of her former status. As for
Rolfe himself, he suspects that the simple life he proposes to
Alma, away from the intricacies of cosmopolitan society, will soon
seem dull to her. Nevertheless he deludes himself.

"From the infinitudes of reverie, her eyes drew near and gazed
upon him — eyes gleaming with mischief, keen with curiosity; a
look now supercilious, now softly submissive; all the varieties of
expression caught in susceptible moments, and stored by a too
faithful memory. Her hair, her lips, her neck, grew present to
him, and lured his fancy with a wanton seduction. In self-defence
— pathetic strategem of intellectual man at issue with the flesh —
he fell back upon the idealism which ever strives to endow a fair
woman with a beautiful soul. . . To depreciate her was simpler,
and had generally been his wont; but subjugation had reached
another stage in him."

The two marry, retreat to a "simple life" in Wales, and there
their son is born. Alma, however, soon longs to return to the
whirlpool: "Her eyes appeared more deliberately conscious of
their depth and gleam; her lips, less responsive to the flying

thought, grew to an habitual expression — not of discontent, but something akin unto it; not of self-will, but something that spoke a spirit neither tranquil nor pliant." The longing becomes overwhelming, the family returns to London, where Alma deludes herself into thinking that her life is still simple and orderly. But by this time "simplicity" has become a caricature, so that the costliest gowns, merely because their lines are "simple," are interpreted by her as a mark of the quiet life. Occasionally she has guilt feelings, but gradually she arrives at the resolve to take nothing seriously. "Sin" becomes a matter of taste, "offense" a denial of sophistication.

" 'I don't take offense, Mrs. Strangeways,' Alma answered with a slight laugh to cover her uneasiness. 'It's so old-fashioned.'

"The hostess uttered a thin trill of merriment. 'One is always safe with people who have humour, dear. It *does* make life easier, doesn't it? Oh, the terrible persons who take everything with tragic airs!' "

It is only when Alma becomes an unwilling accessory to manslaughter that she realizes how shoddy her values have become, but by this time she is too exhausted from her struggles in the whirlpool to benefit for long from her new insight. Like Emma Bovary, she dies from an overdose of laudanum, while those about her still pursue the merry way that Hogarth had depicted a century before in *The Rake's Progress*.

The Whirlpool is Gissing's most accomplished performance in the long novel. Although the characters are many the author never loses control of them, and most of them are shown in relation to Alma and Rolfe, so that there is no impression of supernumeraries cluttering the scene. The characters develop and change, revealing themselves as they react to new people and situations without need of long explanations by the author.

It is not enough to say of the novel, however, that it shows the evidence of more skill than is usual in a novel of Gissing, for

New Grub Street is equally skillful. Perhaps the most memorable thing about *The Whirlpool* is its range, its sweep; in *New Grub Street,* by contrast, there is a lesser sense of panorama. If any one novel of Gissing can be named the keystone of the *Comédie Humaine* that he dreamed of writing after the manner of Balzac, that novel is *The Whirlpool,* for in it all the themes with which Gissing had been obsessed throughout his career are mingled and deepened. It was the final comment of a thoughtful man about man as a social animal.

Perhaps the most shocking theme, of the several Gissing pursues, is the need of most men for approval and gratification, even if self-delusion is the price finally demanded for such favors. Rolfe, the most thoughtful and honest person in the novel, enhances his simple courtship into a full-blown romance, and refuses to admit, for a long time, the force of his sexuality. Alma, far less honest than her husband, is even more deeply committed to self-deception, pretending that a middling ability as a violinist is really talent.

The need of self-knowledge, and the means to acquire it, have always constituted a great theme in English literature. In the nineteenth-century novel, which mirrored and also criticized the teeming and vain seekers after money and power, there is no major author who had not a comment to make: Dickens in *Great Expectations,* Thackeray in *Vanity Fair,* George Eliot in *Middlemarch,* Meredith in *Evan Harrington* or *The Amazing Marriage.* Gissing's *Whirlpool* deserves a place in this fine company, for its theme, and the carrying out, command respect. Gissing has not the wit of Meredith, the humor of Dickens, the charity of Eliot, or the complaisance of Thackeray. There are no faithful Dobbin marrying a wistful Amelia, no Cheeryble brothers, no generous benefactor, not even the one gift which George Eliot grants to depressed favorite characters — talent. In Gissing's novel there is no *deus ex machina,* even when suicide looms; refusal to accept knowledge of self is followed by suicide or that which to

Gissing means suicide of the soul — further vain struggles in the whirlpool.

Technically the novel is a "comedy" in Balzac's sense of the word, for, if Alma dies, Rolfe must go on living. Ironically, too, there is a turn of fortune from bad to improved, and Rolfe returns once more to the "simple life" which his wife had rejected. His very return, however, implies a denial of the special forms of the social contract which the prosperous Englishman of the turn of the century had paraphrased for himself. And so, too, it was in Gissing's private life: he had broken the hold of the usual social bonds.

When he finished *The Whirlpool* Gissing had finished his best work in fiction; what was to come, with the exception perhaps of *Our Friend the Charlatan,* were crumbs from the feast, choice morsels, but not possessed of the former excellence. *The Town Traveller* of 1898 is a close cousin to *The Paying Guest; The Crown of Life* is a duller *Born in Exile;* and *Will Warburton,* published posthumously in 1905, is Biffen's novel realized, *Bailey, Grocer.* As for *Veranilda,* unfinished and published posthumously in 1904, it was the culmination of Gissing's lifelong desire to write a historical novel on the subject of Rome in her decline and fall.

The Crown of Life was not admired by its author, nor by Meredith, who received a presentation copy, nor by the reviewers. The *Athenaeum* summed up the general reaction: "With all the subtlety of this book there is a curious aloofness from life in it." [7] The pity is that the reader has seen the same theme, and seen it developed more satisfactorily, in Gissing's earlier novels. Much forcing is done to bring out conflicts that in the better novels, *The Whirlpool* and *New Grub Street,* were shown more skillfully. For example, the first chapter shows the hero dreaming of the ideal woman as he stares through a shop window at prints and paintings of beautiful women; and throughout the novel he, and Gissing, continue to view people as seen through that very window of rather opaque glass.

There is, too, a stridency, an insistence upon the importance of some characters whom the reader in all honesty cannot take so seriously. Helen Derwent, who to Otway represents the ideal, is neither as interesting as Alma Rolfe nor as warm as Isabel Clarendon; nevertheless Gissing insists upon her charm and all but exhorts admiration. This is another way of saying that the reader cannot accept her graciousness and beauty and intelligence merely because her lover insists upon it, nor can he enjoy the relationship as irony when Gissing insists upon idealization. Minor characters, like Mrs. Borisoff, the "new woman," and the ambitious young man in politics, Arnold Jacks, seem, on the one hand, persons met before, and, on the other hand, persons to be understood more fully. In short, the characterization leaves much to be desired.

There are, of course, the wicked, and enjoyable, Gissing touches, like the description "a semi-detached dwelling in a part of Hammersmith just being invaded by the social class below that for which it was built"; but the major impression left by the novel is that again Gissing was writing only too obviously for "bread money," that he was fatigued and would have benefited from a respite. *The Crown of Life* was neither as good as the past, nor even as the future, and the redundancy by now had become merely tiresome.   *   *   *

Our Friend the Charlatan (1901) recaptured the sparkling Gissing malice that had punctured many an egoist, just as Meredith's had done so brilliantly. Imagine a Godwin Peake more unctuous and less passionate, a still more skillful casuist, and there stands Dyce Lashmar, the most splendid creation of Gissing's last phase. He is "concentrated" ego, for he is unwilling to spill out any of the essence of his personality — in love or in any other relationship. Peake has an occasional confidant, but Lashmar, even in his most intimate relationships, keeps his own confidence. He knows, of course, how to make use of women: "Experience had taught him that he possessed a certain power over women of a certain kind; it seemed probable that Constance belonged to the class; but this was a fact which had no emotional bearing."

Lashmar finds in Lady Ogram, old, vain, wealthy, and shrewd, the very woman to advance him: she controls a "pocket borough" and will advance his candidacy if he pleases her. First he must do intellectual gymnastics and convince his patroness of his brilliance: he reads a French sociologist who divides society into "L'élite and La foule" and he paraphrases the Frenchman's observations while taking credit for originality. Needless to say, he considers himself one of the elite and has a poor opinion of demos: "In the history of the world hitherto, the multitude has had less than its share, the ruling classes have tyrannized. At present it's pretty obvious that we are in danger of just the opposite excess; Demos begans to roar alarmingly, and there will be a poor look out for us if he gets all he wants." Lashmar reads Nietzsche too, but permits himself the luxury of patronizing the German:

"He enjoyed this frank contempt for the average man, persuaded that his own place was on the seat of the lofty, and that disdain of the humdrum, in life or in speculation, had always been his strong point. To be sure, he counted himself Nietzsche's superior as a moralist; as a thinker he imagined himself much more scientific."

Lady Ogram leads Lashmar from one difficult position to the next to prove her power, causing him to offer marriage to two women and then to withdraw the offer, only to be rebuffed at last by both when the consent of either is all that will save his fortunes. The series of ironies that leads to Lashmar's downfall is done brilliantly, the sort of *tour de force* that only Meredith hitherto had been credited with achieving. Lady Ogram dies, and Lashmar's reaction to her death sums up his remarkable character.

"He gazed now and then at the black-palled coffin, and found it impossible to realize that there lay the strange, imperious old woman who for several months had been the centre of his thoughts, and to whom he owed so vast a change in his circumstances. He felt no sorrow, yet thought of her with a certain respect, even with a slight sensation of gratitude, which was chiefly due, however, to the fact that she had been so good as to die. . . He, at all events, had understood and appreciated her. If he became master of Rivenoak, the marble bust should always have an honoured place under that roof."

There is neither tragedy nor romantic comedy in the novel, but there are serious things to be inferred from the witty situations. As one of the more discerning characters remarks, Lashmar had it in him to become one of "those grave comedians who rule the world." It is this reflection which produces admiration for Gissing's clever handling of his subject. Meredith might well have used the novel as an excellent illustration of the uses of "the Comic Spirit."   *   *   *

Compared with *Our Friend the Charlatan, The Town Traveller* and *Will Warburton* are pleasant trivialities, but both of them are technically competent. *The Town Traveller* reminds one of the early sketches of Dickens, full of lively foolish dialogue and gusts of good humor. The reviewers pounced happily upon it as a second proof (after *The Paying Guest*) that Mr. Gissing really did possess a rollicking sense of humor. "Mr. Gissing's is a good study of the temperament of the born flaneur, the natural epicurean." [8] The *Academy* also reprinted one of the best examples in the novel of accurate reportage and humorous overtone. [9] Miss Waghorn introduces her companion to Mr. Gammon, the "hero" of the novel.

"'I've often heard talk of you, Mr. Gammon; glad to meet you, sir. I think it's Berlin wools, isn't it?'

"'Well, it was, sir, but it's been fancy leather goods lately, and now it's going to be something else. You are the Gillingsworth burners, I believe, sir?'"

The plot is of little consequence. It concerns a matter of mistaken identity, a lord and the proprietress of a china shop, and the gossip and quarrels in a lodging house. The good humor and the loquacity of the commercial traveler, Mr. Gammon, are the things that matter, although those who do not know all of Gissing's work still refer to him as "gloomy."

❀　　❀　　❀

Will Warburton and *Veranilda,* both published after Gissing's death, serve an an ironic commentary upon the two poles of his nature, or, as one would say clinically, his "conflict." Will Warburton is a man of decent breeding and studious taste who, after reverses in his modest business, must choose between the genteel drudgery of clerkdom and modest, but independent, comfort as a grocer-proprietor. Were he about to meet death, like the knights in folk tales and ballads who must answer riddles, Warburton could show no more earnestness in making his choice. To be a man behind a counter wearing an apron seems at first unendurable. What will his friends, among them the fashionable painter, say if they hear about his occupation? Nevertheless Warburton's self-reliance is proved: he chooses to be a grocer, independent and useful. After several amusing rebuffs by "friends" who cannot endure the vulgarity of his trade, he accepts his position in life and even finds a wife both clever and unassuming.

As early as 1892 Gissing had been considering a novel about competition among shopkeepers, and even earlier had had Biffen in *New Grub Street* describe a novel about a grocer. It was in 1901, however, that he thought most steadily about his dead father (the memory was to be enshrined in a magazine article in 1902), remembering his father's pride, his scorn for the other shop-keepers in Wakefield, his loneliness. It occurred to him, surely, that his father had enjoyed little peace in his life, in spite of his energetic defenses, like the library of tall books and the botanical articles written for occasional journals. Instead the entire family struggled to prove their importance, their superiority to the neighbors, just as, in novel after novel, the heroes in Gissing's novels chose death rather than low estate in society.

Will Warburton, understood in these terms, represents a cathar-sis, for Warburton, after wrestling mightily with his pride, chooses to be a respectable, if unglamorous, shopkeeper, and practices the "habit" of being content. Above all — the greatest achievement for any protagonist in a Gissing novel — he decides that his former conception of the ideal woman was altogether false, and that simple and kind companionship is the best relationship that he has any hope of establishing.

It seems reasonable, therefore, to infer that Gissing in the last few years of his life was becoming able to look back upon his early years with greater calm and more honesty than it would ever have seemed possible for him to achieve. Too many critics by far have insisted that Gissing the man never came to terms with himself, but, like a squirrel in a cage (the comparison is Mr. Burrell's) [10] proceeded to wear himself out with wasted repetitive motions. *Will Warburton* implies that self-awareness and honesty bring contentment, just as *The Whirlpool* had suggested that in close human relationships, like marriage, the self-awareness of one partner only is not enough for happiness. There are few dramatic encounters in the novel and little action, but the tone is gentle and relaxed, as though all bitterness had been purged.

❖   ❖   ❖

Veranilda is Gissing's half-finished monument to a lifelong wish to write a historical novel about the fall of Rome. In his adoles-cence Gissing had read Gibbon, and in his manhood in London he preferred to go without dinner rather than miss the opportunity to buy a fine edition of Gibbon. He had read Suetonius, and Martial and Tacitus as well;[11] and when he traveled to Italy in 1897–1898, it was to relive the days of old, and, in the monastery of Monte Cassino to store memories that he would use in *Veranilda*.[12] Nevertheless the novel does not represent for Gissing an escape to the glory of antiquity from the sordid reality of the present. The most acute observation in Mr. Frederic Harrison's preface to the novel is that Gissing saw in the fall of Rome in the age of Belisarius and Justinian a parallel to the decline of his own society.[13]

Certainly the characters in *Veranilda* are beset by the same kinds of conflicts that oppress those in Gissing's novels of modern Britain: the heroine comes from an unstable society, the Goths, who had at first been united but later were cloven under the assaults of Byzantium; the hero, Basil, is a Roman aristocrat who debates how best to survive the battle for power between East and West. Lastly there is Marcian, archetype of the man who plays both ends against the middle. He is a man of antitheses, verbal about honor, yet capable of small and silent treachery; a man without passion, yet suddenly capable of lust for the woman loved by his best friend. There is an air of decay in the novel, appropriate to the struggle for survival of debauched and discordant elements in a rotting empire, and the background is as authentic as scrupulous reading and visits to ancient sites could insure that it would be.

The novel cost Gissing immense labor; he wrote it more painfully and more slowly than he had done any other, and must have lamented on his deathbed that he had not been able to bring it to completion. A greengrocer and a Roman aristocrat seem a strange pair simultaneously to emerge from the grave of an English novelist, but the irony of their companionship is the irony of George Gissing's life as a man and as an artist.

Chapter 11

LOVE AND EXILE

In September 1897, Gissing started for the Continent, but spent little time in France. In Italy, in Siena, he paused, deciding to finish there his book on Charles Dickens, a study that would be considered one of the best ever made on the great Victorian. He composed over 2,000 words a day,[1] enjoying the task but looking forward to November when he could begin his Calabrian journey. Siena was not his part of Italy, he declared to Edward Clodd: "I have, I am sorry to say, very little interest in the Renaissance. On the other hand I shout with joy whenever I am brought very near to the old Romans."[2] After finishing his study of Dickens and sending it off to London he left for his tour of Calabria, staying at "terrible Cotrone," once "so splendid that this part of Italy came to be called Greater Greece." But here he became ill, the weak right lung causing him pain and worry.[3] When the acute attack was over, he pushed on to Catanzaro, intent once again upon a book. "It is very plain that I must get to work again. I have materials for a good little book. . . I am at the *toe* of Italy, and as I walk by the sea-shore, I see Sicily opposite, with Mount Etna rising into the clouds, covered with snow."[4] All the impressions of Calabria he husbanded for a book entitled *By the Ionian Sea*, published in 1901.

On December 14 he left Naples and spent the night at Monte Cassino in the great monastery founded by Benedict in 529. He was fascinated by the setting and later used it, much romanticized, in *Veranilda*. "The porphyry pillar, in middle of the court, in which stood statue of Apollo. . . Lights of Cassino just visible, a profound depth. . . Lingering sunset over towards Gaeta, where there is, in clear weather, a glimpse of sea." [5] To his brother Gissing wrote lines of enthusiastic description of the monastery,[6] but in his diary he lamented the meager supper, the endless toil around him: "I grow old, this lenten fare does not suit me. . . The toil, the toil, of that old world! Think of building on these great heights. The old hilly roads mere human Calvaries." [7]

In December he arrived in Rome and remained there until April, not altogether disenchanted, but realizing that he no longer viewed the fabulous land with his former zeal. Italy was superb for "the young and the strong," but for the sick it provided "little comfort" and "many dangers," and he thought with pity of Keats's hopeless trip to Rome.[8] It was the final disappointment that now, when he was best able financially to afford traveling on the continent, his weary body ached for sedentary comforts. It was with little regret that he saw the time come for leaving Rome.

He routed his return trip through Germany in order to see Eduard Bertz, with whom he had not spoken for many years. Bertz had finally succeeded in establishing himself as a literary critic and was dedicating himself to the cause of iconoclasm. Among those he supported were Walt Whitman and his friend of many years, Gissing. The support was of some practical use, for Bertz, having himself published three novels and having formed a profitable connection with Victor Ottmann, the publisher, was now secretary of the Deutscher Schriftseller Verband and a regular contributor to *Das Literarische Echo,* a publication much interested in the contemporary literature of England.[9]

Once more in England, Gissing breathed easily when he learned that in spite of separate living expenses, for himself in Italy and for his family in England, more than £200 remained in his account, in addition to the amount promised by Methuen for the publication of *The Town Traveler.*[10] It was at this time, too, that the publisher Grant Richards made a suggestion that surprised Gissing. Gissing was to permit him all the rights in all his work for the next five years at a price to be determined, one which would be more than the author could get from all other sources of publication.[11] It was the old temptation, a guaranteed modicum of security versus the risk of either great profit or dismal failure. The whole project was finally abandoned.

In May Gissing rented a house in Dorking, carrying out the move with strictest secrecy, for he had no hope of a reconciliation with his wife and was determined to avoid scenes. He was becoming increasingly alarmed over the state of his health, for the doctors in England had diagnosed a diseased condition of the right lung. But on July 6 a new name entered his diary and a new hope entered his life. It was the announcement that Mlle. Gabrielle Fleury had visited him in order to arrange to make a translation of *New Grub Street* into French. He set vigorously to work making cuts in the novel, while she assured him that the *Débats* and the *Temps* were both eager to print the novel in France.

The visits became more frequent; the two dreamed together and talked about wasted years. Mlle. Gabrielle was twenty-nine, intelligent, fluent, in some ways aggressive, but still chained to "Maman." The two read aloud to each other, as Gissing had done before in other poignant moments, but this time self-delusion was not necessary for him to believe that his loved one understood him, for each visit to him in Dorking convinced him only the more that for the first time he was establishing the relationship of which he had dreamed for so many years. Only three months after their first meeting Gissing confided to his diary that the following spring they would live together.[12] It was an impulsive decision, of course, just as his other decisions on love and marriage had been, but this time he found in the woman he had chosen all the qualities that had once seemed out of his reach.

Once again, love and the comfort of having made a basic decision spurred his writing, and he finished *The Crown of Life.* In January, Gabrielle's father died and she was better able to make a decision about the new relationship. Maman was persuaded to adopt a conciliatory attitude, provided that a private marriage take place in France. The ceremony, not recognized under British law, occurred on May 7, 1899.

The year before and the year after the turn of the century passed with such harmony and contentment as Gissing had not known for many years. To his French wife he always referred in the gentlest terms, declaring her beloved by each friend of his who met her.[13] Above all he rejoiced in her sweet voice and her dignity, qualities in women that he had always prized.[14] He remained in Paris with his wife, and usually her mother, except for a visit to England in April. Then, in the summer, the couple decided to rent a villa at Saint Honoré les Bains, Nièvre, where they would remain until autumn and Paris once again.

In Paris Gissing began to unpack the beloved books forwarded from Dorking, but soon the doctors let it be known that a search for a better climate would have to be undertaken: a mountain retreat or sanatorium was strongly recommended. Frightened, the couple went to England so that Gissing could rest in a sanatorium at Nayland in Suffolk. There he remained from May until July of 1901, breaking the monotonous round by occasional visits to H. G. Wells, and once to Henry James in Rye, where the party talked of Turgenev.[15] There was a short visit to Wakefield, where Walter, Gissing's elder son, lived for most of the time, and then a return to France.

He realized now, although it pained him to make the admission, that the remaining years of his life would have to be spent in a pilgrimage to the places that might help his sick lungs. Worst of all was the restriction imposed by the doctors of no more than two hours of work each day. It was a bitter Christmas in 1901, ridden by nostalgia, and spent in Arcachon, Gironde: "I am constantly dreaming over my old walks; I could not now go from Willersey to Broadway and back without exhaustion and fever — a dolorous state of things."[16] The next visit was to Saint Jean de Luz at the foot of the Pyrenees, where the Gissings remained until April of

1903. It was here, in *Basses Pyrénées*, that Gissing made the last attempt to recapture the vigor that had once permitted him to walk twenty miles in a single day.

The record in work of the years after his marriage and his departure from England is that of a man who refused to admit that he ought to take a complete rest. The success of the study on Dickens published in 1898 by Blackie had led to a request that Gissing write a series of prefaces for the Dickens novels. He accepted and finished nine of these for the Rochester edition of Messrs. Methuen, completing the last of the group, the "Christmas Books," in February, 1900.[17] Meanwhile he had finished *By the Ionian Sea* while living in Paris, and then had begun *Veranilda*, the historical novel he had long dreamed of writing. There was also an unpublished novel in his desk drawer, a novel he considered weak.[18] Better than this by far (*Among the Prophets*) was *The Coming Man*, published as *Our Friend the Charlatan*, which Gissing began in May, 1900. When this novel was finished he began the project that he had been considering for a decade.[19] This was *The Private Papers of Henry Ryecroft*, reminiscences of "An Author at Grass" and serialized in the *Fortnightly* beginning in May of 1902. The book had taken nearly two years to complete. Within a few months of publication in volume form, *Ryecroft* went into a third edition, and was "universally read," even in the faraway English colony of St. Jean de Luz.[20] But even after *Ryecroft* Gissing could not stop, for he still needed money. Between November of 1902 and March of 1903, he composed *Will Warburton* and kept on with *Veranilda*. Meanwhile, in the spring of 1901 the French translation of *New Grub Street* was published in volume form after it had appeared in the *Débats*.[21]

The popularity of *Ryecroft* pleased the author, of course, but it did not make him rich. He made note that the publishers of *By the Ionian Sea* were using expensive color plates in the volume,[22] and counted the large number of letters sent him by admiring readers,[23] but still he could not help worrying over what would become of him and his family during a long and costly illness. And what would become of his books after his death? There were complimentary notices in English newspapers and reviews like the long one in the *Academy* for December 29, 1899, but notices were not enough. The sick man feared for his future. He could not afford to undertake the academic studies that most interested him, one on Thackeray, for example, "who be it said between us, appeals much more strongly than Dickens," for he could not afford to work for half a year and receive only a "trifling payment. . ."[24] Now and then Clement Shorter mailed a request for a story for his new *Illustrated Newspaper for the Home*, but Gissing could derive no pleasure from the request: ". . . I shall do my best, as Shorter was kind in the days when he headed legions, but that legend 'For the Home' troubles me and puts restraint upon my imagination."[25] It was as if the ghost of Mrs. Grundy, who had haunted him in the eighties, were there again to plague him.

Worst of all was the realization that try as he might it was too late for him to be a popular author. Years before he had prayed that his "body and brain" would hold out until "the great big stupid public" would accept the work of one who "would fain enlighten as well as amuse." But as late as 1899, in the midst of the Boer War, he wrote despondently:

"It is an evil time enough at present, goodness knows, and one has need to hope for brighter things. But I limit my wishes to individuals. Nations being masses, are brutally stupid, and all one can hope is that any given mass will not bring too heavy a curse on the rest of the world.

"My agent cheers me with his prophecies that no books will be read in England for long enough to come. That *my* books will not be read is a pretty safe forecast; but, on the whole, I imagine that booksellers are not much affected by the war. I see that this and the other novelists have been making their hundred thousand copies lately. It must be a strange feeling, to see one's book really going off like that. Twenty years ago I hoped for it, now I hope no more." [26]

He suspected, too, that publishers looked upon him with some scorn because he was not a popular writer.[27] All that he had left was merely the modest aim of having his novels collected under one imprint; he had quite given up the hope of a fine standard edition, or even supplications for reprint rights. With sad regularity he wrote to James Pinker, his literary agent, asking whether any publisher had been discovered who would buy the available copyrights. It was bad news to hear that the publisher Bullen was leaving the field, for Bullen owned more Gissing titles than did any other single publisher, and Gissing had hoped secretly that Bullen would buy out the other publishers, and so keep most of his work in print. An offer came from Methuen, but Gissing considered it inadequate. Then Heinemann made an offer through James Pinker, which Gissing considered and then rejected.[28] The last desperate idea that he advanced to Pinker was that he write to an American publisher, like Harper's, promising a future book "for *nothing*" if the publisher would buy the rights to the other Gissing books! [29] The thought was the capitulation of a desperate man, and later when he considered his own proposal quite calmly, he must have felt shame for having offered such an inducement to any publisher. Probably the lowest ebb of Gissing's self-confidence was reached the day he learned that a reader for Henry Holt in America had announced that young Mr. Gissing showed promise! The author smarted: "Mr. Holt's reader evidently thinks that I am at the beginning of my literary career! . . . with twenty years of work and more than twenty novels behind me." [30]

Recalling these rebuffs, Morley Roberts later insisted that the mellow sentences in *Henry Ryecroft* were only the dissemblings of a bitter man.[31] Yet the calm self-sufficiency in *Will Warburton* and *Henry Ryecroft* are authentic too, just as the mordant mo-

ments are, for all Gissing's life was a series of swings of the pendulum between self-reliance and despair.

The letters to Edward Clodd present an interesting chronicle
of Gissing's "real" life in his last years, in contrast with the imagi-
nary life of Ryecroft. At the time of writing these letters, from
1895 to 1903, Gissing was no longer dazzled by fashionable society. He had kept up his old friendships with Mrs. Gaussen and
Frederic Harrison, for example, by means of an occasional letter
or visit, and he knew Meredith and Hardy and James and a score
of men in important places, but the one fact that still cut him to
the quick was that after forty years of existence he was still in
exile. His quasi-marriage made it impossible to live a conventional life in England, just as his bad health made it impossible
to live a healthy one. Born in exile, he would die in exile. Yet
he must face the necessity. To Clodd he wrote, "As I have had to
look death in the face, I must not grumble about this expatriation,
if indeed it helps me to live and work for a few years more. My
friends, I trust, will not forget me, and there is always the hope
of a last home in England." [32] He was often oppressed by feelings
of homesickness for his friends and for familiar sights. The Continent, which had been the dream of his youth, seemed now
almost a desert. Thus he wrote to Clodd, "I notice with misgiving
that I cannot find the same delight in travel as of old. My sensi-
bilities are duller." [33] And again, "I miss your talk: I miss it
seriously. For you are one of only two or three people I know
whose talk often goes below the surface of things — who are
capable of intellectual wonder — who do not confuse reason with
materialism — who (rarest thing, perhaps, of all) know how to
joke in earnest." [34]

One of his most earnest jokes was the prospect of the "civilised"
world as he knew it shooting itself to pieces. Fellow rationalists
of his own and an earlier generation shared his fear of rebarbariza-
tion. Remarked Herbert Spencer, for example, in a letter to Grant
Allen, ". . . we are in course of rebarbarisation, and . . . there is

no prospect but that of military despotisms, which we are rapidly approaching." Spencer recommended the formation of "a kind of supreme court of select men to pass opinions of international relations," [35] but Gissing himself had no hope that such a group could stop the course of aggressive wars. "The rebarbarisation of the world goes merrily on." He predicted "continuous war" for the future and was sickened by the news of the day. To ease his troubled mind he turned "as much as possible to the old poets." [36]

But in these last years it was not only the "old poets" that he read. He delighted in *Don Quixote,* having taught himself enough Spanish to read fluently. He read Augustine's *City of God* and mused, "No man ever had such an occasion for moralising as that offered by the fall of Rome before Alaric." [37] And after he had read one of the oldest authors in the western literature of sin and guilt, he turned to one of the newest, whose works were now appearing. He wrote to Joseph Conrad congratulating him upon his work, and declared him to be "the strongest writer — in every sense of the word — at present publishing in English." [38]

He half-realized, perhaps, that Conrad was the herald of a new kind of novel, and that the differences in form would cause many a future critic to label the Gissing novels "obsolete," forgetting that the two men, Gissing and Conrad, have the most basic kinship of all — a deep concern for the honor and guilt in a human soul.

George Gissing died on December 28, 1903, shortly after his forty-sixth birthday. Knowing that his death would be at most a few years away, he must have examined now and then his agnostic's creed, for he was a thoughtful man. The view of religion that he had before his death is best suggested in a letter to Clodd on the occasion of a grandiloquent lecture of H. G. Wells. Gissing, who once had been a militant atheist, did not find it possible to return to orthodoxy even when death was imminent, but both arrogance and mockery had disappeared from his point of view.

"In his [Wells'] lecture to the Royal Institute, he goes, I think, altogether too far, talking about 'eternal' activities of the spirit of man, and defying the threats of the material outlook. Well, let us agree that it is very good to acknowledge a great mystery . . . how to go further than this recognition I know not. That there is *some* order, *some* purpose, seems a certainty; my mind, at all events, refuses to grasp the idea of a universe which means nothing at all.

"But just as unable am I to accept any of the solutions ever proposed. Above all it is the existence of natural beauty that haunts my thoughts." [39]

When he died at St. Jean Pied de Port an English chaplain was at his bedside, and rumor had it that a deathbed conversion occurred, but Edward Clodd has insisted, with more spleen than necessary perhaps, that Gissing did not return in those last moments to the church of his family.

"The falsehood [referring to a notice in the *Church Times* that the novelist had returned to the 'comfort and strength of the Catholic Faith'] was based on the fact that his devoted Gabrielle, thinking that he would be glad to see an English face, asked the chaplain of St. Jean de Luz to call on him. . . Like Mr. Lawrence in the *New Republic,* more probably he [Gissing] would have asked for some passages from the fifteenth and sixteenth chapters of the *Decline and Fall of the Roman Empire*." [40]

The irony of the death bed was the culmination of a life full of ironies. There would be posthumous irony as well, the explanation of Gissing's life by H. G. Wells, who had been at Gissing's bedside shortly before the death, and therefore felt himself qualified, like Morley Roberts, to pass large opinions about his dead friend, and to describe the characters in the novels as "exponent" characters,[41] as if all the Gissing novels were cut from the imperfect cloth of the eighties. But others have been more willing to believe that there was a progression in the novels and a growing artistry. Even Virginia Woolf, who regretted that Gissing, unlike "the great novelist (who) flows in and out of his characters and bathes them in an element which seems to be common to us all," remains "solitary, self-centered, apart" has given him his due. Her refusal ever to give excessive praise makes her judgment all the more commanding.

"With all his narrowness of outlook and meagreness of sensibility, Gissing is one of the extremely rare novelists who believes in the power of the mind — who makes his people think. . . Hence, when we have finished one of Gissing's novels we have taken away not a character, nor an incident, but the comment of a thoughtful man upon life as life seemed to him." [42]

Chapter 12

BELLES-LETTRES
AND CRITICISM

Despite the fact that Gissing's novels outnumber fivefold
his belles-lettres and criticism, the latter have been unequivocally praised while the novels have struggled for recognition.
Indeed Frank Swinnerton in his acidulous study suggests
that Gissing would have done well to write fewer novels and
more essays. "He could not see an incident without spinning from
it — not a story — but a series of reflections. He was an essayist, a
writer upon moral themes; and he began to write novels. What
could be expected from such an equipment?" [1] There are two
volumes, or the equivalent, of criticism of Dickens; two short
articles, "Why I Don't Write Plays" and "Realism in Fiction";
The Private Papers of Henry Ryecroft in the old tradition of
belles-lettres; and *By the Ionian Sea, Notes of a Ramble in Southern Italy.*

One of the few unanimous opinions of Gissing's work has been
that his critical studies of Dickens are excellent. Standard in the
bibliography of Dickensiana are *Charles Dickens: A Critical
Study* (1898) and the series of prefaces Gissing composed for the
Rochester edition of Dickens' novels (Methuen). The Prefaces,
nine of them, plus "Dickens in Memory," the nostalgic essay in
the *Critic* for January, 1902, were collected and reprinted in
Critical Studies of the Works of Charles Dickens (New York,
Greenberg, 1924) and in *The Immortal Dickens* (London, Cecil
Palmer, 1925).

For many years, as the letters and the "Dickens in Memory" bear witness, Gissing had read the work of Dickens, at first with delight and credulity, and later, as a man, with delight and wonder: "Charles Dickens, Alfred Tennyson — these were to me as the names of household gods." [2] He first saw the novels when they arrived in Wakefield in their serial parts and bright wrappers. Then, when he came to London in 1877, he roamed through the streets and places Dickens had made vivid for him. "In time I came to see London with my own eyes, but how much better when I saw them with those of Dickens!" [3] And on the many occasions when he felt exhausted, too weary ever to pick up pen again, he turned to Forster's *Life,* to the account of the indefatigable working to the very end of life. ". . . this it was that stirred me, not to imitate Dickens as a novelist, but to follow afar off his example as a worker." [4] But as he read Forster in the eighties he never imagined that he would be asked to edit the abridged version (Chapman, Hall) after the turn of the century. He recognized, of course, as early as the eighties, that publishers had already classified him as a writer of "proletarian novels," but he had distinguished his aims from Dickens' even at the beginning of his career ". . . I have struck out a path for myself in fiction, for one cannot, of course, compare my methods and aims with those of Dickens." [5] Instead Gissing considered himself at the time of *Workers in the Dawn,* as a scientific Socialist, the "mouthpiece of the advanced Radical party." And later, of course, as he became more clinical in manner, Gissing departed still more daringly from the model of Dickens.

Therefore, when in 1898 the publisher Blackie asked him to write critical essays on Dickens, Gissing set about his task with mingled feelings of affection, envy, and remorse, but during the quiet, busy weeks in Siena, where he worked feverishly upon the study, he permitted himself only such observations as he could term fair-minded. Thus *Charles Dickens, A Critical Study* is neither merely a warm, impressionistic "appreciation" nor a cold and biting attack on earlier Victorian fiction; it is rather the commentary of a self-conscious practitioner of fiction, one of the leaders of the new Realism, with a good knowledge of the history of the novel and with much interest in the art of biography. Like Bourget, whose *Essais de psychologie contemporaine* he had read, Gissing studied the psychology of his subject as it would not have occurred to Forster, with all his gruff reticence, to do. Gissing was fond of using comparisons with other novelists from other backgrounds, and the best antithesis he could find was that of Sir Walter Scott and Dickens.

"Walter Scott, inheriting gentle blood and feudal enthusiasm, resisted to the last the theories of '32; and yet by irony of circumstance owed his ruin to commercial enterprise. Charles Dickens, humbly born, and from first to last fighting the battle of those born in like estate, wore himself to a premature end in striving to found his title of gentleman on something more substantial than glory. The one came into the world too late; the other, from this point of view, was but too thoroughly of his time."

(Later in the study, in the chapter entitled "Art, Veracity and Moral Purpose" Gissing contrasted Scott and Dickens in their response to public taste, noting that Dickens wrote "with an eye steadily fixed upon his publisher's sale-room.")

Gissing does not push his use of "psychological criticism" of Dickens to the lengths pursued by Mr. Edmund Wilson today, for example, but he is quite ready to acknowledge unconscious drives in the writer.

"The landed proprietor of Gadshill could not forget . . . a miserable childhood imprisoned in the Limbo of squalid London; his grudge against this memory was in essence a *class* feeling; to the end his personal triumph gratified him, however unconsciously, as the vindication of a social claim."

The volume is not organized in terms of individual novels; rather, in the fashion which Victorian publishers preferred in books of criticism, there were "catch-all" titles for each chapter, a veritable wastebasket for impressions. "Women and Children" is perhaps the least satisfactory of such chapters, but one of the most stimulating is chapter 4, "Art, Veracity, and Moral Purpose," a chapter in which Gissing probes the allegation that Dickens is a "Realist." Once again his splendid sense of process, of development, in any art form, prevents him from slipping into the familiar clichés about Dickens as Realist, or Romantic, or any of the several confusing claims still made for Dickens by modern critics.

"Dickens might alter his intention, might change his theme; but he never did so with the thought that he was condescending. In this respect a true democrat, he believed, probably without ever reflecting upon it, that the approved of the people was necessarily the supreme in art. At the same time, never man wrought more energetically to justify the people's choice. . .

"Our 'realist' will hear of no such paltering with truth. Heedless of Pilate's question, he takes for granted that the truth can be got at, and that it is his plain duty to set it down without compromise; or, if less crude in his perceptions, he holds that truth for the artist is the impression produced on him, and that to convey this impression with entire sincerity is his sole reason for existing. To Dickens such a view of the artist's duty never presented itself. Art for him was art precisely because it was not nature. . . But Dickens went further; he had a moral purpose; the thing above all others scornfully forbidden in our schools of rigid art. . . But the English novel was at a sorry pass in that day, and doubtless Dickens seriously believed that he had taken a bold step towards naturalism (had he known the word)."

Gissing observes furthermore that Dickens never attained, and doubtless did not want, versimilitude; rather he subjected such characters as Mrs. Gamp to magnificent bowdlerizing.

"Vulgarity he leaves; that is the essence of the matter. . . Vileness on the other hand becomes grotesquerie, wonderfully converted into a subject for laughter. Her speech, the basest ever heard from human tongue, by a process of infinite subtlety, which leaves it the same yet not the same, is made an endless amusement, a source of quotations for laughing lips incapable of unclean utterance."

In the terse manner which Gissing finally achieved in the last decade of his life, both the achievement and the failure of Dickens are summed up:

"This was his task in life, to embody the better dreaming of ordinary men; to fix them as bright realities for weary eyes to look upon. He achieved it in the light of a faultless sympathy, following the true instincts which it is so unjust — so unintelligent — to interpret as mere commercial shrewdness or dulness of artistic perception."

This was a frank confession of the great hallmark of Dickens which Gissing had always wanted to emulate as well as appreciate — a warm and lively sympathy with the mass of men. But if he lacked that virtue, he had at least another which a new aristocracy of readers now appreciated. This virtue was an understanding of a type of modern man only beginning to be examined by European novelists.

"Raskolnikoff . . . a typical Russian, a man of brains maddened by hunger and by the sight of others hungry is the kind of character Dickens never attempted to portray; his motives, his reasonings could not be apprehended by an Englishman of the lower middle class."

The new province, only beginning to be explored, was the domain for only thoughtful and determined men; it was not a province, as Gissing realized, where Dickens and most of his great contemporaries would have felt at home.

The set of prefaces which Gissing composed for the Dickens novels (only six were actually printed in the Rochester edition) are not so fruitful as the earlier study of Dickens, although remarks on individual novels, particularly on *Bleak House,* show awareness of construction which Gissing in his own novels so often neglected. Thus he criticizes the so-called "multiple point of view" of *Bleak House.*

"The object, presumably, of writing a book in this way is to obtain the effect of varied points of view regarding characters and events; but it is of necessity a mistake in art. With a skill much greater than that of Dickens, the device is employed in Daudet's 'Le Nabob' where one still feels that the harmonious construction of the novel is unwarrantably disturbed."

Gissing's criticism of *Bleak House* is at its wry best in the paragraph on the death of Little Jo: "We know that Lord Denman was here quite right; for, though virtue may exist in the ignorant and the poor and the debased, most assuredly the delicacies of virtue will not be found in them, and it is these delicacies on which Dickens so commonly insists." Gissing was nothing if not honest!

          ✿   ✿   ✿

The chapter on "Art, Veracity and Moral Purpose" is not the only place in which Gissing speaks directly on the subject of realism and the problems of his craft in general. Two important articles which have not received the attention they deserve are "Why I Don't Write Plays," an article which appeared in the *Pall Mall Gazette* for September 10, 1892, and "Realism in Fiction" in the *Humanitarian* for July 1895.

Gissing's article in the *Pall Mall Gazette* was requested after the lament of Mr. William Archer over the divorce of literature from drama. Principal novelists of the day were invited by the editors to express their views on the subject, and Gissing's reply is one of the most discerning. Once again he examines the effects of cultural change: he declares the Elizabethan audience superior to the average Victorian audience, and the existing censorship puerile. Nevertheless he comforts himself that the novel is a flexible enough form to make it possible to treat subjects more fully than is possible in dramatic literature.

"Certainly I think it a misfortune that the English mind distinguishes so broadly between a writer for the stage and an artist in narrative fiction. But to say this is merely to lament the social conditions of our time. The acted drama is essentially a popular entertainment. . . When the drama flourished in England, it was by virtue of popular interests, for in those days the paying public was the intelligent public. . . Trash might be produced in abundance, but only because genius and talent are always rare. Conflicts between the artistic sense and motives of self-interest there could — at the happy moments — be little or none. . .

"Conceivably we may some day have a theatre for those who think, quite distinct from the houses sought out by those who are conscious only of crude sensations. But at present we may be grateful that one form of literary art, thanks to the mode of its publication, can be cultivated regardless of the basest opinion. . . The history of culture prepares us to take for granted that a period will have its predominant artistic form, and that of our time is narrative fiction. . . In reading some of Ibsen's plays I have regretted that they *were* plays. 'Hedda Gabler,' for instance, seems to me a strangling of rich possibilities which might have been worked out in the generous scheme of a novel.

". . . To talk about being 'objective' is all very well for those who swear by words. No novelist was ever objective, or ever will be. His work is a bit of life as seen by *him*. It is his business to make us feel a distinct pleasure in seeing the world with *his* eye. Now to be sure — a skillful dramatist does this, up to a certain point. For my own part, I wish to go beyond that point, to have scope for painting, to take in the external world and (by convention, which no novelist has set aside) the unuttered life of the soul. Stage directions and soliloquy will not answer my purpose.

"And again, although my tastes are scarcely pornographic, I wish, when occasion demands it, to write of things that may never be transacted nor discussed *coram populo*."

Gissing's second important critical article, "Realism in Fiction," appeared in July 1895. Only a reader who has wandered in the fog of words produced by the usual steaming debates on realism will appreciate the good sense of Gissing's remarks, the clarity in his use of words. "The novelist works, and must work, subjectively. A demand for objectivity in fiction is worse than meaningless, far apart from the personality of the workman no literary art can exist." Thus the clearing of the air is announced at the beginning.

"When a word has been so grievously mauled, it should be allowed to drop from the ranks.

"Combative it was from the first: Realism, Naturalism, and so on, signified an attitude of revolt against insincerity in the art of fiction. . . Let us have done with the conventional, that is to say, with mere tricks for pleasing the ignorant and the prejudiced. Let the novelist take himself as seriously as the man of science. . . No matter how hideous or heartrending the results, the artist has no responsibility save to his artistic conscience."

To Gissing there are two tests for the value of a novel ". . . first whether it is sincere, secondly, whether it is craftsmanlike."

"It seems to me that no novel can possess the slightest value which has not been conceived, fashioned, elaborated, with a view to depicting some portion of human life as candidly and vividly as is in the author's power.

". . . what the artist sees is to him only a part of the actual; its complement is an emotional effect. Thus it comes about that every novelist beholds a world of his own, and the supreme en-

deavour of his art must be to body forth that world as it exists
for him. The novelist works, and must work subjectively. A demand for objectivity in fiction is worse than meaningless, for apart
from the personality of the workman no literary art can exist.
The cry arose, of course, in protest against the imperfect method
of certain novelists, who came forward in their own pages, and
spoke as showmen; but what can be more absurd than to talk
about the 'objectivity' of such an author as Flaubert, who triumphs
by his extraordinary power of presenting life as he, and no other
man, beheld it. There is no science of fiction.

"Process belongs to the workshop; the critic of the completed
work has only to decide as to its truth, that is to say, to judge the
spirit in which it was conceived, and the technical merit of its
execution.

"Realism, then, signifies nothing more than artistic sincerity in
the portrayal of contemporary life. . . For my own part, I believe
that he (the novelist) must recognize limits in every direction;
that he will constantly reject materials unsuitable to the purposes
of art; and that many features of life are so completely beyond
his province that he cannot dream of representing them. At the
same time I joyfully compare the novelist's freedom in England
today with his bondage of only ten or twelve years ago. . . The
great thing is, that public opinion no longer constrains a novelist
to be false to himself."

❋   ❋   ❋

By the Ionian Sea has always received the limited but steady
support granted to good travel books. Copies are often found in
small libraries in Britain and America where Gissing's other books
are not even listed. Its tone is that of belles-lettres, for although
Gissing travels from place to place, and lists itinerary and names
of persons in the usual manner of travel books, he is less interested
in catalogues than in nostalgic impressions. The style is simple,
with sad cadences. The "ponderous Latinisms" which had marred

the pages of many an earlier book are not in evidence. The opening sentence sounds the keynote, and the mode is sustained.

"This is the third day of scirocco, heavy-clouded, sunless. All the colour has gone out of Naples; the streets are dusty and stifling. I long for the mountains and the sea."

The next day he leaves Naples "by the Messina boat." The city which once filled him with rapture seems now only squalid and somber. The lovely boulevard of Santa Lucia with its fine old houses looks out no longer upon a sparkling bay, but upon garbage dumps and filled-in ground. Even the organ-grinders, whose cheerful music he so much enjoyed, seem to have disappeared: ". . . in a few more years spontaneous melody will be as rare at Naples or Venice as on the banks of the Thames."

Among the most eloquent chapters are "The Grave of Alaric," chapter 3, and chapter 16, "Cassiodorus." In Cosenza Gissing paused at the grave of Alaric, the great leader of the Visigoths who had hoped to make a new and greater Rome, enriched with the children of northern races. Alaric marched south in a path of conquest, hoping to capture Sicily, but at Cosenza he died and with him died the hope of an Italy safe from greedy Byzantium. Cassiodorus, too, saw the dying of a hope; counselor of Theodoric, he failed to stop the tide from the East, and retired to his books.

The twilight in these pages is the light of *Henry Ryecroft*. The reminiscences appeared first in portions in the *Fortnightly* and were entitled "An Author at Grass." Although Henry Ryecroft, the alleged composer, is not quite Gissing himself, he is at least what Gissing was able at some moments to be — one of the rare contemplative souls in a hurrying, screeching century. Ryecroft has lived to middle age, and after a difficult and penury-ridden life he has at last the independent means which enable him to retire to a quiet life in the country. Unlike Samuel Smiles, Ryecroft cannot congratulate himself that his comparative ease com-

pensates for the sufferings of the past. The most that he can say
of his poverty-stricken youth is that at the time his health was
good and that he had "no sense of weakness." "You tell me that
money cannot buy the things most precious. Your commonplace
proves that you have never known lack of it. . . What kindly
joys have I lost, those simple forms of happiness to which every
heart has claim, because of poverty!" No one knew better than
Ryecroft, or Gissing, the delights of material things — not gross
self-indulgence, but the epicurean's daily pleasures. The saddest
note in the book is that of a man not embittered, but certainly
wounded, by past deprivations. "Mentally and physically I must
be much older than my years. At three-and-fifty a man ought not
to be brooding constantly of his vanished youth." But one of the
delights recollected in tranquility is his joy at rustication in
Devon after so many years of toil in London. "So intense was my
delight in the beautiful world about me that I forgot even myself; I enjoyed without retrospect or forecast; I, the egoist in
grain, forgot to scrutinize my own emotions, or to trouble my
happiness with others' happier fortune."

Ryecroft admits that he is neither a democrat nor a worshipper
of science, although his rejection of both make him unpopular.

"We are in a transition stage, between the bad old time when
only a few had academic privileges, and that happy future which
will see all men liberally instructed. Unfortunately for this argument education is a thing of which only the few are capable;
teach as you will, only a small percentage will profit by your most
zealous energy. On an ungenerous soil it is vain to look for rich
crops. Your average mortal will be your average mortal still: and
if he grows conscious of power, if he becomes vocal and self-
assertive, if he gets into his hands all the material resources of
the country, why, you have a state of things such as at present
looms menacingly before every Englishman blessed — or cursed —
with an unpopular spirit."

And of science Ryecroft writes,

"Oh, the generous hopes and aspirations of forty years ago! Science, then, was seen as the deliverer; only a few could prophesy its tyranny, could foresee that it would revive old evils and trample on the promises of its beginning. This is the course of things; we must accept it."

The last sentence, "This is the course of things; we must accept it," is the epitome of the mood of *Ryecroft,* just as it is the epitome of such dissimilar books as *The Whirlpool* and *Will Warburton,* and the letters to Clodd. Staunch opinion was possible — scorn and hatred altogether impossible. There was a growing realization that he, Ryecroft, as he Gissing, had condemned some things too heartily. Thus Ryecroft asks the reader to reconsider Puritanism (against which Gissing had rebelled in his early manhood):

"It is time that we gave a second thought to Puritanism. In the heyday of release from forms which had lost their meaning, it was natural to look back on that period of our history with eyes that saw in it nothing but fanatical excess. . . Now, when the peril of emancipation becomes as manifest as was the hardship of restraint, we shall do well to remember all the good that lay in that stern Puritan discipline, how it renewed the spiritual vitality of our race, and made for the civic freedom which is our highest national privilege."

The mood of *Henry Ryecroft* is not merely *fin de siècle.* It is one of the remaining signs of sanity in the present that the book has maintained its popularity and that it has so often been reprinted, for these are idylls from an age of brass, by a man who read his Theocritus in both Sicily and Lambeth. There are few modern men who can write belles-lettres without sounding pompous or even flatulent, and Gissing is one of the few. Nor can he be included among the "cranky" Victorian rationalists, as quaint as the tintypes which preserve in sepia their stern faces, for he read enough and thought enough to attempt to be a Humanist without the great postulate of the immanent dignity of man. Like a latter-day Burton he "anatomized" the ego, although he was often made unhappy by what he saw. And in making his study of Ryecroft, he also made one of himself, exposing the wild and cruel iconoclasm of youth, taking a stand, even if an unpopular one, in the present, and looking forward to a future in which peace and sanity were possible only in terms of individual responsibility, not group delusions.

Chapter 13

RETROSPECT

For a man so little known and published, Gissing has suc-
ceeded remarkably in being many things to those who interest
themselves in him. To the lover of the classics, he is "George Gissing, Classicist," a man of scholarly temper and recondite information. To the self-educated, self-conscious businessman (and this
man often turns out to be a collector of Gissing), the trials and
tribulations of Gissing mean more than any question of style. To
the Marxist, Gissing is valued as a prosecutor of capitalism. To the
Positivist critics of the brand of H. G. Wells, Gissing is an interesting example of the dangers of a classical education for a naïve
young man. To the weary modern Humanist who is wary of ex-
tremes and yearns for a Golden Mean, Gissing is an admirable
example of Moderation. The Humanist finds admirable a man who
attacked the vices of industrialism while lamenting the "human
Calvaries" that ancient and more splendid cultures allotted to
their masses; he respects the man who did not believe in Christmas but who would have thought it infamous to convert the day
into a "Fir-Tree Festival."

Each of these admirers of Gissing has a different reason for
showing interest, but all together constitute a small cult, united
in their belief that Gissing deserves attention for his compelling personality rather than for any craftsmanship. The
classicist goes out to buy *Sleeping Fires,* the social reformer hails
Thyrza or *Demos,* the worried, literate businessman prefers *New
Grub Street,* but few care to assess Gissing's standing in the history of literature. Interest in Gissing thus becomes occult, and

one either "likes" the mordant stories as one has a taste for persimmons, or one does not.

The temptation to withhold a verdict is of course understandable. It is an old wives' tale among the French that Englishmen lend a special odor to their novels; that is, so many English novels bear the taint as well as the gift of strong individuality, even eccentricity. Or as Thackeray would say, the man who moves the puppet wants to show what an important fellow he is, even if the puppets suffer for it. The taint of the puppet-mover was strong in Victorian fiction, and Gissing belonged to the tradition. Lavishly he poured the details of his own life into his dramas, thus setting many a reader on the trail of a *roman à clef*. Stridently he insisted upon giving his opinions, and these were voluminous, even when the characters were not able to carry the extra burden. It took a long time before he learned that the reader does not have to be clubbed into attention.

The fact that Gissing did learn many lessons is not fully appreciated even by his admirers. They continue to prefer their favorite novel, even if it is from the point of view of craftsmanship one of the weaker books. The moral can only be that a strong personality will hold a reader even if the hold has all the subtlety of a hammer lock. Gissing has the attraction most people feel in the spectacle of a frail man bullied by adversaries, a spectacle that Gissing presented, with varying degrees of skill, time and again. The attraction is a fundamental one, rooted as it is in the fear of powerful beings, but it is not necessarily enough to assure for Gissing an important place in literary history. Indeed the man in the side show who walks barefoot among the crocodiles makes his livelihood by evoking the same response. The difficult question must be faced, therefore, of whether the force of Gissing's life experience can be the final justification for the preservation of his novels.

Curiously enough, although a very sensitive stylist, Virginia Woolf was satisfied that Gissing's worth lay in one achievement —

"the comment of a thoughtful man upon life as life seemed to him"; but in her approval there is the implication that his technique cannot, and need not, withstand critical examination. Unfortunately, however, although the comment of thoughtful men is usually worth reading, that comment is not always best suited to the novel. Indeed, Frank Swinnerton went so far as to praise Gissing primarily as an essayist, a writer of belles-lettres who went misguidedly into the novel.

Thoughtful Gissing was always (indeed his intellectualization goes sometimes to such lengths that one is reminded of the wicked comparison of the elephant who picks up peas), but he learned only gradually to distinguish between thoughtfulness and polemics. In *Workers in the Dawn,* his first novel, *The Nether World* of the eighties or even *In the Year of Jubilee* of the nineties, he insists upon interrupting, like a shrill conductor on a tour of the slums, to make sure that his point is not overlooked. The insistence constitutes the comment of a thoughtful man, but is not welcome reading. To the observer of Gissing, therefore, one of the first signs of maturity is diminution of shrillness, and by the time of *Eve's Ransom,* stridency has almost disappeared. The reader makes inferences about characters and their problems and Gissing merely tells the story.

The major achievement of Gissing is that he learned to move his story easily, no simple feat, for the novelist steeped in the Victorian tradition of plot and subplot hardly recognized the clean sweep of a story. One of the signs of the more skilled novels of Gissing is, then, the "clean" story line. Salvation today can no longer be by purple passage alone, despite the assurance of John Morley, a contemporary of Gissing, that a passage in *Demos* was one of "the most beautiful in modern literature." Instead the main design of each novel must be sought, the "defined shape," as Mr. Percy Lubbock called it in his *Craft of Fiction,* and in the search Gissing's achievement becomes visible. It is true that Gissing knew more about the craft of fiction by the end of his life than

he knew in 1880, but this admission is not the same as saying that
the novels of the last period are better than those of the mid-
nineties. *The Crown of Life* of 1899 is no match for *New Grub
Street* of 1891; the revised version (1895) of *The Unclassed* is
not a great improvement over the cumbersome version of 1884.
The useful question to ask of Gissing's work is not "What year?"
but "What design?"

The design that Gissing used most often was the solitary figure,
a little more than life-size, forced into a succession of relationships consisting usually of a central intimate relationship and a
multiplicity of ephemeral relationships. The juxtaposition is often
arranged so that the intimate relationship constitutes the only
security for the chief character, the only permanence in a world
of flux. Thus, when the "permanent" relationship is shown to
deteriorate the devastation of the protagonist is complete, for the
world now seems all motion and force, hostile to him. It is no
accident that Gissing gave as title to so many of his novels the
name of the chief character, and usually to the extent that he
remembers whose story it is, to that extent is the presentation
successful. For Gissing's novels, in spite of grandiloquent asides,
are essentially domestic novels of a narrow range, and they fare
best when the scene is not cluttered and the conflicts of the protagonist are clearly defined.

The most skilled novels of this design are *New Grub Street,
Born in Exile, The Whirlpool,* and *Our Friend the Charlatan.* In
each of these novels the construction is simple, the focus indisputable. *The Whirlpool* is the most complex of the group, but a
careful reading makes it clear that the decline and fall of Alma
Rolfe is the main narrative theme, to which the accompanying
remarks of Alma's husband make a counterpoint.

There are, unfortunately, several novels in which the central
design is lost, in which Gissing is so seduced by competing characters that he forgets the "story line." These are the novels that
most readily show themselves obsolescent. *Workers in the Dawn*

is a book of scattered interest in which the picaresque story of a waif in the tradition of *Great Expectations* could have been poignant if it had been less cluttered and less shrill. In the novels, *In the Year of Jubilee* and *The Emancipated,* Gissing cannot decide whose story is central; in *The Odd Women* he deliberately avoids concentration upon a central character and tries his best to give a clinical picture of a family, only to lose the narrative in complicated intrigue involving a character originally intended to be secondary.

The sheep are not difficult to separate from the goats, but several novels are difficult to classify, for by any careful test of design they are shown to be deficient. Nevertheless, as in *Demos,* in which the author adulates the character whom most readers find a sham, or as in *Thyrza* and *The Nether World* when subplots get out of hand — a few novels survive by brute passion rather than by skill. These are the novels in which one endures some tedium for the sake of a fresh or daring conception of character. These are the novels in which one is at once most rewarded and most disappointed.

There is a variation in the chief form of a Gissing novel, and *Eve's Ransom* shows the variation at its best. In this story, instead of covering time in the leisurely fashion of the novel over a period of years, Gissing chooses a point in time from which the chief character and the reader can look back into the past and forward into the future. Thus the moment when the hero receives an unexpected sum of money is the one in which the grubbiness of the past seems the most hateful and the seductions of the future the most compelling. The point in time and the sudden necessity for decision are the tests for the novelette, in which number of words becomes a secondary consideration. *Denzil Quarrier,* which superficially resembles *Eve's Ransom* in brevity, does not really belong in the same category, since the management of sequences in time is not different from that in much longer novels. Thus it seems no more than the scenario of a political novel which would be worked out in an immensely superior form in *Our Friend the Charlatan.*

Although the design of most Gissing novels is a simple one, there is variety in the way of looking at the world. In the novels in which Gissing's perceptions and those of his protagonist are almost the same, as in *Born in Exile,* there is a harmony which makes unnecessary any insistence by the author in his own person. Occasionally, however, Gissing can convey a double visibility of the world — from his own point of view and from that of the chief character — without awkward interruptions. *Our Friend the Charlatan* is a good example of such skill.

Design, point of view — these Gissing learned to use. Language itself, supposedly the essential substance in the craft of fiction, was a constant problem. In *The Private Papers of Henry Ryecroft,* in which Gissing assumed the guise of the contented legatee at pasture in Wessex, the form he chose helped him to achieve a felicity of language that was seldom his to command. The most recent tribute to the language of *Henry Ryecroft* was paid in 1953 by Cyril Connolly:

"... it lingers near the edge of preciosity (so common in the nineties) but never trips over. A keen, exact eye for the details of the countryside, an astringent critical gift, a vein of satire, a touch of epigram keep the mixture light, crisp and sparkling, yet set like a jelly in the mellifluous prose." [1]

In the novels, unfortunately, Gissing's language is often heavy and dull. Such passages are all the more disagreeable because they jostle urbanities on the one hand and superb descriptive passages on the other.

On the whole, Gissing's ear for dialogue was true. Much of the dialogue in *A Life's Morning* reads like a parody of George Moore, as do portions of *The Emancipated* and *Sleeping Fires,* but when Gissing is at his best he conveys the muscular vernacular of the nether world and the lower middle class with an authority that is indisputable; and when he knows his sophisticated characters well from prototypes in real life, such characters as Isabel Clarendon or Harvey Rolfe, he is equally at ease and equally effective.

Gissing's belles-lettres seem to be in a safe position. *Henry Ryecroft* will doubtless go through one printing after the other, and it is proper that modern pastoralism, in sweet and felicitous language, should be so rewarded. No apologia therefore is needed for Gissing the essayist, just as no garland is needed for the man. The literate, even though in small bands, have taken care of such homage.

Gissing's reputation as a standard English novelist is at the mercy not only of critics but also of publishers. The fiftieth anniversary of his death has brought his work into the public domain, and perhaps more publishers will be tempted to reprint it. The important question is whether the best of Gissing will reach the public gaze, or whether the state of things will continue in which *Isabel Clarendon* remains out of print while lesser novels are brought forth. Certainly Gissing's reputation must rest upon a half-dozen novels, and not upon all twenty-two. To ascertain the best, no search for purple passages provides an adequate test. Indeed the explorer might best stop looking for nuggets in the Victorian mines and examine instead the depth and construction of the mines themselves.

The final labels for the commodious and dusty baggage of Gissing's lifetime are difficult to choose. He was above all a professional, writing for "bread money," even if a few novels seem the work of an amateur. He knew that his background made unlikely any extraordinary success in the fashionable world; yet he refused to make self-pity an obsession and eventually learned to see himself and others, for the purposes of fiction, "in the round." In his last years he had no illusions about the trade he had chosen and counseled a friend not to attempt a livelihood by writing unless he were prepared for the worst hardships. He made a duty of curiosity, and as an educated man (for to be truly that was his aim in life), made himself at home in past cultures, through reading and travel, and in the society of his time.

He probably had a sound opinion of the value of his work; as he eventually decided about George Eliot's fiction, "intellectual power" was not the only criterion for good writing; "imaginative light" and grace with words were also necessary. Nevertheless he believed, correctly, that his work would continue to be read by the few thoughtful people who would accept the strange fiction that is neither tragedy nor comedy. Gissing could not write tragedy because he found even his heroes unpredictable: in his most tragic moment, a Gissing hero is as likely to sneeze or look ridiculous as to say magnificent words. Similarly, Gissing could not write high comedy (although capable of premeditated buffoonery), for he was not amused by the plight of man before natural and social forces. Preferring, as he told Edward Clodd, the "joke in earnest" which is too bitter for most men, with wry smile and dry tears Gissing the writer was forced to play the role of the grave comedian.

APPENDIX

Six volumes of Gissing's short stories have been published. *The Sins of the Fathers* (1924) and *Brownie* (1931) are collections of stories written in the seventies, whereas the others are representative of Gissing's mature work — *Human Odds and Ends* (1898), *The House of Cobwebs and Other Stories* (1906), *A Victim of Circumstances* (1927), and *Stories and Sketches* (1938).

The collection of 1938 (Michael Joseph, Publisher) is especially interesting because it reprints the earliest stories (except for the American ones) like "Phoebe" and "Letty Coe" as well as those of the nineties. Some of the stories are, in the words of Alfred C. Gissing, "mere crescendos of heaped up misfortune . . ." but most of them are more economical and more skillful than one would expect after the verboseness in many of the novels. Gissing seems well suited to the demands of the short story, and seems to lose in that form his tendency to interrupt and digress.

"Lou and Liz" is an example of the simplest construction — a day in the lives of two Cockney girls, a day a little more memorable than other days because it brings the temporary return of a long-lost husband. But the day ends in the usual fashion with no husband and no prospect of a different tomorrow. The tone is that of *The Nether World*. "One Way of Happiness" shows the same simplicity in construction, but this time the group is larger. The action in "Lou and Liz" extends through a day — that in the latter story, through a holiday weekend in Brighton. Now, too, the class is the "respectable" vulgar. The story reads remarkably like Thackeray, but Gissing wrote others, less acidulous, about similar people: "Fleet Footed Hester," is, for example, a bizarre but cheerful story of a girl who prefers running to walking. It is Dickens in its extravagant moments, but the basic mood is "realistic."

Probably the best example of the control which Gissing had in the nineties over the form of the short story just as he had it in the novel is "The Honeymoon." The method of conducting narrative is altogether modern. The story opens with the wife's opinion, gently tolerant, of her husband's good fortune in winning such a bride, moves quickly to the husband's inner thoughts on his marriage; then there is a brisk dialogue in which the wife's conceit is shattered, and a swift denouement — the wife's feigned suicide in order to frighten her husband, her humiliation and submission to superior intelligence.

Most of the stories show a high degree of technical competence, and to dismiss them as mere vignettes of two classes, the proletariat and the lower middle class, is like dismissing Maupassant because he wrote about so many Normans.

BIBLIOGRAPHY

I PRINCIPAL EDITIONS OF GISSING'S WORKS *

Workers in the Dawn, 3 vols., London, Remington, 1880; 2 vols., New York, Doubleday, Doran, 1935.

The Unclassed, 3 vols., London, Bentley, 1884; 1 vol., rev. ed., Lawrence & Bullen, 1895; Routledge, 1905; Sidgwick, Jackson, 1911; Benn, 1930.

Isabel Clarendon, 3 vols., London, Chapman, 1886.

Demos, 3 vols., London, Smith, Elder, 1886; Harper, 1886; Dent, Wayfarer Library, 1915; Eveleigh, Nash & Grayson, 1928, 1936.

Thyrza, 3 vols., London, Smith, Elder, 1887; Eveleigh, Nash & Grayson, 1927.

A Life's Morning, 3 vols., London, Smith, Elder, 1888; Home & Van Thal, 1947; Eveleigh, Nash & Grayson, 1928, 1938. *Cornhill* Magazine, January–June 1888.

The Nether World, 3 vols., London, Smith, Elder, 1889; Eveleigh, Nash & Grayson, 1928.

The Emancipated, 3 vols., London, Bentley, 1890; Lawrence & Bullen, 1893; Sidgwick, Jackson, 1911.

New Grub Street, 3 vols., London, Smith, Elder, 1891; Nelson, 1907; Eveleigh, Nash & Grayson, 1927, 1938.

Denzil Quarrier, London, Lawrence & Bullen, 1892; Sidgwick, Jackson, 1911; New York, Macmillan, 1892.

Born in Exile, 3 vols., London, A. & C. Black, 1892; Nelson, 1907.

The Odd Women, 3 vols., London, Lawrence & Bullen, 1893; Sidgwick, Jackson, 1911.

In the Year of Jubilee, 3 vols., London, Lawrence & Bullen, 1894; Sidgwick, Jackson, 1911; Watergate Classics, 1947.

Eve's Ransom, London, Lawrence & Bullen, 1895; Benn, 1929. *Illustrated London News* (a Saturday weekly) Jan. 5, 1895–March 30, 1895.

The Paying Guest, London, Cassell, 1895.

Sleeping Fires, London, T. Fisher Unwin, 1895, 1927.

The Whirlpool, London, Lawrence & Bullen, 1897; Stokes, 1897; Hodder & Stoughton, 1911.

Human Odds and Ends, Stories and Sketches, London, Lawrence & Bullen, 1898.

The Town Traveller, London, Methuen, 1898.

---

* Unless there is an indication to the contrary, editions are single volumes.

Charles Dickens, A Critical Study, London, Blackie, 1898; New York, Dodd, Mead, 1898.

The Crown of Life, London, Methuen, 1899; Stokes.

By the Ionian Sea, Notes of a Ramble in Southern Italy, London, Chapman, 1901; Jonathan Cape, 1933; Travellers Library.

Our Friend the Charlatan, London, Chapman, 1901.

The Private Papers of Henry Ryecroft, London, Constable, 1903; New York, Dutton; Modern Library, *n.d.*

Veranilda, London, Constable, 1904; Dutton, 1905; Oxford "World Classics," 1929.

Will Warburton, London, Constable, 1905; New York, Dutton.

The House of Cobwebs and Other Stories, London, Constable, 1906.

An Heiress on Condition, Philadelphia, 1923. Privately printed for the Pennell Club.

Sins of the Fathers and Other Tales, Chicago, Pascal Covici, 1924.

Critical Studies of the Works of Charles Dickens, New York, Greenberg, 1924, with Bibliography of Gissing by Temple Scott.

The Immortal Dickens, London, Cecil Palmer, 1925. Contents are largely those of preceding collection, except for the Bibliography.

A Victim of Circumstances and Other Stories, London, Constable, 1927, with preface by Gissing's younger son, Alfred C. Gissing; Boston, Houghton Mifflin.

A Yorkshire Lass, New York, 1928. Privately printed.

Selections Autobiographical and Imaginative from the Works of George Gissing, London, Jonathan Cape, 1929.

Brownie, New York, Columbia University, 1931.

Stories and Sketches, London, Michael Joseph, 1938.

II MISCELLANEOUS WRITINGS, NOT REPRINTED IN BOOK FORM

"Notes on Social Democracy, I," *Pall Mall Gazette,* Sept. 9, 1880; Part II, Sept. 11, 1880, both unsigned.

"The New Censorship of Literature," *Pall Mall Budget,* Dec. 19, 1884, pp. 12–13. A signed letter of Gissing is reprinted in part. It is this letter which provoked the attack by *Punch* on Jan. 3, 1885.

"On Greek Accent in Verse," *The Times* (London), Feb. 25, 1891, signed.

"Why I Don't Write Plays," *Pall Mall Gazette,* Sept. 10, 1892, signed.

Letter in London *Academy,* March 19, 1898, from Rome, protesting an article entitled "Mr. George Gissing at Home."

III DIARIES AND LETTERS
A. *Manuscript Sources*
Yale University Library:
Notes G. R. G. 1877 [90 p.]
Early Poems and Verse-Plays
Youthful Notes on Drawing
Reminiscences of My Father 1884
Letters, to the Gissing family, to Eduard Bertz, and others
Concerning the George Matthew Adams Collection see *The Yale University Library Gazette*, XVI, 1942, pp. 47–50, by Richard F. Niebling
New York Public Library, Henry W. and Albert A. Berg Collection
My Clerical Rival, Holograph, undated
School Drawing Book
Miscellaneous holograph notes made during childhood
Diary 1887–1903
Letters, Berg, Howe, and Pforzheimer groups

B. *Books and Articles*
Letters of George Gissing to Members of His Family, London, Constable and Company, 1927, Collected and Arranged by Algernon and Ellen Gissing.

Adams, George Matthew, "How and Why I Collect George Gissing," *Colophon*, Part XVIII, September 1934.

Bulletin of the Boston Public Library, November and December, 1947, XXII, seventeen letters written to Ellen Gissing; see November 1947, p. 325.

Letters to Edward Clodd from George Gissing, London, 1914. Printed for Thomas J. Wise, for private circulation, thirteen letters, from May 5, 1885, to Oct. 17, 1903. Nine of these were published, with variant spellings, in Clodd's *Memories*, Chapman and Hall, London, 1916.

Two Letters from George Gissing to Joseph Conrad, London, 1926. Printed for the First Edition Club; Christmas Day 1902, May 9, 1903.

Letters to an Editor, by George Gissing, London, 1915. Privately printed for Clement Shorter.

Gosse, Edmund, *Questions at Issue*, London, 1893, contains a letter from Gissing "on the estimate in which poetry is held by the lower classes."

IV BIOGRAPHICAL AND CRITICAL STUDIES
Bateson, M., "Mr. George Gissing," *The Guardian*, Jan. 6, 1904.
Bennett, Enoch Arnold, *Fame and Fiction*, London, 1901.
Bjorkman, Edwin, *Voices of Tomorrow*, New York, 1913, pp. 224–239.
Brewster, Dorothy, and Burrell, Angus, *Modern Fiction*, New York, 1934.

Cazamian, Madeleine L., *Le Roman et Les Idées en Angleterre*, L'Influence de la Science, Paris, 1923.

Colles, W. Morris, "George Gissing," *The Academy and Literature*, London, Jan. 9, 1904, p. 40.

Dolman, Frederick, "The Novels of George Gissing," *National Review*, October 1897, pp. 258–266.

Fehr, B., *Die Englische Literatur des XIX und XX Jahrhunderts*, Berlin, 1923.

Follett, H. T., and W., *Some Modern Novelists*, New York, 1918.

Frierson, William C., *L'Influence du Naturalisme Français sur les Romanciers Anglais de 1885 à 1900*, Paris, 1925.

Gapp, Samuel Vogt, *George Gissing, Classicist*, Philadelphia, 1936.

Gissing, Alfred C., "George Gissing — Some Aspects of His Life and Work," *The National Review*, London, August 1929, pp. 932–941.

Gissing, Ellen, "George Gissing, A Character Sketch," *The Nineteenth Century*, September 1927, pp. 417–424.

Gissing, Ellen, "Some Personal Recollections of George Gissing," *Blackwood's Magazine*, May 1929, p. 653 ff.

Gladstone, W. E., " 'Robert Elsmere' and the Battle of Belief," *The Nineteenth Century*, May 1888, pp. 766–788.

Greenebaum, Elizabeth, "George Gissing," *The History of the Novel in England*, Robert Morss Lovett & Helen Sard Hughes, eds. Boston, 1932, pp. 362–369.

Harrison, Austin, "George Gissing," *The Nineteenth Century and After*, London, September 1906, p. 453 ff.

Harrison, Frederic, "Preface," *Veranilda*, London, Constable, 1904.

James, Henry, *Notes on Novelists, With Some Other Notes*, New York, 1914.

Leavis, Q. D., "Gissing and the English Novel," *Scrutiny*, June 1938, pp. 73–81.

McKay, Ruth Capers, *George Gissing and His Critic Frank Swinnerton*, Philadelphia, 1933.

Masterman, C. F. G., *In Peril of Change*, London, 1905.

More, Paul Elmer, *Shelburne Essays*, Fifth Series, New York, 1908. "Introduction," *The Private Papers of Henry Ryecroft*, New York, Modern Library, n.d.

Nicoll, Sir William Robertson, *A Bookman's Letters*, London, 1913.

The Outlook, London, Jan 2, 1904, "George Gissing," anon.

Owens College Union Magazine, "George Robert Gissing," January 1904, pp. 80–81.

Roberts, Morley, *The Private Life of Henry Maitland*, London, 1912; rev. ed., 1923.

Rotter, A., *Frank Swinnerton und George Gissing, Eine Kritische Studie*, Prague, 1930.

Seccombe, Thomas, *Dictionary of National Biography*, Second Supplement, London, 1912, II, pp. 114–116.

"Introduction," *House of Cobwebs*, London, 1906.

Shafer, Robert, "The Vitality of George Gissing," *American Review*, V, 1935, pp. 459–487.

"Introduction," *Workers in the Dawn*, New York, 1935.

Sichel, Edith, "Two Philanthropic Novelists," *Murray's Magazine*, April 1888, pp. 506–518.

Stearns, George A., "George Gissing in America," *The Bookman*, New York, August 1926, pp. 683–686.

Swinnerton, Frank, *George Gissing, A Critical Study*, London, 1912; rev. ed., 1923.

Times Literary Supplement, London, "Gissing's Academic Career," May 20, 1944, p. 252.

Waugh, Arthur, "George Gissing," *Fortnightly Review*, London, February 1904, p. 244 ff.

Weber, Anton, *George Gissing und die Soziale Frage*, Leipzig, 1932.

Wells, H. G., "The Novels of Mr. George Gissing," *Contemporary Review*, London, August 1897, p. 192 ff.

"George Gissing, An Impression," *The Monthly Review*, London, August 1904, pp. 160–172.

Experiment in Autobiography, New York, 1934.

Weygandt, C., *A Century of the English Novel*, New York, 1925.

Williams, H., *Modern English Writers 1890–1914*, London, 1918; 3rd ed. rev., 1925.

Williamson, George C., "George Gissing," *The Academy and Literature*, London, Jan. 9, 1904, p. 46.

Woolf, Virginia, "Introduction," *By the Ionian Sea*, London, 1929, 1933.

Yates, May, *George Gissing, An Appreciation*, Manchester, 1922.

Young, W. T., *The Cambridge History of English Literature*, XIII, Cambridge, 1917, ch. 14.

NOTES

CHAPTER 1. REVALUATION

1. "Gissing the Rod," *Punch*, LXXXIX, Jan. 3, 1885.
2. Angus Burrell, *Modern Fiction*, with Dorothy Brewster, p. 37.
3. Q. D. Leavis, "Gissing and the English Novel," p. 79.
4. *Letters of George Gissing to Members of His Family*, A. and E. Gissing, eds.
5. Thomas Seccombe, "Introduction," Gissing's *House of Cobwebs*, p. viii.
6. The tables of Gissing's annual earnings are reproduced in George Matthew Adams, "How and Why I Collect George Gissing."
7. *Athenaeum*, June 22, 1901, full column review.
8. Feb. 26, 1880, to Algernon, Yale University Library.
9. *Letters*, p. 42, Jan. 26, 1879, to Algernon.
10. Anton Weber, *George Gissing und Die Soziale Frage*, p. 17; B. Fehr, *Die Englische Literatur des XIX und XX Jahrhunderts;* W. Spemann, *Goldenes Buch des Weltliteratur*, Berlin, 1912, pp. 322–323.
11. *Academy*, March 2, 1895.
12. Robert Shafer, "Introduction," Gissing's *Workers in the Dawn*, p. xxxix.
13. *Academy*, May 15, 1897.
14. Virginia Woolf, "Introduction," *Selections Autobiographical and Imaginative from the Works of George Gissing*, with Biographical and Critical Notes by his Son, London, Jonathan Cape, 1929, p. 12.
15. June 8, 1880, to Algernon, Yale University Library.
16. Nov. 9, 1878, to Algernon, Berg Collection, N. Y. Public Library.
17. *Letters*, p. 141, June 23, 1884, to Algernon.
18. *Letters*, p. 86, Nov. 22, 1880, to Algernon.
19. "The New Censorship of Literature," *Pall Mall Budget*, XXXII, Dec. 19, 1884, pp. 12–13.
20. For an account of the trial of 1888, see the *Pall Mall Gazette*, March 24, 1888 and May 10, 1888; also E. Vizetelly, *Emile Zola*, London, 1904, pp. 256–286.
21. *Bulletin of the Boston Public Library*, November 1947, p. 335, April 1, 1890, to Ellen.

CHAPTER 2. EARLY INFLUENCES

1. H. G. Wells, "George Gissing, An Impression," p. 161.
2. George Gissing, "Dickens in Memory," *The Critic*, January 1902, p. 49.
3. MS, Yale University Library.

4. *Letters,* p. 347, May 20, 1896, to Algernon; see also *A Biographical Index of Deceased British Botanists,* 1st ed. 1893, 2nd ed. 1931, pp. 123–124; also *Journal of Botany,* IX, 1871, p. 96.

5. Subsequent quotations, on experiences of childhood, are from MS Reminiscences, Yale University Library.

6. *Letters,* p. 4; Diary, Sept. 10, 1870.

7. MS, Berg Collection, N. Y. Public Library.

8. *Letters,* Appendix C, p. 403.

9. MS, Berg Collection, N. Y. Public Library.

10. *Ibid.*

11. From an unpublished letter to the biographer, from Mr. Stanley Wood, a son of Mr. James Wood, the headmaster.

12. *Philadelphia Inquirer,* May 11, 1931, noted in Samuel Vogt Gapp, *George Gissing, Classicist,* p. 20.

13. MS, Yale University Library.

14. *Letters,* p. 8, to his mother, May 5, 1872.

15. A. S. W., "George Robert Gissing," *Owens College Union Magazine,* pp. 80–81.

16. *Letters,* p. 9, April 19, 1873, to his mother.

17. April 23, 1873, to Bowes, from catalogue of George Grasberger, Philadelphia, December 1930, item no. 54.

18. MS, Yale University Library.

19. *Introductory Lectures on the Opening of Owens College,* Manchester, 1852.

20. *Owens College Union Magazine,* p. 81.

21. Morley Roberts, *The Private Life of Henry Maitland.*

22. Roberts, pp. 26, 27.

23. *Charles Dickens, A Critical Study,* p. 223.

24. Burrell, p. 18.

25. Feb. 26, 1880, to Algernon, Yale University Library.

26. July 1, 1879, to Algernon, Yale University Library.

27. Oct. 26, 1884, to Algernon, Berg Collection, N. Y. Public Library.

28. Sept. 13, 1888, to Ellen, *Bulletin of the Boston Public Library,* December 1947, p. 376.

29. *Letters,* p. 12, Oct. 5, 1876, to William.

30. *Ibid.*

31. *Letters,* p. 17, Nov. 13, 1876, to Algernon.

32. *Letters,* p. 19, Jan. 28, 1877, to Algernon.

33. MS Diary, Yale University Library, gives the itinerary, beginning in March 1877.

34. *Letters,* p. 58, Feb. 7, 1880, to Algernon.

35. MS Diary, Yale University Library.

36. June 16, 1879, to Algernon, Berg Collection, N. Y. Public Library.

37. March 2, 1897, to Algernon, Yale University Library.
38. *Letters*, p. 97, May 4, 1881, to Algernon.
39. *Letters*, p. 47, Aug. 20, 1879, to Algernon.
40. *Workers in the Dawn*.
41. *Letters*, p. 19, Jan. 28, 1877, to Algernon.
42. In *Letters*, p. 32, the editors declare the legacy to be "about five hundred pounds." However, the sum which Gissing mentions as his capital is £300. See letter of June 16, 1879, to Algernon, Berg Collection, N. Y. Public Library.
43. *Letters*, p. 75, June 15, 1880, to Algernon.

CHAPTER 3. POVERTY AND DISGRACE

1. Edward Clodd, *Memories*, p. 172.
2. *Letters*, p. 30, May 22, 1878, to Algernon. By March 1882 Gissing had ten pupils, *Letters*, p. 108, to Margaret.
3. See marriage register, London Parish of Saint James, Hampstead Road, Oct. 27, 1879.
4. *Letters*, p. 22.
5. July 1, 1879; Feb. 26, 1880, to Algernon, Yale University Library.
6. June 30, 1880, to Algernon, Yale University Library.
7. Oct. 31, 1882, to Algernon, Yale University Library.
8. Oct. 6, 1882, to Algernon, Yale University Library.
9. Feb. 14, 1885, to Algernon, Yale University Library.
10. March 9, 1879, to Algernon, Berg Collection, N. Y. Public Library.
11. March 23, 1879, to Algernon, Berg Collection, N. Y. Public Library.
12. *Letters*, p. 42, Jan. 26, 1879, to Algernon.
13. *Letters*, p. 40, Jan. 19, 1879, to Algernon.
14. June 16, 1879, to Algernon, Berg Collection, N. Y. Public Library.
15. *Dictionary of National Biography*, p. 114.
16. Dec. 21, 1880, to Algernon, Yale University Library.
17. *Letters*, p. 83, Nov. 3, 1880, to Algernon.
18. April 17, 1887, to Bertz, Yale University Library.
19. May 2, 1880, to Algernon, Yale University Library.
20. Dec. 21, 1880, to Algernon, Yale University Library.
21. June 13, 1883, to Algernon, Berg Collection, N. Y. Public Library.
22. Sept. 2, 1883, to Algernon, Yale University Library.
23. March 21, 1884, to Algernon, Yale University Library.
24. MS agreement, Yale University Library.
25. *Letters*, pp. 77, 78, July 22, 1880; Harrison's letter is quoted by Gissing.
26. *Letters*, p. 80, Aug. 20, 1880, to Algernon.
27. *Letters*, p. 85, Nov. 18, 1880, to Algernon.
28. *Letters*, pp. 88, 89, Jan. 16, 1881, to Algernon.
29. *Letters*, p. 49, Oct. 22, 1879, to George from William.

30. Nov. 9, 1878, to Algernon, Berg Collection, N. Y. Public Library.
31. *Letters*, p. 69, Spring 1880, to Algernon.
32. *The Positive Philosophy of Auguste Comte*, by Harriet Martineau, 2 vols., pref. to 2nd ed., London, Trubner, 1875.
33. Comte, Preface to 1829 edition, *The Fundamental Principles of the Positive Philosophy*, ed. Edward Spencer Beesly, London, *n.d.*
34. *Letters*, p. 84, Nov. 11, 1880, to Algernon.
35. *Letters*, p. 92, Feb. 11, 1881, to Algernon.
36. Jan. 30, 1881, to Algernon, Yale University Library.
37. *Letters*, p. 41, Jan. 26, 1879, to Algernon.
38. Oct. 6, 1882, to Algernon, Yale University Library.
39. Leslie Stephen, "Philosophic Doubt," *Mind*, A Quarterly Review of Psychology and Philosophy, V, April 1880, pp. 180–181.
40. May 9, 1880, to Algernon, Yale University Library.
41. *Letters*, p. 40, Jan. 19, 1879, to Algernon.
42. May 9, 1880, to Algernon, Yale University Library.
43. *Letters*, p. 37, Dec. 5, 1878, to Algernon.
44. *Letters*, p. 41, Jan. 26, 1879, to Algernon.
45. *Letters*, p. 28, Feb. 12, 1878, to Algernon.
46. *Letters*, p. 27, Feb. 12, 1878, to Algernon.
47. *Letters*, p. 92, Feb. 11, 1881, to Algernon.
48. Oct. 6, 1882, to Algernon, Yale University Library, cf. *Letters*, p. 120.
49. *Letters*, p. 118, July 12, 1882, to Margaret.
50. June 7, 1882, to Algernon, Yale University Library.
51. *Letters*, p. 126, May 12, 1883, to Margaret.
52. *Letters*, p. 122, Feb. 14, 1883, to Algernon.
53. August 25, 1884, to Algernon, Berg Collection, N. Y. Public Library.
54. *Letters*, p. 102, July 28, 1881, to Algernon.
55. July 10, 1881, to Margaret, Berg Collection, N. Y. Public Library.
56. Dec. 7, 1879, to Algernon, Berg Collection, N. Y. Public Library.
57. Nov. 21, 1879, to Algernon, Berg Collection, N. Y. Public Library.
58. April 15, 1878, to Algernon, Berg Collection, N. Y. Public Library.
59. April 17, 1887, to Eduard Bertz, Yale University Library.
60. *Letters*, p. 95, March 13, 1881, to Algernon.
61. *Letters*, p. 97, May 4, 1881, to Algernon.
62. Oct. 31, 1882, to Algernon, Yale University Library.
63. MS Diary, from 1887 to the year of Gissing's death, is in N. Y. Public Library, Berg Collection. See entry for March 1, 1888.
64. Nov. 21, 1879, to Algernon, Berg Collection, N. Y. Public Library.
65. *Letters*, p. 103, Aug. 8, 1881, to Algernon.
66. *Letters*, p. 115, May 18, 1882, to Algernon.
67. *Letters*, p. 128, July 18, 1883, to Algernon.
68. *Letters*, p. 114, May 7, 1882, to Algernon.

CHAPTER 4. A YOUNG MAN'S FIRST BOOKS

1. *Letters,* p. 83, Nov. 3, 1880, to Algernon.
2. *Saturday Review,* Jan. 19, 1861.
3. David Daiches, *The Novel and the Modern World,* Chicago, University of Chicago, 1939, p. 5.
4. *Literature at Nurse,* London, 1885.
5. "The Art of Fiction," *Longman's Magazine,* September, 1884.
6. Mary Ellen Chase, *Thomas Hardy from Serial to Novel,* Minneapolis, University of Minnesota, 1927.
7. Vizetelly, p. 286.
8. Edmund Wilson, "The Two Scrooges," *The Wound and the Bow,* New York, Houghton Mifflin, 1941.
9. John Forster, *Life of Dickens,* III, pp. 368–369.
10. Forster, *Dickens,* II, p. 434.
11. William Henry Wills, *Charles Dickens as Editor,* New York, 1912, p. 168.
12. *Ibid.,* p. 247.
13. Lawrence Hutton, *Letters of Charles Dickens to Wilkie Collins,* New York, 1892, p. 139.
14. Amy Cruse, *The Victorians and Their Books,* London, Allen and Unwin, 1935, p. 55.
15. *Letters,* p. 56, Jan. 25, 1880, to Algernon.
16. "Bleak House," *The Immortal Dickens,* p. 234.
17. The edition published by Doubleday, New York, 1935, with an introduction by Robert Shafer, indicates passages which Gissing wished to delete (for only a portion of the novel).
18. Burrell, p. 18.
19. *The Unclassed,* London, Lawrence & Bullen, 1895.
20. *Athenaeum,* June 28, 1884.
21. *Academy,* June 28, 1884.

CHAPTER 5. BETWEEN TWO WORLDS

1. *Letters,* p. 122, Feb. 13, 1883, to Algernon.
2. Nov. 2, 1883, to Margaret, Berg Collection, N. Y. Public Library.
3. *Letters,* p. 131, Sept. 15, 1883, to Margaret.
4. Diary, Aug. 6, 1891, Berg Collection, N. Y. Public Library.
5. June 13, 1883, to Algernon, Berg Collection, N. Y. Public Library.
6. *Ibid.*
7. May 3, 1883, to Algernon, Yale University Library.
8. March 7, 1883, to Algernon, Berg Collection, N. Y. Public Library.
9. Aug. 25, 1884, to Algernon, Berg Collection, N. Y. Public Library.
10. Oct. 26, 1884, to Algernon, Berg Collection, N. Y. Public Library.
11. *Letters,* p. 150, Oct. 26, 1884, to Margaret.
12. Sept. 1, 1884, to Algernon, Yale University Library.

13. Oct. 26, 1884, to Algernon, Berg Collection, N. Y. Public Library.
14. Oct. 27, 1885, to Algernon, Yale University Library.
15. Nov. 24, 1884, to Algernon, Yale University Library.
16. Aug. 25, 1884, to Algernon, Berg Collection, N. Y. Public Library.
17. Sept. 7, 1884, to Algernon, Berg Collection, N. Y. Public Library.
18. *Letters*, p. 141, June 23, 1884, to Algernon.
19. *Letters*, p. 142, quoted in Gissing's letter of June 25, 1884.
20. Dec. 2, 1884, to Algernon, Berg Collection, N. Y. Public Library.
21. "The New Censorship of Literature," *Pall Mall Budget*, XXXII, pp. 12–13.
22. Aug. 9, 1883, to Margaret, Berg Collection, N. Y. Public Library.
23. *Letters*, p. 170, October 1885, to Algernon.
24. *Letters*, p. 171.
25. Nov. 9, 1885, to Algernon, Yale University Library.
26. *Letters*, p. 172, Oct. 31, 1885, to Algernon.
27. Nov. 24, 1885, to Algernon, Yale University Library.
28. *Letters*, pp. 168–169, Sept. 22, 1885, to Algernon.
29. Feb. 14, 1885, to Margaret, Berg Collection, N. Y. Public Library.
30. Dec. 28, 1886, to Algernon, Berg Collection, N. Y. Public Library.
31. *Letters*, p. 31, May 22, 1878, to Algernon.
32. Tentatively dated May 1885, to Ellen, *Bulletin of the Boston Public Library*, November 1947, pp. 329–330.
33. H. G. Wells, "George Gissing, An Impression," p. 163.
34. Diary, March 26, 1888, Berg Collection, N. Y. Public Library.
35. *Letters*, p. 156, April 10, 1885, to Margaret.
36. *Letters*, p. 158, "Thursday" [June, 1885], to Ellen.
37. Nov. 22, 1885, to Margaret, Berg Collection, N. Y. Public Library.
38. Feb. 15, 1886, to Margaret, Berg Collection, N. Y. Public Library.
39. *Letters*, p. 180, May 8, 1886, to Ellen.
40. *Letters*, p. 177, March 22, 1886, to Algernon.
41. *Letters*, p. 182, June 13, 1886, to Margaret.
42. *Letters*, p. 182, July 31, 1886, to Margaret.
43. *Letters*, p. 185, Aug. 20, 1886, to Ellen.
44. *Letters*, p. 183, July 31, 1886, to Margaret.
45. *Letters*, p. 185, Sept. 27, 1886, to Margaret.
46. Dec. 16, 1886, to Algernon, Berg Collection, N. Y. Public Library.
47. Dec. 28, 1886, to Algernon, Berg Collection, N. Y. Public Library.
48. *Letters*, p. 189, January 1887, to Ellen.
49. *Ibid.*
50. *Letters*, p. 192, May 6, 1887, to Margaret.
51. *Letters*, p. 198, Aug. 25, 1887, to Ellen.
52. *Letters*, p. 195, June 13, 1887, to Algernon.
53. *Letters*, p. 204, Nov. 13, 1887, to Margaret.

54. *Letters,* p. 196, July 8, 1887, to Ellen.
55. *Letters,* p. 197, July 10, 1887, to Algernon.
56. Diary, Jan. 1, 1888, Berg Collection, N. Y. Public Library.
57. *Letters,* p. 208, Feb. 16, 1888, to Algernon.
58. Diary, March 1, 1888, Berg Collection, N. Y. Public Library.
59. *Letters,* p. 214, Diary, May 8, 1888.

CHAPTER 6.   NOVELS OF MANOR AND OF SLUMS

1. *Letters,* p. 147, Sept. 1, 1884, to Algernon.
2. Seccombe, p. xiv.
3. *Athenaeum,* June 19, 1886.
4. *Academy,* July 10, 1886.
5. *Letters,* p. 164, Aug. 9, 1885, to Algernon.
6. *Athenaeum,* Dec. 8, 1888.
7. *Letters,* p. 177, March 1886, to Algernon.
8. *Letters,* p. 176, March 14, 1886, to Ellen; *Letters,* p. 181, May 21, 1886, to Ellen.
9. See Gapp, *George Gissing, Classicist.*
10. *Athenaeum,* May 7, 1887.
11. Seccombe, p. xviii.
12. *Ibid.*
13. Dec. 16, 1886, to Algernon, Berg Collection, N. Y. Public Library.
14. W. E. Gladstone, " 'Robert Elsmere' and The Battle of Belief," p. 787.
15. Diary, June 17, 1888, Berg Collection, N. Y. Public Library.

CHAPTER 7.   MARRIAGE AND MISANTHROPY

1. George J. Romanes, *Animal Intelligence,* International Scientific Series, 3rd ed., London, Kegan, Paul, 1883; listed in Diary, June 3, 1891, Berg Collection, N. Y. Public Library.
2. Paul Bourget, *Essais de psychologie contemporaine,* Paris, Alphonse Lemerre, 1885; referred to in Diary, Oct. 24, 1889, Berg Collection, N. Y. Public Library.
3. Diary, May 24, 1888, Berg Collection, N. Y. Public Library.
4. Diary, June 20, 1888, Berg Collection, N. Y. Public Library.
5. Diary, Oct. 6, 1888, *Letters,* p. 226.
6. *Letters,* p. 217, June 17, 1888, to Ellen.
7. Diary, Sept. 29, 1891, Berg Collection, N. Y. Public Library.
8. Aug. 9, 1885, to Algernon, Yale University Library.
9. Sept. 11, 1889, to Algernon, Berg Collection, N. Y. Public Library.
10. Diary, June 3, 1888, *Letters,* p. 215.
11. Diary, Oct. 14, 1888, *Letters,* p. 227, but Plitt is mentioned by name only in the MS.
12. Diary, Dec. 25, 1888, Berg Collection, N. Y. Public Library.

13. *Letters*, p. 258, Dec. 17, 1888, to Margaret.
14. *Ibid.*, p. 260.
15. Dec. 17, 1888, to Margaret, Berg Collection, N. Y. Public Library, excerpt not in *Letters*.
16. Jan. 21, 1889, to Mrs. Algernon Gissing (Katie), Berg Collection, N. Y. Public Library.
17. Diary, April 2, 1889, *Letters*, p. 282.
18. Diary, Oct. 5, 1889, Berg Collection, N. Y. Public Library.
19. Diary, Nov. 9, 1889, Berg Collection, N. Y. Public Library.
20. Diary, Dec. 11, 1889, Berg Collection, N. Y. Public Library.
21. *Letters*, p. 297, Nov. 29, 1889, to Algernon.
22. *Letters*, p. 306, Jan. 22, 1890, to Algernon. Shortridge is mentioned by name in MSS.
23. *Ibid.*, p. 307.
24. *Letters*, p. 308, March 16, 1890, to Algernon.
25. *Ibid.*
26. Diary, June 20, 1890, Berg Collection, N. Y. Public Library.
27. April 1, 1890, to Ellen, *Bulletin of the Boston Public Library*, November 1947, p. 335.
28. April 3, 1890, to Ellen, *Bulletin of the Boston Public Library*, December 1947, p. 376.
29. Diary, Aug. 6, 1890, Berg Collection, N. Y. Public Library.
30. Diary, Aug. 11, 1890, Berg Collection, N. Y. Public Library.
31. Diary, Sept. 16, 1890, Berg Collection, N. Y. Public Library.
32. Diary, Aug. 23, 1890, Berg Collection, N. Y. Public Library.
33. Roberts, p. 140.
34. All entries in the diary for Edith Underwood begin in the autumn of 1890.
35. Jan. 11, 1891, to Algernon, Berg Collection, N. Y. Public Library.
36. Diary, Dec. 5, 1890, Berg Collection, N. Y. Public Library.
37. *The Author*, "Organ of the Incorporated Society of Authors," July 1, 1891, p. 43.
38. Diary, May 27, 1891, Berg Collection, N. Y. Public Library.
39. Diary, Aug. 7, 1891, Berg Collection, N. Y. Public Library.
40. Diary, Oct. 6, 1891, Berg Collection, N. Y. Public Library.
41. Diary, Aug. 15, 1891, Berg Collection, N. Y. Public Library.
42. Diary, Nov. 25, 1891, Berg Collection, N. Y. Public Library.
43. Diary, Jan. 23, 1894; Sept. 8, 1894; Berg Collection, N. Y. Public Library.
44. See *The Society of Authors, A Record of Its Action from Its Foundation*, by Walter Besant, published by the National Society of Authors, 1893.
45. Diary, Jan. 12, 1895, Berg Collection, N. Y. Public Library.
46. Diary, note for end of year, 1894, Berg Collection, N. Y. Public Library.
47. Diary, Nov. 20, 1896, Berg Collection, N. Y. Public Library.

48. March 1, 1902, to Edward Clodd, in *Letters to Edward Clodd from George Gissing.*

49. Sept. 22, 1895, to Algernon, Yale University Library.

50. Diary, Sept. 15, 1895, Berg Collection, N. Y. Public Library.

51. Edward Clodd, *Memories,* p. 165.

52. Diary, June 6, 1895, Berg Collection, N. Y. Public Library.

53. Edward Clodd, *Grant Allen, A Memoir,* London, Grant Richards, 1900, p. 42.

54. Joseph McCabe, "Austin Harrison," *A Biographical Dictionary of Modern Rationalists,* 1920.

55. Joseph McCabe, *Edward Clodd, A Memoir,* London, John Lane, 1932, p. 214.

56. Diary, June 19, 1892, Berg Collection, N. Y. Public Library.

57. Miss Collet is first mentioned in the diary on March 14, 1892. Gissing's sister Ellen had sent him a clipping concerning Miss Collet's lecture to the London Ethical Society on his work. Miss Orme of Tulse Hill also volunteered help: Diary, Sept. 17, 1897.

58. *Letters,* pp. 344–345, Diary, Dec. 25, 1895.

59. Diary, April 28, 1896; Aug. 9, 1896, Berg Collection, N. Y. Public Library.

60. The incident occurred in February, but was recorded in the diary on June 2, 1897.

61. Edmund Gosse, *Questions at Issue,* New York, Appleton, 1893, pp. 325–331 (Appendix) in which Gissing's letter to Gosse is printed. Gosse's paper "Tennyson — and After" is printed on pp. 177–198.

CHAPTER 8.   THREE LATER NOVELS

1. Leavis, p. 80.

2. *Athenaeum,* May 9, 1891.

3. May 26, 1887, to Margaret, Berg Collection, N. Y. Public Library.

4. *Athenaeum,* May 28, 1892.

5. *Academy,* July 23, 1892.

6. *Ibid.*

CHAPTER 9.   REGRESSION

1. *Academy,* April 9, 1892.

2. *Athenaeum,* May 27, 1893.

3. *Saturday Review,* Jan. 19, 1895.

4. *Athenaeum,* Jan. 12, 1895.

CHAPTER 10.   "THE GENRE OF NERVOUS EXHAUSTION"

1. *Letters,* p. 166, August 1885, to Algernon.

2. May 6, 1901, to H. D. Davray, Berg Collection, N. Y. Public Library.

3. *Saturday Review,* April 18, 1896.

4. *Athenaeum,* Jan. 25, 1896.

5. *Academy,* May 15, 1897.

6. Shafer, p. xxxix.

7. *Athenaeum,* Nov. 18, 1899.

8. *Academy Supplement,* Sept. 10, 1898.

9. *Ibid.*

10. Burrell, p. 37.

11. *Letters,* p. 351.

12. See ch. 24 of *Veranilda.*

13. Frederic Harrison, "Preface," Gissing's *Veranilda.*

CHAPTER 11. LOVE AND EXILE

1. *Letters,* p. 354, Oct. 12, 1897, to Algernon.

2. Edward Clodd, *Memories,* Nov. 6, 1897, p. 168.

3. *Letters,* p. 355, Nov. 26, 1897, to son Walter; Diary, Dec. 4, p. 357.

4. *Letters,* p. 359, Dec. 7, 1897, to Ellen; p. 360, Dec. 11, 1897, to Ellen.

5. *Letters,* p. 361, Diary, Dec. 14, 1897.

6. *Letters,* p. 363, Dec. 15, 1897, to Algernon.

7. *Letters,* p. 361, Diary, Dec. 14, 1897; Dec. 15, p. 363.

8. *Letters,* p. 364, Jan. 23, 1898, to Ellen.

9. Bertz was a regular contributor from Potsdam to *Das Literarische Echo.* In the volume for October 1899–October 1900, see his article, "Die Neue Ethik," pp. 90–94, which describes the impact of Darwin and Nietzsche upon modern ethics. Gissing may have read the article, as he read many of Bertz's writings. Certainly in *Our Friend the Charlatan* he shows acquaintance with similar ideas.

10. Diary, March 7, 1898, Berg Collection, N. Y. Public Library.

11. Diary, April 20, 1898, Berg Collection, N. Y. Public Library.

12. Diary, Oct. 15, 1898, Berg Collection, N. Y. Public Library.

13. Clodd, *Memories,* Jan. 8, 1902, p. 177.

14. Roberts, p. 222; also Diary, May 7, 1899, Berg Collection, N. Y. Public Library.

15. *Letters,* p. 377, June 25, 1901, to Ellen.

16. *Letters,* p. 379, Dec. 28, 1901, to Algernon.

17. *Letters,* p. 368, Diary, Feb. 19, 1900.

18. *Letters,* p. 368, Diary, Feb. 14, 1900.

19. Clodd, *Memories,* Jan. 8, 1902, p. 178.

20. *Letters,* p. 392, March 21, 1903, to Ellen.

21. *Letters,* p. 383, Diary, April 14, 1902.

22. *Letters,* p. 375, Feb. 17, 1901, to Clara Collet.

23. *Letters,* p. 393, March 25, 1903, to Margaret.

24. Clodd, *Memories,* Sept. 1, 1898, p. 170.

25. Clodd, *Memories,* Nov. 7, 1899, p. 172.

26. *Letters,* p. 366, Dec. 29, 1899, to Clara Collet.

27. Clodd, *Memories,* Nov. 7, 1899, p. 172.

28. Oct. 6, 1900, to James B. Pinker, Berg Collection, N. Y. Public Library.

29. Oct. 27, 1900, to James B. Pinker, Berg Collection, N. Y. Public Library.

30. Nov. 29, 1900, to James B. Pinker, Berg Collection, N. Y. Public Library.

31. Roberts, p. 255.

32. Clodd, *Memories,* March 1, 1902, p. 179.

33. Clodd, *Memories,* Nov. 7, 1899, p. 173.

34. Clodd, *Memories,* May 6, 1900, p. 174.

35. Clodd, *Grant Allen,* p. 198.

36. *Letters,* p. 371, July 8, 1900, to Clara Collet.

37. Clodd, *Memories,* June 16, 1903, p. 188.

38. *Letters,* p. 391, Dec. 24, 1902, to Clara Collet.

39. Clodd, *Memories,* March 1, 1902, p. 179.

40. Clodd, *Memories,* p. 195.

41. H. G. Wells, "The Novels of Mr. George Gissing," p. 197.

42. Woolf, p. 13.

CHAPTER 12.   BELLES-LETTRES AND CRITICISM

1. Frank Swinnerton, *George Gissing, A Critical Study,* p. 36.

2. Gissing, "Dickens in Memory," *The Critic,* January 1902, p. 47.

3. *Ibid.,* p. 50.

4. *Ibid.,* p. 51.

5. *Letters,* p. 83, Nov. 3, 1880, to Algernon.

CHAPTER 13.   RETROSPECT

1. Cyril Connolly, "The Legacy of Gissing," *The Sunday Times* (London), Jan. 25, 1953.

INDEX